WOMEN PLAYWRIGHTS

The Best Plays of 2001

Edited by D.L. Lepidus

CONTEMPORARY PLAYWRIGHTS
SERIES

SK
A Smith and Kraus Book

A Smith and Kraus Book
Published by Smith and Kraus, Inc.
177 Lyme Road, Hanover, NH 03755
www.SmithKraus.com

First Edition: November 2002
10 9 8 7 6 5 4 3 2 1
Manufactured in the United States of America

Cover and text design by Julia Hill Gignoux, Freedom Hill Design

The Library of Congress Cataloging-In-Publication Data
Women playwrights : the best plays of 2001 / edited by D.L. Lepidus
p. cm. — (Contemporary playwrights series)
ISBN 1-57525-296-1
1. American drama—women authors. 2. American drama—20th century. 3.
Women—drama.
I. Smith, Marisa. II. Series: Contemporary playwrights series.
PS628.W6W668   1994
812'.540809287—dc20
94-10071
CIP

WOMEN PLAYWRIGHTS
The Best Plays of 2001

SMITH AND KRAUS PUBLISHERS
Contemporary Playwrights / Full-Length Play Anthologies

Humana Festival '93: The Complete Plays
Humana Festival '94: The Complete Plays
Humana Festival '95: The Complete Plays
Humana Festival '96: The Complete Plays
Humana Festival '97: The Complete Plays
Humana Festival '98: The Complete Plays
Humana Festival '99: The Complete Plays
Humana Festival 2000: The Complete Plays
Humana Festival 2001: The Complete Plays
Humana Festival: 20 One-Acts Plays 1976–1996

New Dramatists 2000: The Best Plays by the Graduating Class
New Dramatists 2001: The Best Plays by the Graduating Class

New Playwrights: The Best Plays of 1998
New Playwrights: The Best Plays of 1999
New Playwrights: The Best Plays of 2000

Women Playwrights: The Best Plays of 1992
Women Playwrights: The Best Plays of 1993
Women Playwrights: The Best Plays of 1994
Women Playwrights: The Best Plays of 1995
Women Playwrights: The Best Plays of 1996
Women Playwrights: The Best Plays of 1997
Women Playwrights: The Best Plays of 1998
Women Playwrights: The Best Plays of 1999
Women Playwrights: The Best Plays of 2000

If you require prepublication information about forthcoming Smith and Kraus books, you may receive our semiannual catalogue, free of charge, by sending your name and address to *Smith and Kraus Catalogue, PO Box 127, Lyme, NH 03768.* Or call us at (800) 895-4331, fax (603) 643-1831. www.SmithKraus.com.

CONTENTS

CONTENTS

FOREWORD

I am told that production of plays by women has fallen off in recent years. This may be so, but when I began this project for Smith and Kraus, I found an extraordinary variety of fine plays by women that had been produced by America's professional theaters, both in New York and not in New York.

Saint Lucy's Eyes, for instance, was developed by the Cherry Lane Alternative in New York City, then given a full production by the Women's Project. This production then transferred back to Cherry Lane Theatre, Off-Broadway. It's a funny, poignant play that deals with, in an unusual manner, the hot-button subject of abortion. *The Syringa Tree,* by Pamela Gien, also had a successful Off-Broadway run. It's a beautifully written one-woman play about growing up white in South Africa during the apartheid era. Like the best one-person plays, the actress plays various roles, often bringing the story into the present-tense realm of drama, as opposed to narrative. As of this writing, *Deux Mariages: Romola and Nijinsky* has not been produced in New York, though the excellent Primary Stages has it on its schedule for the 2002–2003 season.

But what about the other plays in this volume? No New York City plans for them so far. Don't buy into the myth — cultivated by the New York hotshots — that the "best" plays are the ones done in New York. New York is, after all, merely America's most prominent regional theater. Mary Lathrop (*The Visible Horse*), Gina Barnett (*T for 2*), Jennifer Laura Paige (*Notes*), and Barbara Lhota (*Romance* and *Strangers*) have all had significant productions of their work outside New York, and all are worthy of your attention.

Smith and Kraus has published their annual anthology of new plays by women for many years now. If you enjoy this book, I hope you'll take a look at some of the other volumes in this series — and keep an eye out for the 2002 book, which I'm putting together even as I type.

D. L. Lepidus

INTRODUCTION

Whenever I sit on a panel of playwrights, the question of gender comes up. Everyone wants to hear me talk about what it's like to be a woman playwright. People know that it's different from being a male playwright—and by the way, no one ever asks the guys on the panel what it's like to be a male playwright. Male playwrights are normal. Women playwrights are not.

Usually when I'm asked about being a "woman playwright," it's by some ferocious and proud young woman, who wants me to dish about how horrible it is to be discriminated against on the basis of my gender. Actresses often want to talk about it, because they're still frustrated that there are so many fewer parts available to them than there are to their male counterparts. Artists of color want to talk about it because they feel that like women, their stories have been marginalized by the theatrical culture. Sometimes people want to know why women's plays are so bad, completely forgetting for a moment that a lot of the plays written by men are bad, too. But the general assumption seems to be that women need to be let in more. The hope is that as women playwrights and directors become more central to the system, storytelling in America will be invigorated with the passion of people whose stories have not yet been told.

This movement toward storytelling, which centralizes on a woman's heroic journey, unfortunately is still a bit of a struggle. The 2001 NYSCA study on the status of women playwrights and directors in the American theater was a bit of a sad eye-opener. Prominent critics and producers admitted an institutionalized prejudice against women's voices does exist. The number of plays produced by American women playwrights on American stages is shockingly low.

But we have in our hands another volume of new plays that proves once again that all these disappointments and obstacles are nothing in the face of an artist's will and spirit. We have in our hands a volume of beautiful plays written by people who happen, among the many other qualities of their humanity — gay and straight, young and old, black and white — to be women.

My good friend Marlene Meyer, a gifted playwright and sage, once said to me, "You're not a woman writer. They don't know *what* you are." Male playwrights are playwrights. We're witches, or madwomen, or feminists, or something else unspeakably unnatural. It is not a distinction we make for ourselves; we just write. But as long as it is being made for us, I choose to celebrate it.

I don't have any problem being a woman writer. I don't think it qualifies or narrows my understanding of the world I live in, the world I write about. The perspective is different and I celebrate that, as do all the women whose work appears here in this exceptional volume.

And so, I celebrate this book, I celebrate these writers, and I celebrate their plays.

Theresa Rebeck
playwright

Deux Mariages:
Romola and Nijinsky

By Lynne Alvarez

To Craig Slaight,
without whom this piece and many others would not exist.

THE AUTHOR

Lynne Alvarez arrived in New York in 1978 planning to be a hot-shot poet. On a whim, she accompanied a friend to a gathering of Hispanic writers at the Puerto Rican Travelling Theatre. At thirty-one, she had never had a thought of writing a play, but she was now hooked.

Lynne wrote three plays under the auspices of Miriam Colon and the Puerto Rican Travelling Theatre; *Graciela,* which was presented at the Puerto Rican Travelling Theatre, *Mundo,* which premiered at IATI Theatre Off-Broadway in 1983; and the third play, *The Guitarron,* earned Lynne an NEA Fellowship and premiered in 1984 at St. Clements Theatre in New York.

Lynne was a member of New Dramatists for seven years where she wrote *Hidden Parts* (1981), which won the Kesselring Award in 1983. She also wrote *The Wonderful Tower of Humbert Lavoigent* (1983), which won two awards: The Le Compte De Nouey Award in 1984 and an FDG/CBS Award for Best Play and, later, Best Production at Capital Repertory Company in Albany, New York in 1984/85. The same year, The Actors Theatre of Louisville commissioned a one-act play, which became the full-length play, *Thin Air: Tales from a Revolution. Thin Air* premiered at the San Diego Repertory Company in 1987 and won a Drama League Award and a Rockefeller Fellowship in 1988. Lynne won a second NEA Fellowship in 1989/90. She was worked extensively with ACT and both its Conservatories, which have premiered *The Reincarnation of Jaime Brown, Eddie Mundo Edmundo,* and *Analiese.* In 2000, Smith and Kraus published a collection of her early plays.

Lynne has also done commissioned translations and adaptations: *The Damsel and the Gorilla or The Red Madonna* by Fernando Arrabal for INTAR in 1988 and Tirso de Molina's *Don Juan of Seville* for Classic Stage Company in 1990. Her translations of three plays by the Mexican playwright Felipe Santander were published by Smith and Kraus in 2002. Lynne's musical adaptations of the children's stories *Rikki-Tikki-Tavi* and *The Pied Piper of Hamlin* were produced by The Repertory Theatre of St. Louis in 1991 and 1992 respectively, and her adaptation of . . . *And Now Miguel* was commissioned and premiered by the Lincoln Center Institute in 1995.

She is currently working on a new play *Hunter Hunted* and is the recipient of grants from The Peter Sharp Foundation and Works & Process.

AUTHOR'S NOTE

Of course, I am fascinated by dance for the usual reasons — the beauty of the movements, the physicality of the dancers, the rhythm, the music, the ensemble, and so on — but as a playwright what has fascinated me most is that dance can hold an audience rapt without using words and many times with no plot. What is the secret? Why does the cobra's dance mesmerize the mouse? I wanted to experiment with this — the use of movement and silence as a presence on stage. When the dancer Nijinsky's diaries were republished in their unabridged form several years ago, I knew I had found the perfect subject matter for the kind of play I was interested in writing. I could use dancers and dance and yet explore the intricacies of love and sexuality through character and plot. What's more, the story took place in an almost heartbreakingly irretrievable period of color and innocence — the years leading up to the First World War.

However, I didn't want to explore the Nijinsky/Diagheliff duo yet again nor write a bio-epic of Nijinsky's life and madness. What fascinated me was his two-week courtship aboard a ship sailing to South America of the woman who became his wife for the next thirty years: Romola de Pulsky. She bore him two children and supported him through his years of madness, exile, and two World Wars.

The questions posed by his actions were obvious. Did he love her? Was he homosexual? Bisexual? Sexual at all? Was he deranged? Did she ruin his dance career? His life? However the questions I had about Romola de Pulsky were not so obvious. No one in the dance world then or afterward had much good to say about her — she was portrayed as an arriviste on the dance scene, a socialite, and worst of all — a dilettante who was demanding, ignorant, and perhaps destructive of his genius. I wanted to know what the chemistry was; who was this young girl (she was nineteen at the time) who boldly smoked cigarettes but was a virgin; who was well-heeled, well-traveled, but so innocent about love; who directed her energies — unlike her mother who was a great Hungarian actress — toward something less abstract than art? What happened on the *Avon* that so bound Romola and Nijinsky to each other?

ORIGINAL PRODUCTION

Bat Theater Company presented *Deux Mariages* on May 31, 2001. It was directed by David Levine, with choreography by Daniel Gwirtzman, and featured the Daniel Gwirtzman Dance Company at The Flea Theater. Actors were Doug Barron, John Daggett, Lindsey Dietz, Adam Feldman, Jack Fitzpatrick, Fiona Gallagher, Cary McWilliam, Thomas Nieto, Christa Scott Reed, Valda Setterfield, and Satomi Shikata.

Set by Marsha Ginsberg. Lights were by Lap Chi Chu, costumes by Naama Greenfield, original music composed by Brendan Connelly, with producer Tonya Canada. James Ball, Jr. was the stage manager, and Eve Udesky was Assistant Director.

CHARACTERS

ROMOLA DE PULSKY: 20, Dancer in the Corps de Ballets in the Ballets Russes

VASLAV NIJINSKY: 21, Soloist and star of the Ballets Russes

BARON DIMITRI DE GUNSBOURG: 45, Russian aristocrat, acting director of Ballets Russes on tour

EMILIA MARKUS: 40, Great Hungarian classic actress and Romola's mother

SERGEI DIAGHELIFF: 45, Creater and director of the Ballets Russes, formerly Nijinsky's lover and mentor

ANNA: 40, Romola's companion/attendant

VASSILY: 60, Nijinsky's valet

FOUR DANCERS: 3 women, 1 man, play all other roles including the man with the pipe, the ship's captain, maids, waiters, prostitutes, couples on the boat, dancers, regardless of gender

SETTING

Place is variously: a ballroom in St. Moritz, Switzerland; aboard the ship *Avon* traveling to South America; a church in Buenos Aires. Sets are optional.

TIME

Time is both 1913 and 1919.

DEUX MARIAGES: ROMOLA AND NIJINSKY

ACT I
Scene One
Le Deuxième Mariage (*Le Mariage avec Dieu*)

January 19, 1919. A private home. St. Moritz, Switzerland. A night sky. Instead of stars we gradually realize there are a variety of eyes overhead: some blinking, some staring, some human and others of animals. Nijinsky is in a circle of light. He is wearing practical clothes. Far upstage right in another spot of light is a dancer dressed as Nijinsky. He dances. At some point during Nijinsky's speech, he turns and turns and turns and turns and turns and disappears. Nijinsky speaks simply to the audience.

NIJINSKY: I used to deceive my wife because I had too much semen. I had to ejaculate. I like whores, but I did not ejaculate into them. I have lots of semen and I keep it for another child. I hope I will be presented with the gift of a boy. God is a prick who breeds with one woman. I am a man who breeds children with one woman.

I used to give my wife roses that cost five francs a piece. I brought her roses every day, twenty, thirty at a time. I loved giving her white roses. Red roses frightened me. I loved her terribly. But I already felt death. My wife wept and wept. She suffered. I wanted a simple life. I loved Tolstoy. I loved the dance. I wanted to work. I worked hard. I was like a draft horse, whipped until it fell and all its guts dropped out its ass. I lost heart. I noticed I wasn't liked. I weep and weep. I love Tolstoy. I love Russia although I am a Catholic Pole. I will work on a farm. I will practice masturbation and spiritualism. I will eat everyone I can get a hold of. I will stop at nothing. I will make love to my wife's mother and child. I will weep, but I will do everything God commands me.

No. No. I do not love anyone. I am evil. I wish to harm everyone and be good to myself. I am an egoist. I am not God. I am a beast and predator.

How dare you disturb me? I am not a machine. I will dance when I feel like it! You are stupid. You are stupid. You are beasts. You are meat.

You are death. I feel God. I feel God. You came to be amused, but God wants to arouse you. I will dance frightening things. See? I can mimic a crazy person like my brother, Stassik. I can be a whore, an old Jew with peyes, a cripple, an aristocrat. Who says workmen are good? Workmen are as depraved as aristocrats. They have less money. They drink cheap wine. My stomach is clean. I do not like meat. I saw how a calf was killed. I saw how a pig was killed. I saw it and felt their tears. I could not bear it. See? I can dance like a dying pig, like a dying czar, like a soldier creeping in the shadow of the gate and shot — "unh" — in the snow. Silence! *(He executes violent, angry movements.)*

Ay, I feel God. He loves me. I love him. Today . . . Today . . . Silence! Silence! Today is the day of my marriage with God!

(A bustle of activity. The lights up, sounds of seawater lapping at a large ship. Perhaps gulls. The prostitutes dance on as does the captain of the ship. There is a ship's railing. Couples gather. One of the prostitutes puts on a maid's apron and begins scrubbing the deck with a mop and pail. Vassily enters with a barre, a white towel, and a watering can. He sets up the barre, sprinkles water on the stage. Nijinsky goes to the barre to practice. There is "oohhhhing" and "ahhhhing" as he passes. People gather to watch him. The Baron is there with the man with the pipe. Anna enters and finds Romola. She and the man with the pipe exchange glances.)

Scene Two
Le Premier Mariage (*Le Mariage de Coeur*)

Romola and Anna walking on deck.

ROMOLA: Of course he's extreme, Anna. He's a genius and he's Russian. What would you expect? He's beautiful.
(The Englishman smoking a pipe walks by. The maid follows, still cleaning. Perhaps polishing something.)
ANNA: I think I will learn to smoke a pipe.
ROMOLA: I can't believe you like that Englishman. He's so . . . common!
ANNA: Ssshhh!
ROMOLA: He doesn't understand Hungarian! No one understands Hungarian. Come over here. Look at the ocean. It's endless.
ANNA: It moves too much.
ROMOLA: And the sun. I wish I could be naked as a child and get brown all

over. I want to look like a native from some exotic place . . . I'd walk through the streets in costume. I can't wait until we get to Buenos Aires.

ANNA: With all those dark men following you whispering obscenities.

ROMOLA: Yes!

ANNA: I'm going to follow my Englishman.

ROMOLA: No, Anna. You can't leave me.

ANNA: Yes. I can. I'm not going to end up a pruney old maid with an unscathed hymen . . . like some people.

ROMOLA: Le Petit!

ANNA: Please.

ROMOLA: You can't leave. I need you. How do I look?

ANNA: Awful. You've never looked worse.

ROMOLA: Is he looking at me?

ANNA: No.

ROMOLA: Wait! *(She lights a cigarette.)*

ANNA: I smell camel dung.

ROMOLA: Turkish.

ANNA: Blow the smoke the other way.

ROMOLA: Is he watching yet?

ANNA: No.

ROMOLA: What's he doing?

ANNA: He's stopped practicing and Vassily is wiping his armpits.

ROMOLA: I want to kiss him there and in that cleft under his lower lip where no one else has ever kissed him before. *(She blows out a plume of smoke and Vassily approaches angrily.)*

VASSILY: Away! Away! Go. Very bad!

ROMOLA: What did he say? He speaks French like a barking dog.

ANNA: He wants us to leave.

ROMOLA: Yes, Vassily. All right. *(She puts out her cigarette with great show. The maid comes over hurriedly and sweeps it up.)* Vassily, the inevitable. Like a little old lady with his little towel and his watering can. He probably accompanies Vaslav to the loo and wipes his bottom.

ANNA: Hush.

ROMOLA: They don't understand Hungarian either!

ANNA: Well, don't say their names. They understand that!

ROMOLA: How rude. He hasn't given me a glance. I can't stand it. You'd think he never saw me before. And it was so much fun in Budapest when he mistook me for the prima ballerina of the Hungarian Opera. With that Tartar face and ill-fitting clothes, he looked like some poor Japanese student, but he moved like a tiger — so soft and fierce. I allowed him to kiss my hand. Remember? Now he's impossible! I'll show him I can ignore him too. *(She laughs.)* Of course, first he has to notice me!

God — I'm sure the first time he does notice me again will be when I fall on my face on the dance floor during rehearsal. Oh, please — Miraculous Jesus of Prague, Divine Child — be with me every minute when the time comes. Let me move like a feather, like an angel, like a drum, like Karsavina, at least. I know the only way to his heart is through the dance. *(She cries.)*

ANNA: Romola, don't suffer. Nothing has happened yet.

ROMOLA: I know. But I can already see his sly derisive smile.

(Romola drags Anna off. The Madonna picks up her pail and with the Baby Jesus under one arm, leaves. Vassily drapes a towel around Nijinsky, takes up the barre and watering can, and they exit together. The stage is empty. We hear the slow rise and fall of the ocean against the ship. A couple walks by. The woman is angry and precedes the man. The man follows, pleading with her, smoking a pipe. Lights down. We see three separate cabins aboard the Avon. Nijinsky is getting a massage. Anna and Romola are changing clothes. Baron de Gunsbourg is putting the final touches on his toilette, he is humming parts of The Fire Bird *as he dresses. He stops to conduct when he comes to an especially lively passage and then continues dressing, watching himself in the mirror.)*

Scene Three

In his cabin, the Baron has on a white linen suit. But something is missing. He looks around and picks up a brightly colored shawl and wraps it around his waist, admires himself, and exits. He makes his way to Nijinsky's cabin. Nijinsky is sitting on the massage table as the masseur gathers up his things. The masseur has a "tic." When the masseur's back is turned, Nijinsky studies his movements and tries to reproduce them. There is a knock on the door.

BARON: May I come in? It is I, Dimitri.

NIJINSKY: I'm just finishing my massage. What's the matter?

BARON: I can't bear to be alone.

NIJINSKY: It's only an hour to dinner.

BARON: I know, I know.

(Vassily opens the door and the Baron enters. Vassily gives a slight bow and leaves. The Baron notices Vaslav imitating Romola's gesture from Scene I.)

BARON: What is it? What's wrong? Vaslav, are you having a fit? Oh, I see you're doing one of your studies. Well, you do look just like that man, but why would you want to? You should do me. Oh, no, no, no that would be too pathetic. But tell me, how do I look? I tried this sash for a bit of color and dash, as we are going to South America. Olé. Oh, I can just imagine what your dear Sergei would say, "Dimitri, you look like an aging whore." Odd, I don't miss him, but I'm always quoting him. How indelicate. Personally, I think this separation from Sergei will do you wonders, not that I don't understand your relationship. I had one myself, very romantic, rose petals on the bed, that sort of thing. But, I knew it was doomed. He would always arrive from Kiev with this very small valise. I'd take one look at that small valise and think, "He's already planning to leave." I felt deserted as soon as he arrived.

NIJINSKY: Please don't talk about love, Dimitri. I am feeling too good.

BARON: Yes, of course. Passion is nothing but an inferno.

NIJINSKY: Except for dance.

BARON: Oh, dance. Yes, of course. You are so brilliant!

NIJINSKY: You are so transparent. What is it you want, Dimitri?

BARON: Your happiness. Your completeness. I think it's time you rethought your relationship with Diagheliff . . . I think Sergei has lost his edge. He didn't really appreciate your choreography the way he should. I adored *Sacre* and *Jeux* . . . Although I admit not many others did. And he wasn't very fond of *L'Apres Midi*. He actually said, "I refuse to give that thing in Paris. It's not a ballet. I will dismiss the company before I give it again . . . " Is that painful? I'm so sorry. But I, on the other hand, thought it was majestic. You know it almost makes me think of starting another company . . . I know how deathly tired you are of all that intrigue. Sergei runs the Ballets Russes like a Caliph's court, full of favorites and concubines. We should start a small company where we could achieve some interesting results, don't you think? No. No. No. No. Don't answer me now. Think about it. In the meantime, let's play. I have it in mind to introduce you to someone who is quite mad for you.

NIJINSKY: I'm not interested. Thank you, Baron.

BARON: Come. Come. The cure for disenchantment is love. If you're interested in girls, there's a beautiful girl on board I think you should meet. She's taken every opportunity to drape herself in front of you. You must have noticed.

NIJINSKY: The blue-eyed girl?

BARON: Yes, yes. That's her.

NIJINSKY: Is she a dancer?

BARON: In the Corps de Ballet, I believe.

NIJINSKY: But the Corps de Ballet is not in first class and this girl has a cabin near mine.

BARON: Oh, she's very rich. Her mother is a great classical actress, the premier actress of Hungary, actually. Some say she is as great as Bernhardt. *(Whispering.)* She was the seventh child of a button manufacturer.

NIJINSKY: The blue-eyed girl?

BARON: No, her mother. But she became a great actress and married de Pulsky, an aristocrat, which in turn made her very wealthy, which in turn made Romola, that is the blue-eyed girl, a beneficiary of the money. What I am trying to say is, she has money and she paid for her own cabin and you should meet her.

NIJINSKY: Does she dance well?

BARON: I can't say. I've never seen her dance. She's only just joined the company for this tour.

NIJINSKY: I could never be interested in anyone who wasn't a beautiful dancer.

BARON: She's quite pretty and has eyes like sapphires. Oh, for heaven's sakes, why limit yourself to prima ballerinas?

NIJINSKY: Because for me, dancing is the highest thing.

BARON: Ach! It's a good thing I'm not an artist or I'd kill myself. You need light. You need gaiety. And perhaps she is a good dancer. Who knows? I will introduce you.

NIJINSKY: We've already met.

BARON: How strange. She never greets you. You never greet her. Do you hate her then?

NIJINSKY: No, I make a display of not noticing her.

BARON: For heaven's sakes, why? She's from a very good family.

NIJINSKY: You seem awfully determined that we should meet. And why is that, Dimitri? Do you want me to fall in love and run away with her? Away from Sergei? Straight into your arms?

BARON: No, I would never presume . . .

NIJINSKY: I am the Ballets Russes. I will not desert her. As for the girl, I enjoy provoking her to flirt. It's always a privilege to watch someone do what they do best. I'm perfectly happy, Baron. I only want to observe love like a beautiful painting of a landscape. It's enchanting and I don't have to inhabit it.

BARON: So, you don't love girls.

NIJINSKY: I was madly in love with a girl once.

BARON: Don't tell me.

NIJINSKY: Dark, beautiful Maria Gorshkova — a dancer, of course. My mother was violently opposed. *(Imitating his mother.)* "She can't be serious about you. You're a boy, you're eighteen, and she's a woman! She's trying to turn your head for the sake of her career. You'll see. One day you'll take her in your arms and she'll love you — but only on condition that she dances with you." It was like a knife in my heart. I was furious. I broke glasses. I threw the samovar on the floor and swore that not only did I love her, but I would marry her! And then . . . it happened exactly as my mother told me. I had my arms around Maria and was about to kiss her when she whispered coyly, "Vatza, promise me you will insist on dancing a *pas de deux* with me." That cured me of love for girls.

BARON: So you don't love girls anymore.

NIJINSKY: Now, I am like Christ. I love all people.

BARON: I'm much too shallow for that. I can only love two or three at a time.

NIJINSKY: You're terribly shallow, but very clever; you play dumb like a wolf does so the poor lamb will ignore it. So, I leave you to your motives and ask you to take me on deck and show me how to smoke a pipe like a proper Englishman. *(Nijinsky dresses.)*

BARON: A pipe? What makes you think I know . . . ? Oh . . . Ohhhhh. Yes, oh, so you saw me with that lovely gentleman. He's quite impressive and he knows everything about Indian ruins. He's been hunting with a minor maharajah. He's wild about animals, so sensitive. He told me he would give his soul if, just once, he could watch an elephant drink. He's offered to take me on safari through the jungles of the Amazon — but I can't possibly go. Suppose the relationship is brief? Safari clothes are so costly and it would be a perfect waste of money to have them made if the relationship were brief. I mean, where else could I use them? Certainly not with my wife.

(They exit. The lights fade on one cabin and slowly brighten over Romola's. She is kneeling before a figure of the Madonna carrying a small child with a large golden halo. Romola is absorbed in prayer and crosses herself and then remembers something and kneels again. The Madonna looks down and notices this. She hands the infant Jesus to Romola, who is startled, and then pleased. The Madonna begins to dance.)

Scene Four

Romola is kneeling. The Madonna finishes her dance. She disappears behind a wall. A stately woman in high renaissance dress enters. She parades around Romola until Romola looks up from her prayers.

EMILIA: Well? Who am I?

ROMOLA: Mother!

EMILIA: No, no, no. You know the game. Who am I?

ROMOLA: I'm no longer a child.

EMILIA: That's debatable. But let's not quibble. This is such a good game. Indulge me or I won't go away. Who am I?

ROMOLA: You're Ophelia from The Royal Theater's 1912 production of *Hamlet*. A very old Ophelia.

EMILIA: If you look as good at my age, you will kneel down and kiss the earth with gratitude. Now what did I do?

ROMOLA: You murdered my father.

EMILIA: Your father had killed himself, but I am talking about the play. In the play, what did Ophelia do?

ROMOLA: She went mad and drowned herself.

EMILIA: Why?

ROMOLA: She was in love and it wasn't reciprocated.

EMILIA: I rest my case.

ROMOLA: Like Papa.

EMILIA: I'm getting tired of this.

ROMOLA: Well, you decided to show up here.

EMILIA: No, as usual you have it wrong. You called me — just to torture me. *(Pause.)* I wish you didn't worship your father . . .

ROMOLA: He died for love. He was a hero.

EMILIA: You were a child. You didn't really know your father. He was unstable and unpredictable. On a good day, I would say he was a tragic figure, sort of a Don Quixote with a dim sense of reality. On a bad day, I would call him a fool. And when he was drunk . . . I hated it when Karoly was drunk and wanted to make love. . . . There were things you wouldn't know as a child . . .

ROMOLA: I knew you threw parties when he was sending you piteous letters from England.

EMILIA: Yes. Parties that old men in Budapest will remember with pleasure twenty years from now.

ROMOLA: You destroyed him. You wouldn't go to him. Of course, you couldn't, could you? After all, you can only act in Hungarian, so how could you leave? No one understands Hungarian!

EMILIA: I know that's what you think.

ROMOLA: It's what I know. What I've seen. I'll never be like you.

EMILIA: You mean by chasing a man you can never have? You may despise me, but I am your mother and I warn you, as your mother, as a woman of the world, Nijinsky's friendship with Diagheliff is more than a friendship. You see, he can't possibly be interested in you!

ROMOLA: Diagheliff is not on this ship. Nijinsky is alone.

EMILIA: Romuschka — He's not alone. None of us is ever alone. . . . Do you really think there can be only two people alone in a room or in a bed. Believe me. What I wouldn't give for a moment's peace alone in bed . . . But no — all our past piles in next to us and grabs the covers and knees our backs and makes loud demands. I assure you, Diagheliff is as present as you are.

ROMOLA: Nijinsky will learn to love me if I dance. He loved Karsavina when he was a boy.

EMILIA: Then dance. At least you'll get a career out of the relationship. Who would have thought it possible, watching Maestro Cechitti turn purple trying to make you dance properly that you'd be dancing with the Ballets Russes!

ROMOLA: I'm in the last row of the Corps de Ballet, Mother. And then only because so many dancers refused to go to this *pays de negres* to be eaten alive by jungle animals.

EMILIA: Nonsense. It's the greatest company on earth and you've done it in two years! Who knows what's next — prima ballerina, ballerina assoluta!

ROMOLA: Why is it you say such nice things, but you make me feel like a failure?

EMILIA: I have no idea!

ROMOLA: Public acclaim can't be the only measure of success.

EMILIA: Of course not.

ROMOLA: You say that. But that's not what you believe.

EMILIA: What we believe.

ROMOLA: Are all mothers so self-centered they can only see their daughters as extensions of themselves?

EMILIA: Now what did I do?

ROMOLA: Jesus of Prague, Divine Child, when the time comes, save me please . . .

EMILIA: Praying is useless. Work is the only answer.

ROMOLA: Work, work, work. You sound like Chekov.

EMILIA: Yes, I do. He writes such lovely parts for women . . . *(Overacting.)* "I am so weary. If I could rest . . . rest! . . . Ah, I am a seagull . . . No, not right. I am an actress . . . I am a seagull . . . no, I am a pimple on the ass of God." There! I almost made you smile!

ROMOLA: I won't let you charm me, Mother.

EMILIA: All right, then hate me — but don't be a fool.

ROMOLA: Like my father!

EMILIA: Romola!

ROMOLA: Go away!

EMILIA: *(Takes up the Baby Jesus and exiting, imitates Romola scathingly.)* Please . . . Please . . . Divine Child . . .

(Anna has just reappeared. She begins to straighten things in the room.)

ROMOLA: Go away! Get out of here!

ANNA: Go away? Go away? And here I thought you wanted to know if your precious Vaslav was on deck. Well, he is, and, for your information, you only have ten more days to steal his heart. And, you needn't be rude to me because you're in a bad mood. *(She exits.)*

Scene Five

Romola and Anna are sitting on deck chairs. Romola is daydreaming with a book in her lap and Anna is carefully putting on lotion. The man with the pipe walks by. He greets both ladies but he is eyeing Anna.

MAN WITH THE PIPE: Good day, mademoiselles. Lovely morning.

ANNA: A fine day to you, too, monsieur.

(Their eyes linger.)

MAN WITH THE PIPE: This equatorial sun is terribly hot, don't you think?

ANNA: Have we crossed the equator, then?

MAN WITH THE PIPE: No. Tonight. Is this your first time?

ANNA: First time . . . ?

MAN WITH THE PIPE: Crossing.

ANNA: Oh, yes, and yours?

MAN WITH THE PIPE: My third.

ANNA: Oh.

MAN WITH THE PIPE: Yes, they'll give you little silk flags of all the nations that touch the equator . . . yes . . . well, ladies, enjoy your morning. *(He continues to walk.)*

ROMOLA: Was that him?

ANNA: Who?

ROMOLA: Please. I saw that look pass between you. If you ask me, he was altogether too familiar.

ANNA: Yes, I'll go tell him at once. *(She gets up.)*

ROMOLA: I can't believe you're going to follow him?

ANNA: What? You think you're the only one who can flirt with a stranger? I have no time to lose.

ROMOLA: But what do you know about him?

ANNA: He's shown interest in me. He's English and he smokes a pipe. I'll tell you more about him when I get back. Ta!

ROMOLA: Go! Leave me alone then, you hussy!

(Anna exits in the direction of the man. Romola takes up a book. Two women walk by in deep discussion.)

WOMAN 2: Pickles and vodka?

WOMAN 1: But he has an estate.

WOMAN 2: Ahh, the legendary well-kept church, the pious peasants, the alley of limes. I suppose you can't resist.

WOMAN 1: I don't know. The village is backward, the peasants are drunk, and the roads are impassable.

(The women sit. Romola is restless. The Baron and Nijinsky enter and Romola ostentatiously raises her book to read. The Baron is laughing as Nijinsky is imitating the man with the pipe.)

BARON: Yes, yes that is him! I swear it is him down to the annoying way he holds his pipe. He is pretentious, isn't he? I don't know why the English are so determined to be thought eccentric. I mean, did he think it was attractive? All those bizarre stories about mysterious fires and prominent social figures beaten to death with polo mallets? I refuse to take him seriously.

NIJINSKY: He seemed to like you well enough.

BARON: Please! And when he said, "Dimitri, if you ever want to commit suicide, do it in my arms . . . " Oh, look, there's that lovely girl. Shall we say hello?

(He doesn't wait for a response and heads over to Romola who feigns distraction. Nijinsky goes to the ship's rail. He is followed by two of the prostitutes.)

BARON: What are you reading, my dear?

ROMOLA: Baron, you startled me. Monsieur Nijinsky.

(Nijinsky smiles.)

ROMOLA: *Anna Karenina.*

(The Baron takes it and shows it to Nijinsky.)

BARON: Look, she is reading a Russian novel, *Anna Karenina.*

ROMOLA: I'm afraid it's in French. I don't speak or read Russian.

BARON: Why bother? Anyone you would care to know speaks French. *(Nijinsky has wandered away.)* Even my friend here speaks a little . . . now where did he go? Let me introduce you.

ROMOLA: Never mind, Dimitri. He obviously is more interested in the ocean.

BARON: Oh, you know how he is . . . the artiste.

ROMOLA: No, Baron, really don't bother.

BARON: Why? Are you afraid of him? He may be *Le Dieu de la Dance* onstage, but off stage he's a charming young man.

ROMOLA: I'm not afraid of him.

BARON: Good. Then let me present him to you.

ROMOLA: I don't care to, Baron. Thank you.

BARON: Don't be silly. You admire him.

ROMOLA: Do I?

BARON: Please! He's captivating. We all admire him. He won't harm you. I promise and we are great pals.

ROMOLA: No. I'm just sick of it. I've been presented to him over and over again and he never remembers me.

BARON: Vaslav Fomitch.

(Nijinsky approaches smiling.)

BARON: So! Monsieur Nijinsky, permettez-moi de vous présenter Mlle. De Pulsky. Her mother is the greatest classical actress in Hungary.

(Romola extends her hand and Nijinsky takes it.)

BARON: Mlle. De Pulsky is a very talented dancer in our Corps de Ballet.

NIJINSKY: Yes.

ROMOLA: Yes . . . Yes . . . Well. Monsieur Nijinsky, I must thank you.

NIJINSKY: Thank me?

ROMOLA: Oh, yes, for *Printemps*, for *Sacre.*

NIJINSKY: You are welcome.

ROMOLA: You've made dance the highest art. Never lose your nerve!

NIJINSKY: *(Turns to the Baron for a translation.)* Nerve?

ROMOLA: All great work begins as blasphemy!

(The Baron goes to translate, but Nijinsky stops him.)

NIJINSKY: *(To Baron.)* She understands me, Dimitri! I think she understands.

(He smiles at Romola.)

ROMOLA: *(To the Baron.)* Did he comment?

BARON: Well, he did say . . .

NIJINSKY: No! Ask why she has a cabin near me.

BARON: I can hardly ask that!

NIJINSKY: I want to see her blush.

BARON: I won't be a party to insult. Now speak French, you're being so rude!

(Nijinsky turns away and taps his foot annoyingly.)

BARON: But, really . . .

(Nijinsky places his foot on the arm of her deck chair and ties his shoe. Romola looks at his shoe and then his calf, and when she looks up, he is looking down at her and smiling, watching her look at his leg.)

BARON: You know, I must tell you. We've decided to have a costume ball this evening to celebrate crossing the equator. I hope you'll come. Perhaps I shall be an odalisque and, Romola Carlovna, I have a brilliant idea for you. You are so slim. You almost look like a boy if you hide your hair and I will loan you a pair of my green silk pajamas.

ROMOLA: And what will you wear, Monsieur Nijinsky?

(A figure wearing a large head of Diagheliff walks up to Nijinsky. No one else sees him. He takes off the head, which is a replica of his own.)

DIAGHELIFF: Vatza, really! *(He walks away.)*

NIJINSKY: Sergei? What? *(He follows him leaving the Baron stranded.)* Wait!

BARON: *(Laughs uneasily.)* Yes, well, you know how he is. Well then — when you write her — regards to your mother. Brrrrr, she is a lioness, isn't she? *(Anna returns.)* Good day, Anna. *(He exits.)*

ROMOLA: Anna, guess what? Le Petit came over and flirted with me and I looked into his eyes. They're slanted, just like my pet Siamese. His eyes aren't green as I thought onstage. They're a soft, soft brown, like velvet.

(Eyes appear in the sky like stars. As the lights darken, some are cats' eyes, others are human. Some stare, some blink. We see Nijinsky asleep in his cabin.)

Scene Six

The giant eyes, blinking and non-blinking become even more pronounced. We can make out Nijinsky's figure lying on the bed and another figure in formal attire sitting at the foot of the bed. The figure reaches over and pours some water from a flask at Nijinsky's bedside. Nijinsky stirs. He is still dressed in his practice clothes and reaches blindly for the water.

DIAGHELIFF: Is this what you're looking for?

(Nijinsky is horrified and doesn't move.)

DIAGHELIFF: One really shouldn't nap in the afternoon. It's such a heavy sleep and one becomes so disoriented, don't you think? *(He hands the glass to Nijinsky who drinks from it.)* But my dear, you know you wanted to see me. I'm never out of your thoughts and I hate to admit it, but you're scarcely out of mine. Here. Drink. Drink.

NIJINSKY: You have a new boy anyway. Go away. *(Nijinsky gulps down some water and lights some lights.)*

DIAGHELIFF: Funny, but I'm still here. Perhaps, you've lost control of your mind. Ah, mon cher, careful, you are beginning to remind me of your crazy brother, Stassik. Pour soul. *(He looks around the cabin.)* Those eyes are making me nervous. You're not becoming paranoid, are you? *(Diagheliff snaps his fingers and the eyes disappear.)*

NIJINSKY: I know what an eye is. An eye is a theater.

DIAGHELIFF: Shush, Vatsa, shush.

NIJINSKY: I am sick at heart, Sergei. I am tired of intrigue and intrigue. I want to be a monk and build a simple house. I want to go to Siberia and preach to the peasants and work the land. I want to be a tree and its roots. I want to live simply, in isolation.

DIAGHELIFF: You must stop reading that old lunatic, Tolstoy. All this "philosophy." You are really getting boring, Vatza. I wanted you to take some time off, but for God's sake, use it creatively. Remember we must do something new for Paris this year. Tolstoy! You would go back to the Stone Age at a time when we can't be less modern. No! Futurism, cubism — the soul splintered from the universe — these are the last words. I will not let the position of artistic leadership slip away from me.

NIJINSKY: It's too late. You've already become a theatrical lackey. You, the visionary, the God of art, are now terrified of causing the least scandal.

DIAGHELIFF: You only say this because I thought your ballet *Jeux* was a complete failure. Even your *Sacre du Printemps* is not a real ballet . . . and *L'Apres Midi* — an eleven-minute ballet that needs a hundred hours of rehearsal. My God. All our friends of the Ballets Russes agree with me. It would be a mistake to encourage you further as a choreographer.

NIJINSKY: *Jeux* was not entirely successful. But, *Sacre* was important.

DIAGHELIFF: But the public, the paying public booed it.

NIJINSKY: It's new. It was not understood.

DIAGHELIFF: Vatza, Vatza. A painting or a piece of a music might be misunderstood at first or unappreciated for a long time, maybe a hundred years, but a ballet? A ballet must be received by the public today and tomorrow or else it is doomed to obscurity. Come, come, you know how much

I have done for you. I have given you three ballets to choreograph and *Jeux* and *Sacre* are not the kind of ballets that can sustain the successes of the Ballets Russes. You must understand that I have a great obligation.

NIJINSKY: But not to me.

DIAGHELIFF: Of course to you, darling. In fact, Fokin is composing some new ballets and I want you to look at them and give me your opinion. That is, if you have time. I must remember to tell that idiot, De Gunsbourg, to keep that little Hungarian flirt away from you. That imbecile. Does he really think he can separate the two of us with a socialite? He's plotting to have his own company again, but I am hardly worried. That man couldn't run a flea circus.

NIJINSKY: I don't think as little of women as you do, Sergei.

DIAGHELIFF: My poor little saint.

NIJINSKY: There is a difference between what I do for others and what I do for myself.

(Three dancers dressed as prostitutes dance out laughing raucously and approach first Nijinsky and then turn to fawn over Diagheliff, who treats them with bored indifference.)

DIAGHELIFF: Really?

NIJINSKY: Those long solitary walks in Paris? I was looking for whores. I wanted beautiful, healthy girls. Sometimes I fucked whores every day. I found a room in small Paris hotel. Once I made love to a woman who had her period. Then I went to you because I knew it would disgust you. I lied to you. I became you, a fake, a fraud. You dye you hair black so no one will know you are old, but I know you're old. I see that disgusting black cream you leave on the pillowcases and the lock of hair you dye white just to be noticed — it has turned yellow. Yellow. You have two false front teeth and when you take them out, you look like a wicked old woman. And that monocle you wear is only for effect. Your eyes are perfect. Deceit is your art. Deceit and sex.

DIAGHELIFF: You didn't seem to mind the sex, as I recall. Actually, as I was telling Prince Lvov when he passed you on to me, I was quite gratified by all the nice tricks he taught you. He was a very athletic young man, wasn't he?

NIJINSKY: He understood love. He wrote love poems. He was beautiful. He thought you would be useful to me.

DIAGHELIFF: Yes. His was a great love. He passed you around like a used penny. And I — who corrupted you, who used you — as you claim — made you a god. Le dieu de la danse. Vatza, you are a great artist, a gentle soul. Who else can appreciate you as I do?

NIJINSKY: You appreciate me like a painting in a museum. But, museums are graveyards! They are tidy. They are dead. Beauty for me isn't tidy. It's not pretty. Beauty is feeling in a face. Beauty is a hunchback. I like hunchbacks. I like ugly people. I am an ugly man with feeling. I dance hunchbacks and straight-backs. I am the artist who loves all shapes and all kinds of beauty.

DIAGHELIFF: Then you must love me, too.

NIJINSKY: I have found a girl. She has flaxen hair, her nose is long and straight. It has character. Her eyes are alive. I want to fuck her.

DIAGHELIFF: What are doing, Vatza? I am worried to death about you.

NIJINSKY: Of course. You, who thought I was boring and stupid. Who was ashamed I would speak and humiliate you in front of your brilliant friends. I hated you. But, I put up a pretense. I knew without you my mother and I would starve. I wasn't mature enough for life. But I loved the Ballets Russes. I gave my whole heart to the Ballets Russes. I worked like an ox. I lived like a martyr. I killed myself for the dance, but I am tired. Tired. For you, I pretended I was rested, cheerful — so that you, Diagheliff, would not be bored. But I was so tired. I was tired, tired. Tired of you showing that Nijinsky is your pupil in everything. I was tired of looking for love when there was nothing. You all thought I wanted praise, compliments. I hate compliments. I only love. You love fame, you love boys, you love a beautiful body, and you love objets d'art. You are wicked. You are crazy. I carry you with me like a stone, like a cross I can't put down. Leave me alone so I can breathe. I am going to the New World. I will have a new life and will do what God asks me.

DIAGHELIFF: Good, good. Take a year off. Take some time. *(He exits.)*

(Vassily enters.)

VASSILY: Vatza. *(He fills a glass with water.)*

NIJINSKY: *(Sobbing.)* You are not wicked. I will weep for you if you are ever hurt. I do not like you, but you are a human being and I love all human beings. I have no right to judge. The judge is God and he will whisper in my ear what do, what to do . . .

VASSILY: Vatza, Vatza, here drink. There is nothing to be afraid of. Nothing. Shall I make more light in the room?

NIJINSKY: *(Drinking with great thirst.)* What? No.

VASSILY: Here. Let me wipe your face. You're sweating. You had a dream? You had a nightmare? . . . There . . . there, all will be well, you'll see. Do you still want to go to the costume ball? Yes? Let me lay out your choices. You should never sleep in the afternoon. It is a heavy, unhealthy sleep. I will open a porthole. Here . . . drink, Vatza. Water will cleanse you.

NIJINSKY: We can't go traveling around the world forever like a caravan of gypsies. We shall never be able to create real artistic work that way. We belong to Russia. We must go home and work there.

END OF ACT I

ACT II
Scene One

We hear the end of a dance tune and voices of a crowd. A tango is begun. Suddenly, we see a figure spotlighted center stage. The figure is dressed in classic tango clothes, only the right half is dressed as a man, the left half is dressed as a woman. We begin with the male half turned toward the audience so that, at first, we believe it is only a man dancing. There is a dramatic turn and then the female side is turned toward the audience. The man/woman does a solo tango in which he first seduces a man and then a woman. Another couple joins in the tango. They all tango.

As the tango is ending, Nijinsky enters. He is not in costume but in evening clothes looking very elegant. The lights come up and we see a circle of grotesquely costumed party goers. Diagheliff with the large papier-mâché head is there also. Someone is dressed as a bird of paradise and another as a gargoyle. Nijinsky is very interested in the steps of the tango.

The tango ends and a bolero begins. Couples pair off. The Diagheliff head approaches Nijinsky. The head is removed and we see the Baron underneath.

BARON: Good evening. Good evening. How handsome you look, but you're not in costume. Or are you? Let me guess, you're disguised as a gentleman. Just joking. Just joking. As you can see, I've come as a monster — our dear Sergei. I must say this head is very hot. No wonder he's hot-headed. Speaking of which, I hope you are still thinking over my proposal. You could work independently. We could build a new theater. Didn't you say you wanted a round theater like the Greeks?

NIJINSKY: Like an eye.

BARON: Yes. Yes. An eye. An eye. Exactly, the cyclopean eye, all seeing. Brilliant. Am I not Sergei incarnate? Well, no business. When I hear music . . . ah . . . I simply must dance. Do I look like an idiot? Don't tell me if I do. I'm having too much fun! But, you must dance too.

(The Baron disappears into the crowd and grabs a partner. Romola enters alone. She is wearing an elegant evening dress and her hair is carefully done. She and Nijinsky nod to each other, but stand silently a little ways apart watching the crowd. Finally, Nijinsky moves closer.)

NIJINSKY: Good evening, mademoiselle.

ROMOLA: Good evening, Monsieur Nijinsky.

(There is much gesturing and pantomime between them to make themselves understood.)

NIJINSKY: Beautiful dress.

ROMOLA: Thank you.

NIJINSKY: Like me, no costume . . .

ROMOLA: I want to feel pretty, not disguised.

NIJINSKY: For stage. I become other. Golden. Tragic. Tonight only myself.

ROMOLA: Me too.

(They smile at each other. They are silent and watch the dance then. They both speak at once.)

ROMOLA: Do you enjoy . . .

NIJINSKY: I must tell you.

ROMOLA: Go on. You must tell me . . . What?

NIJINSKY: No you.

ROMOLA: All right. Do you enjoy this Argentine music?

NIJINSKY: Very much. I learn tango. Very dramatic. You teach?

ROMOLA: I don't know it. I've never been to Buenos Aires before.

(The half man, half woman approaches Nijinsky.)

MAN/WOMAN: Senor Nijinsky, I am so honored. I want to prostrate myself before the altar of your magnificence. I want to tell you how noble, how utterly handsome and graceful you are, yet inexorably masculine. Your greatness humbles us all.

NIJINSKY: *(To Romola.)* I'm sorry . . .

ROMOLA: She said she was delighted to meet you.

NIJINSKY: *(Nijinsky extends his hand, which the woman grabs and kisses.)* You dance very well.

MAN/WOMAN: I hear you love all dances. The tango is queen among dances and, if you like, I will teach you. Yes? *(They look at Romola.)*

ROMOLA: She'd like to teach you to tango. You see, what you wish for comes true.

NIJINSKY: Now?

ROMOLA: Yes.

NIJINSKY: I love to learn, but later. Tell her please.

ROMOLA: Si, le gustaría bailar el tango, pero mas tarde.

MAN/WOMAN: Later then. *(She turns the masculine side to him and then the feminine side.)* You can dance with whomever pleases you most. *(She exits.)*

ROMOLA: She said later is fine.

NIJINSKY: You speak Spanish?

ROMOLA: A little.

NIJINSKY: My French — terrible, like savage. You speak Russian?

ROMOLA: Not a word. I don't suppose you speak Hungarian?

NIJINSKY: I am sorry.

ROMOLA: I'm Hungarian. From Budapest.

NIJINSKY: Am Polish and Russian.

ROMOLA: My father's family is from Poland.

NIJINSKY: You speak Polish? I speak Polish.

ROMOLA: No. My father's family left Poland a hundred years ago.

NIJINSKY: Ah.

ROMOLA: Yes.

> *(They fall silent again. Nijinsky offers Romola his arm.)*

NIJINSKY: Shall we? Away from lights, see sky better.

> *(Romola is enchanted. She takes his arm. They walk a few steps, but it is the dancers who sweep offstage, leaving them alone. The stars brighten and the music grows faint.)*

ROMOLA: Have we crossed . . . *(Gestures.)* crossed the equator?

NIJINSKY: Yes.

ROMOLA: Then, this is a new sky I've never seen before.

NIJINSKY: The New World.

ROMOLA: They say there are new constellations. *(She indicates the stars.)* New stars that can't be seen from the Northern Hemisphere.

NIJINSKY: You know stars?

ROMOLA: No. Do you know the constellations?

NIJINSKY: No.

ROMOLA: I can't believe this!

NIJINSKY: What this?

ROMOLA: Nothing.

NIJINSKY: Tell me, you love dance?

ROMOLA: Dance? Oh, dance. I'm only in the chorus.

NIJINSKY: But Ballets Russes Chorus! Good. You love dance?

ROMOLA: I love dance, but . . .

NIJINSKY: If comes from the heart — is good. Others more virtuosi. Yes. But heart gives grace.

ROMOLA: It can't be only the heart you need. You work hard at it. Endlessly. I hoped . . . I thought that grace might be acquired.

NIJINSKY: Acquired?

ROMOLA: Learned.

NIJINSKY: Ah, yes, hard work, but grace learned goes so far . . . then stops. Grace born. Grace born has no end . . . end?

ROMOLA: No limit. Limitless grace.

NIJINSKY: So serious. But now we laugh. I show you Dimitri. So vain in his looks because he has none. Now Dimitri in love . . . and here comes man with pipe. *(He mimics Dimitri.)* I do perfect Dimitri.

ROMOLA: Yes.

(He walks away suddenly.)

NIJINSKY: I'm tired of lies.

ROMOLA: What lies?

NIJINSKY: You only here with me because I am famous.

ROMOLA: No.

NIJINSKY: Yes. World imitates. Foolish women copy costumes. They put eyes like this *(Indicates slanted eyes.)* with black pencil so look like me . . . Nijinsky, Ballets Russes — Ooooh-la-la. I am rich now. Famous. If not — you never here with me. Truth!

ROMOLA: The truth. When I first saw you — you were already rich and famous, so I can't say what I'd have done if you'd been different.

(Nijinsky stares at her for a moment and then kisses her suddenly.)

NIJINSKY: I love truth.

ROMOLA: And you? You probably think I'm very rich — now don't you?

NIJINSKY: Yes.

ROMOLA: I'm not very rich. Only a little.

(Nijinsky laughs.)

NIJINSKY: Ahhh — so maybe now we be like Tolstoy, my hero, and wife Sofia.

ROMOLA: You'll drive me crazy. What does Tolstoy have to do with us?

NIJINSKY: Tolstoy, a God of truth. In life. In spirit. With truth everything simple. Clear. Pure. I aspire, I dream to live like him. He and wife — no secrets, no dark. Everyday — they write . . . uh . . . diaries . . . diaries. Every night share diaries. Every thought. No secrets. To me, this is peace. And you?

ROMOLA: I don't think I can be so mercilessly candid.

NIJINSKY: Yes. You. I believe you can! I begin. No secrets. Now I tell you . . . I am Catholic because born Polish. But really, am Russian, Russian soul — eat bread, cabbage soup. I love Russia. I miss Russia too much.

ROMOLA: I'm Catholic too.

NIJINSKY: Yes! Yes! . . . so much to tell, my mother . . . her mother . . .

ROMOLA: *(Trying to follow his train of thought.)* Your grandmother.

NIJINSKY: Yes. My grandmother die, starve herself. Die screaming.

ROMOLA: How terrible.

NIJINSKY: You must know!

ROMOLA: What?

NIJINSKY: Stassik, my brother . . . is crazy . . . ugly. *(He imitates Stassik.)* Am good mimic, but great dancer. In dance, I make Stassik beautiful. We talk dance. You are dancer. I must see you dance. If dance, must dance beautifully. I give lessons so you dance more beautiful.

ROMOLA: No. No. I would never even think to ask you.

NIJINSKY: I am not critic. I am teacher. I hate critics. Critics believe public is stupid. Critics think to explain art to stupid public. I hate critic. Critic is death. Calmette, in Paris, he hate my *Faun*. My *Faun* obscene he say. But, never I think obscene. I compose alone, with love. But, Sergei believe critic . . . Sergei is . . . *(Pantomimes being stuck.)*

ROMOLA: Sergei Diagheliff?

NIJINSKY: Never mind.

(Three prostitutes walk by and flirt outrageously with Nijinsky. He is momentarily distracted. Romola, of course, does not see them. The music grows a bit louder and we hear faint sounds from the dance.)

ROMOLA: Monsieur Nijinsky?

NIJINSKY: Yes.

ROMOLA: Are you all right?

NIJINSKY: I want to say to you, before.

ROMOLA: Yes? What were you going to say?

NIJINSKY: You beautiful eyes, but is nose I like.

ROMOLA: My nose?

NIJINSKY: Has character. Now know why. Is good straight Polish nose.

(A couple from the dance strolls by. Then the rest of the dancers sweep in. The Baron disengages himself and approaches Romola and Nijinsky.)

BARON: Where have you been? You don't know what a stir you've caused. Everyone is talking. So interested. So worried. You, Romuschka are a gold digger and you, Vaslav are a fickle flirt . . . or is it the other way around?

ROMOLA: I'm afraid that I have a headache that's quite painful. I must find Anna.

BARON: What? I have said something terrible. Why do I do this? Don't go. Ignore me. Have fun. Ah, but, Vatza, can you imagine Sergei? He would be livid. He would be drunk with so many of his English Scotches by now, but so polite. Would kill you with politeness. But none of us have to worry. He's not here. He's terrified of boats and the ocean. My, ever since a gypsy told him he would die at sea . . .

NIJINSKY: Excuse me, Mademoiselle, Baron. *(He goes to the Half-Man/Half-*

Woman and asks her to dance. She begins to teach him the tango. The pros-titutes also set themselves to learn.)

BARON: My dear, he's Russian . . .

ROMOLA: I must go to bed, Dimitri. Forgive me.

BARON: But I haven't told you about the other gossip. Poor Maicherska. Did you see? She insisted on displaying her lovely shoulders, even with a tremendous love bite on one of them. She tried to say that a washstand had fallen on her, but no one believed her.

ROMOLA: You must tell me everything . . . tomorrow.

BARON: *(As he exits with Romola.)* I won't hear of it. I shall walk you to your cabin. But, did you hear? One of the busboys cut off the last digit of his ring finger to impress his girlfriend? Such cries. We all ran to steerage to see, but, of course, all one could see was this poor girl clutching a rag with a few drops of blood on it. So, perhaps I have exaggerated . . . *(He exits with Romola.)*

Scene Two

Romola and Anna are in Romola's cabin getting ready to go to breakfast. Vass-ily approaches with a large bouquet of white roses. Two maids rush by, one is carrying clean towels.

VASSILY: *(Muttering.)* It will be me! Me! I will be the one who answers the door and lies to her annoying face that you're not in! What do you care if you tire of her or not? This one, that one, this one, that one. What am I, a doorman, a pimp? Wait! You'll see her dance, your heart will drop to your boots and I, Vassily, am here to pick it up and close the door in her face. Achhh . . . *(He knocks loudly on Romola's door. Anna answers.)*

ANNA: Yes?

VASSILY: *(Vassily thrusts the flowers into her arms.)* Here! *(He walks away a few paces. Anna closes the door, a bit puzzled. She looks for a note.)*

ROMOLA: Who is it?

ANNA: Vassily.

ROMOLA: Oh, let me see. What beautiful roses. Anna, Le Petit is flirting with me. With me! Isn't it wonderful? You can make little velvet bags and fill them with petals and I can sleep with them in my bed. My bed. *(She lies down provocatively.)* How do I look?

ANNA: Like your mother interviewing a new actor!

ROMOLA: I hate you. You're terrible.

(Vassily knocks again at the door. Romola jumps up. Anna opens it. He hands her an envelope. As Anna goes to shut the door, he holds it open.)

VASSILY: She is very sly, but I know what she is up to. I see everything. How she talks louder when he enters a room so he'll notice her. How she waits to come out her door until he's in the hallway. She can never understand him. Never. He was born to dance. She is nothing. She will never know his true heart. My God, she will ruin him. Sergei Diagheliff will have a heart attack. It is the end of the Ballets Russes. Finis! *(He is almost in tears. He exits.)*

ANNA: *(Yells after him.)* Moujik! *(She slams the door.)*

ROMOLA: So, who was that?

ANNA: Vassily.

ROMOLA: Again? What did he say?

ANNA: Don't ask me. I don't understand a word of that barbaric language. All I understood was "finis" and he gave me this. It's for you, of course.

ROMOLA: "Finis"? What does he mean finished? *(She opens the letter quickly.)*

ANNA: Go ahead. Read it to me.

ROMOLA: Just a minute while I read it. *(She smells it.)* Mmm. It has his cologne, Guerlain, I believe.

ANNA: I prefer the smell of pipe tobacco and a good energetic walk around the deck. *(Referring to the note.)* If it's in French, you can be sure the Baron wrote it.

ROMOLA: Oh.

ANNA: What does it say?

ROMOLA: He says "forgive me." But I have nothing to forgive him for. What could he mean?

ANNA: Ask him.

ROMOLA: He's sorry he kissed me. He won't be seeing me again. "Finis." What else could it mean?

ANNA: Perhaps these are the only words he knows in French. Let's see. He's misspelled "forgive." Personally, I think he's indulging in a nasty tendency to gain strength from other people's uncertainty! But endless speculation is absurd when three words could set it straight. I can't stand it. Let's go to breakfast.

ROMOLA: I can't face him.

ANNA: Please. I'm starving and Nijinsky has already left. I heard his door close.

ROMOLA: If he ignores me when I pass his table, I'll die. I'll know he meant good-bye. The humiliation. Everyone will see it. No, I can't possibly go.

ANNA: Young love is so enervating. You really must come out and eat something.

ROMOLA: You go. I must dance.

(Anna exits as Romola begins to practice intensely.)

Scene Three

Dining room. The captain is greeting people. Two women are in front. One is older and wears a Bohemian costume with lots of jewelry. The other is quite short.

BOHEMIAN WOMAN: My concepts of society are more developed now. I look at Karl Marx as a very intelligent charismatic revolutionary.

CAPTAIN: Wasn't Karl Marx a Jew?

BOHEMIAN WOMAN: I'm not recanting.

(The two women whisper. The Baron arrives.)

CAPTAIN: Good morning, Baron.

BARON: Morning, morning.

CAPTAIN: Have the fresh oranges. Wonderful. Those monkeys in Sicily picked them.

BARON: Gibraltar has the monkeys. Sicily has the oranges.

CAPTAIN: My mistake. I thought those little dark creatures picking oranges in Sicily were monkeys. *(He laughs alone.)*

(Anna arrives and then Rupert close behind her. He offers her a single flower. The Baron tries discreetly to get his attention, but Rupert ignores him.)

ANNA: Rupert. How dear of you. I hope you slept well.

RUPERT: Why is that man staring at me?

ANNA: Perhaps he thinks he knows you. *(She gives a little wave to the Baron, who looks away.)* That's Baron de Gunsbourg. He's quite charming, I assure you.

RUPERT: He seems odd, but no matter. How would you like to stroll with me and watch the sun dancing fire off the waves?

ANNA: I'd love to, but I haven't had breakfast yet.

RUPERT: Yes, I see.

ANNA: I'm not rejecting you.

RUPERT: Good. Then, perhaps later this morning.

ANNA: That would be lovely.

RUPERT: Your English is astonishingly good.

ANNA: Why thank you.

RUPERT: Yes, well . . . May I watch you eat?

ANNA: What?

RUPERT: I just thought . . . The truth is, I find your mouth delectable and want to watch you . . . well, move it.

ANNA: You're making me quite self-conscious.

RUPERT: Sorry.

ANNA: Yes.

RUPERT: Should I go then?

ANNA: You can stay, but don't stare at my mouth.

RUPERT: Oh, no. I wouldn't think of it.

CAPTAIN: *(Loudly.)* He may be the God of Dance, but I prefer Opera. Ah, Wagner — there is a god!

(Anna is a bit distracted.)

RUPERT: There is a favor I'd like to ask.

ANNA: Yes.

RUPERT: The question's been bothering me. Kept me up in fact. And you, being a woman, well, I'm sure you would know this sort of thing.

ANNA: I'd love to help.

RUPERT: Such fine elocution from such a lovely mouth. Sorry. I got carried away. Sorry.

ANNA: Yes.

RUPERT: The question I have is this — well, it's something my aunty told me. She said women put all kinds of sweet things inside themselves so animals will lick them down there. Is that true?

ANNA: What!? *(She slaps his face and leaves. He follows sheepishly as Romola arrives.)*

RUPERT: Oh dear, don't make a fuss.

(She takes out a handkerchief and wipes her eyes. The captain sees Anna is upset and goes over to her.)

CAPTAIN: May I help you, Mademoiselle? Is something wrong?

ANNA: Loving someone you don't know is a knife in the heart. But I suppose — if a man is twisted or damaged — it's better to know that now.

Scene Four

It is late night. Romola is pacing the deck. She has been crying. A couple passes and she turns away. A waiter with a bottle of champagne rushes through. Romola sits on a deck chair in the dark and lights a cigarette. Nijinsky enters.

NIJINSKY: Mademoiselle.

ROMOLA: *(Startled, Romola is torn between wanting to run away and putting out her cigarette. She does neither.)* Go away.

NIJINSKY: Romola.

ROMOLA: What?!

NIJINSKY: If smoke, no good for dance. *(Mimes coughing.)*

ROMOLA: Leave if it bothers you. *(She turns so he can't see her face. She blows a plume of smoke.)*

NIJINSKY: Eyes red.

ROMOLA: Please, Monsieur Nijinsky.

NIJINSKY: You like me little, so can't say, Vaslav?

ROMOLA: We hardly know each other.

NIJINSKY: True. We walk and know better.

ROMOLA: No, thank you. *(She puts out her cigarette.)*

NIJINSKY: You cry?

ROMOLA: No.

NIJINSKY: I see. But, I think you cry. I think. I think . . . *(He kisses her lightly.)* You cry for me?

ROMOLA: Yes, so?

NIJINSKY: We walk.

ROMOLA: Please spare me and leave. Well, leave! Or do you think I'm so desperate that common decency won't work with me? You're probably right, I'm like one of those silly girls who steal your underwear after a performance. And yes, I've done that too. I've rummaged around in your hotel at Monte Carlo — like an opium addict after cash . . . I snatched a little pillow they said your mother had made which you slept on every night. So there! I stole it! I sleep with it. So — laugh at me!

NIJINSKY: *(Laughing.)* I'm sorry. You speak too fast. You love a pillow?

ROMOLA: You're impossible. You understood every word I said.

NIJINSKY: No. Please, please. Not words. But, you I understand. I feel you. You feel me, too, no? So. *(He takes her hand and puts it through his arm.*

They walk. He points to the sky.) That? So bright. The Southern Cross. See, I have learned. New World.

(They watch the sky in silence or a moment. We hear the water against the hull of the moving ship.)

NIJINSKY: Modern people say no God. Everything "matter in motion." I believe God. Some people God wants . . . *(Gestures.)* . . . together. In the Stars. *(He holds their hands out together. He points to her ring finger, and then to his.)* Romola?

ROMOLA: Yes.

NIJINSKY: Do you want? Voulez-vous? Vous et moi?

ROMOLA: You and I?

NIJINSKY: Yes.

ROMOLA: Married?

NIJINSKY: Oui.

> *(Extended pause between them. A group of four approach. Three women draping themselves over the arm of a tall man in a top hat. The women are laughing.)*

NIJINSKY: You — first woman I love.

ROMOLA: The first woman?

NIJINSKY: Yes.

ROMOLA: The truth.

NIJINSKY: Only you. *(He kisses her hand.)* Vous et moi — Oui.

ROMOLA: Yes. Oh, yes. I'll marry you!

> *(Nijinsky kisses her hand again, then kisses her.)*

ROMOLA: We must telegraph everyone.

NIJINSKY: Not everyone.

ROMOLA: My mother?

NIJINSKY: Yes. Yes.

ROMOLA: Your mother.

NIJINSKY: We tell Baron.

ROMOLA: And the captain for the wedding?

NIJINSKY: No captain. Real wedding. Before God. In Church.

ROMOLA: Yes. In church. A dress! I have no papers! *(She embraces him.)* I knew you had a kind heart. I saw you dance so many, many times. I knew your genius, your nature, everything! Anyone who dances as you do must have a loving heart!

NIJINSKY: I am sorry . . .

ROMOLA: But, Monsieur . . . what do you want from me?

NIJINSKY: From you . . . ?

ROMOLA: Monsieur.

NIJINSKY: Yes?

ROMOLA: Why did you write "forgive me" on the note with your flowers?

NIJINSKY: *(Laughs.)* Dark mood. Russian mood. But at heart — am joyous Pole. So! Now — only beautiful notes. I go write — dancing like Pavlova. *(He imitates Pavlova and glides offstage.)*

END OF ACT II

ACT III
Scene One

Religious chanting; a giant painted cornucopia is background, showing ballerinas spilling out of it. Most are painted but there are two live ballerinas posed as part of the backdrop.

Stage left is an altar of white roses. A priest. We see the wedding at the same time we see Romola's preparations for the wedding.

Nijinsky stands before the priest, as does the Baron. Emilia is dressed exotically and tragically as Medea. Emilia approaches Romola.

EMILIA: Ouff — don't tell me you're wearing blue. It's very unlucky.

ROMOLA: For the love of God!

EMILIA: You know who I am today, or do I need to show you my bloody knife?

ROMOLA: Why would you come to my marriage as Medea, mother?

ANNA: Turn. Shoulders straight.

EMILIA: Marriage can be vicious . . . and tedious. I wouldn't wear blue if I were you. *(Emilia drifts back to the wedding, crossing paths with two ballerinas who rush in.)*

BALLERINA I: Katrina is having hysterics because Nijinsky is marrying you. And, with all the men on board, she has to faint in my husband's arms.

BALLERINA II: Congratulations! I am so happy. So happy for you. I always knew Nijinsky wasn't like that. Let me see your ring. *(She does.)* Very pretty.

BALLERINA I: For my part, I would rather be a mistress. The Aga Kahn sent Marushka seven leopard skins and a gold and ruby belt because she had the sniffles. Of course, Marushka is a prima ballerina.

BALLERINA II: Ouff! Don't tell me you're wearing blue. That's very unlucky.

(They exit whispering together and return to the wedding.)

ROMOLA: I can't stand this dress.

ANNA: Why not? We're almost finished.

ROMOLA: I hate it. I won't wear it. Blue is bad luck.

ANNA: So, now you're superstitious?

ROMOLA: Now is not the time to tempt the gods. I want a white dress. With lace and pearls.

ANNA: Well, you can't wear pearls either, then.

ROMOLA: Why not?

ANNA: Some say they're unlucky too.

ROMOLA: Then I won't get married at all. Forget it!

ANNA: You don't mean that.

ROMOLA: Why not? Who knows what marriage is! . . . I know — I'll write in a note. Yes — find me some note paper. I'll write him. Ah, yes, I'll begin . . . "Forgive me . . . "

ANNA: Sit. Breathe deeply. Now, what's wrong, Romuschka? What has you in this state?

ROMOLA: I'm going to die of fear.

ANNA: Is it the sex?

ROMOLA: No, no, no.

ANNA: He still loves Diagheliff?

ROMOLA: There's something worse. Oh, God — it's terrible.

ANNA: Your menstruation. It always comes at the worst times!

ROMOLA: Don't be stupid!

ANNA: It's stupid of you to keep me guessing. So die of fear. Go ahead. Then I won't have to drive myself crazy trying to find a white dress in two days!

ROMOLA: What's the use. It's a farce.

ANNA: Roma — he loves you.

ROMOLA: But he hasn't seen me dance.

(Anna exits and returns with a cream-colored dress. At first, Romola refuses to put it on, but then grudgingly lets Anna dress her. Nijinsky is at the wedding. The Baron arrives and whispers to him. He checks his watch. Romola arrives. The Baron takes her arm and leads her to Nijinsky. Emilia arrives alone dressed as Medea.)

EMILIA: September 10, 1913. Ladies and gentlemen, *(Indicating the wedding.)* the Tower of Babel. The priest is speaking Latin; Romola, Hungarian; the Baron, Russian; and Le Petit Nijinsky, Polish. I have a headache and I'm not even invited.

(The priest and the others act as a chorus with Romola and Nijinsky as soloists. The priest says the words, the chorus chants them softly while Romola and Nijinsky respond to the priest.)

PRIEST: I, Romola, will stay with you, Vaslav, in happiness and misfortune, in health and sickness till death do us part.

FEMALE CHORUS: *(Chanting.)*
I will stay with you
I will stay with you
With you
With you
In happiness and misfortune
Till death

Death
Death
Do us paaa-art!

MALE CHORUS:
I will stay with you
With you
With you
In happiness and misfortune
Till death
Death
Death
Do us paaa-art!

ROMOLA: I, Romola, will stay with you, Vaslav, in happiness and misfortune, in health and sickness till death do us part.

PRIEST: I, Vaslav, will stay with you, Romola, in happiness and misfortune, in health and sickness till death do us part.

BARON: I, Vaslav, will stay with you, Romola, in happiness and misfortune, in health and sickness till death do us part.

NIJINSKY: I, Vaslav, will stay with you, Romola, in happiness and misfortune, in health and sickness till death do us part.

PRIEST: You may now exchange the rings.

(Romola is almost in tears. She holds out her hand. It is shaking. The Baron gives Nijinsky the ring, which he slips on her finger. The Baron hands Romola a ring, which she slips on Nijinsky's finger as well. He brings her hand to his lips and kisses it.)

PRIEST: In the name of The Father, The Son, and The Holy Spirit, I now pronounce you man and wife. Let no man put asunder whom God has joined today.

(They all cross themselves. Everyone rushes to congratulate the bride and groom. There is much kissing and embracing. The guests leave except for Anna who wheels in a lone bed. She undresses and gets in and falls asleep. The three ballerinas change costume in full sight of the audience and become three prostitutes. They exit and return with a gaily decorated table with a wrapped present on it. Now we see two isolated areas: one with the bed and the other with the table. Overcome with curiosity, one of the prostitutes makes a move to open the present. Another one slaps her.)

Scene Two

Hotel suite in Buenos Aires. Romola and Nijinsky enter. The prostitutes are eating from a table and stop guiltily when the two enter.

NIJINSKY: Our rooms.

ROMOLA: Our rooms.

(They quickly separate and explore the room.)

ROMOLA: Look — a cold supper.

NIJINSKY: Anna sent.

ROMOLA: A view of the park. I love palm trees.

NIJINSKY: Yes. Paris with palms.

ROMOLA: Yes. Almost.

NIJINSKY: *(Indicates a small pile of gifts.)* For you. From me.

ROMOLA: I love presents. Shall I . . . ?

NIJINSKY: *(Brings over glasses and champagne.)* Champagne?

ROMOLA: Wait!

NIJINSKY: What?

ROMOLA: I'll pour for you. *(She does.)*

NIJINSKY: *(He kisses her neck.)* Maia jeiia.

ROMOLA: What does that mean?

NIJINSKY: My wife.

(They smile. Nijinsky dips a finger in the champagne and makes the sign of the cross on her face.)

NIJINSKY: I bless, "Together forever through fire and water."

ROMOLA: Is that something holy?

NIJINSKY: *(Laughs.)* No. In Polish. In hard times, my family say this.

ROMOLA: My family says, in Hungarian mind you, *(She dips her finger and makes the cross on his heart.)* "May this blessing preserve you from all evil." There! You're safe! Now what shall we do?

NIJINSKY: We marry fast. Now — everything slow. *(He kisses her.)*

ROMOLA: Except the presents. Do you have what I bought you?

NIJINSKY: Yes. *(Exits. One prostitute is curious and follows him. He returns with a silk robe. Romola is trying to decide which present to open.)*

ROMOLA: Put it on. Does it fit?

(Nijinsky starts to put it on over his clothes.)

ROMOLA: No. You have to take your jacket off. *(She takes his jacket off.)* And your cravat and cummerbund. *(When she gets to the cummerbund, she backs away.)* . . . I'll let you do it.

(He tries on the robe.)

ROMOLA: You look like the emperor of . . . *(She pulls the skin near her eyes to make them slant.)* . . . of Mongolia!
(They both laugh. The prostitutes make their eyes slanted as well and look at each other and are amused.)

NIJINSKY: *(He picks out a large box.)* For you.

ROMOLA: No. I like this one!

NIJINSKY: That one tomorrow!

ROMOLA: Tomorrow? Why? What's in it? No. I think this is exactly the one I must open today! *(She takes a smaller present and opens it.)* A book! A picture book. It's Chinese. How exotic.

NIJINSKY: It is very old.

ROMOLA: Look how beautiful it's made. All the figures are hand painted. The writing's so black, but it's Chinese. I can't read it.
(One of the prostitutes goes to look at the book and bursts out laughing. Another elbows her. The three look closely at the pictures and then two assume a sexual position. The third checks the book and directs them. Romola looks more closely at the book.)

ROMOLA: They're having sex!
(A prostitute looks and directs the other two into another more flamboyant position. It is difficult, all three consult the book and try again.)

NIJINSKY: I wanted for . . . You are offended.

ROMOLA: No. It's funny. It's fascinating . . . once you get used to it.

NIJINSKY: Like you. *(He kisses her. They kiss and become passionate. He takes off his tie and cummerbund. He helps her out of her dress. He has her stand in her underclothes. They kiss again. He turns her gently around and kneels and caresses her buttocks softly and rests his head against her. Diagheliff enters.)*

DIAGHELIFF: Have you forgotten, you're the god of dance? Get off your knees and get some rest and, for God's sake, make her shave her pubis! *(He exits. Nijinsky rises.)*

ROMOLA: What? But where are you going? Vaslav. Vaslav? We must sleep beside each other.

NIJINSKY: *(Kisses her hand.)* Forgive me. *(He goes to one bedroom and closes the door.)*

ROMOLA: But . . . only people who fall asleep and wake up together really belong to each other.

Scene Three

Romola is doing warm-up in her room. She is in practice clothes. In another part of the stage we see a barre and a piano where an accompianist is playing Stravinsky. He falters. Nijinsky, in practice clothes but with his face made up, pounds the piano.

Vassily knocks on Romola's door and when she answers motions for her to follow him.

VASSILY: Come?

ROMOLA: Where?

VASSILY: Monsieur Nijinsky. Practice.

ROMOLA: Rehearsal isn't for two hours !

(Vassily shrugs.)

ROMOLA: He wants to see me dance?

(Vassily shrugs.)

ROMOLA: Now?

VASSILY: Yes.

ROMOLA: *(Looks around wildly.)* I can't.

VASSILY: Good. *(He smirks and leaves.)*

ROMOLA: *(Runs out after him, crossing herself repeatedly.)* Oh, God . . .

(In the rehearsal room, Vassily enters and waits for Nijinsky to finish.)

NIJINSKY: No. What are you thinking? Stop! *(He paces.)* It's presto prestissimo. One and two and three and four five, one and two and three and four five. You're playing like you're dragging a dead horse behind you. I can't believe you've played for the greatest dancers of the Ballets Russes. One and two and three and four five. Play it as Stravinsky wrote it. He is a musical genius, you are not!

(Romola enters, ready to greet him. Nijinsky ignores her.)

NIJINSKY: Enough! We have an opening tonight. Do you want to ruin everything? Go practice where I can't hear you. Prestissimo, prestissimo, cretin! Go ahead. Go!

(Vassily is about to speak with Nijinsky when the Baron pops in.)

BARON: *(Popping in for a minute.)* The girls are hysterical. We opened the trunks and the dresser packed only left shoes. And Arkady has a splinter in his foot and can't dance. All the doctors are at Mass. Oh, yes, they're sanding the stage floor so we can't possibly get in until four . . . which really means seven if we're lucky. It's a disaster. Why am I doing this? . . . Sorry to bother you. *(He exits.)*

(Romola enters out of breath and she and Vassily exchange venomous glances.)

ROMOLA: *(Steps close to Nijinsky and whispers.)* You sent for me.

NIJINSKY: Vassily, come here. Please ask Mlle. Rambert to come down in an hour. We'll practice our *pas de deux.*

VASSILY: I would like to watch this practice.

NIJINSKY: I don't care particularly what you like this morning, Vassily.

VASSILY: Very good, sir. An hour then? Won't you need two or three — with her?!

NIJINSKY: Vassily! Go!

(Vassily bows and exits.)

ROMOLA: He loathes me. He was the only person in the entire company who didn't come to our wedding.

NIJINSKY: Forget about it. It's nothing. We have an opening tomorrow. An opening is everything. One chance to win an audience. There are no second chances. What was I thinking? I should have seen you dance sooner!

ROMOLA: You're speaking Russian, Vaslav.

NIJINSKY: The dance needs precision, refinement. The slightest deviation, the smallest undue tension in the rhythm of the movement, any small mistake can destroy the whole composition. The dance becomes a caricature.

ROMOLA: Vaslav, I can't understand you.

NIJINSKY: I give lesson. Go to the barre. Warm up.

(Romola goes to the barre and begins warm-up exercises. Nijinsky watches. She falters. She corrects herself. Emilia and Diagheliff enter. Diagheliff is being very gallant. He bows and lets her enter first. He is in evening dress and to go out, and Emilia is costumed as an Egyptian. They shush each other and laugh together softly, but stand to one side and watch.)

NIJINSKY: Hold. Heel forward!

ROMOLA: It won't move. My leg is already turned out.

NIJINSKY: Leg not turned out. No. Wrong. It is not heel. Movement begins here! *(He adjusts her pelvis.)*

ROMOLA: In my pelvis. Here?

NIJINSKY: Yes. Yes. Pelvis move forward, then heel correct. Yes. There. Very good.

DIAGHELIFF: What did you expect? An artist to share your heart and soul? My poor Vaslav. Tsk, tsk, tsk.

EMILIA: She's quite good and quite beautiful.

DIAGHELIFF: Madame, she has no rhythm. A dancer without rhythm is a freak.

NIJINSKY: *Battement tendu.* Point the toe. Stretch. Stretch. Hold. *(To Diagheliff.)* You're jealous of my beautiful bride. Admit it, Sergei.

DIAGHELIFF: Do you really know what it means to cross me, Vatza? And to cross me like this? For a cow? I could almost cry for your ignorance.

NIJINSKY: . . . Now side, to back, to side, to front . . . repetez. *(To Diagheliff.)* You will be happy for me even though you can't love this way. She is brutal and sweet. Her eyes are blue green like the sea at Lido. Think of the Lido, Sergei, where you find all your beautiful little Italian boys stretched out on the beach, powdered with sand as if they are delectable blini covered with sugar. You will forgive me.

DIAGHELIFF: You'll make babies, not ballets!

NIJINSKY: *(To Romola.)* Close to fifth position. Close. No. No. No. *(He adjusts her foot.)* Close. Fourth.

(She loses her balance.)

NIJINSKY: *Porte-bras.* Shoulder drop. Drop . . . Neck long. *(He adjusts her.)* Developez à la seconde. High, more high. No. Not hip. Hip down! Feet arch. Hold.

(She stumbles.)

NIJINSKY: On floor now.

ROMOLA: Do you want to see my part of the *pas de trois?*

NIJINSKY: No. Walk.

ROMOLA: Walk?

NIJINSKY: Yes. Walk now.

ROMOLA: Have I done something wrong? I want to dance for you now.

NIJINSKY: No. Walk, please. Away. Stop. *(He takes first one hand and then the other and shakes it hard.)* Loose. Now walk. Not in danse de style. Fingers close. Natural. *(He takes her hand again and shakes it harder.)* For beautiful hands, watch children. Children natural always. Concentration. Romola!

ROMOLA: *(To her mother.)* Am I doing badly?

EMILIA: *(Staring at Diagheliff.)* Who wouldn't with all this faggotry!

DIAGHELIFF: Bury her in the back of the Corps de Ballet, please. I could kill that idiot Gunsbourg. This is all his doing. But, you haven't slept with her, you can have an annulment. *(He turns back.)*

NIJINSKY: Stop. You work too hard.

ROMOLA: You told me to work hard!

NIJINSKY: Dance not work. You are too tight. You move like cripple.

ROMOLA: I'm about to die from nerves. Of course I'm tight, but you can't understand because you're a machine, not a human being!

NIJINSKY: Dance never tight. *(He does a few steps to demonstrate. He speaks in Russian out of frustration.)* You see? Dance is simple. Like one breath and then another. Every step, every action is separate, but it must seem inevitable. You see? Like the natural and harmonious consequence of all previous action.

ROMOLA: Please speak French, Vaslav.

NIJINSKY: Ach! *(He walks away.)*

ROMOLA: Mother, what have I done?

EMILIA: It's what I've done. Oh, Romola, you know he will be insane.

ROMOLA: Don't say that. How can you say that?

EMILIA: Can't you see?

ROMOLA: He's an artist that's all and he's Russian!

EMILIA: He's furious. His pupils are dilated and he reeks like an animal.

ROMOLA: He has the face of a primitive god.

EMILIA: His grandmother went mad and starved herself to death —

ROMOLA: So? Papa killed himself and I'm not insane.

EMILIA: He has a brother who sits drooling in a lunatic asylum.

ROMOLA: Stassik fell two stories and damaged his head. Everyone knows that.

EMILIA: You want to be his nursemaid the rest of your life. Is this what you aspire to do?

ROMOLA: We'll have a beautiful life. Vaslav will be besieged with admirers on every continent. I will give my life for him and we will be so happy and fulfilled. I wish you could be happy for me and not tell me your cruel intentions as if they were prophecies.

EMILIA: I've failed you. How tragic. I only wanted to save you from one disillusionment and now I've thrown you into the path of another.

ROMOLA: What are you talking about?

EMILIA: Your father. Your damn father. I let you worship him. I let you delude yourself that love was his God and his life was a noble sacrifice. You were devastated when he died. You worshipped him. I wanted to preserve your love for him like a relic from a totally destroyed world. It made you so happy to think that somewhere in this world love was pure and endless and tragic. But it's not true. It's a lie. Your father didn't die for love. He died for greed. He embezzled money. There was a great scandal.

ROMOLA: That's a lie! You could have saved him.

EMILIA: It wasn't I who placed a gun in his hand and made him blow his brains out. It was his so-called friends in Budapest who gave him the revolver and suggested he end his life honorably!

ROMOLA: You're lying. You can't stand to see me happy, can you?

EMILIA: If he had cared for either of us, he would have lived. You see my terrible mistake? You now think love is like art where you live and die for a moment of terrible perfection. You think this man is normal. Don't. Please. But to measure love by art — let me tell you if he equates the two then he is heartless or mad. This about this. Leave him and if you get pregnant — have an abortion.

(Emilia waits for Romola's response. Romola approaches Nijinsky.)

ROMOLA: My *pas de trois?*

(Emilia exits.)

NIJINSKY: *(Not looking at her.)* Dance. Dance. You may weep, but you must work. Even for the very back row of the Corps de Ballet. Dance. An artist must have one goal, one goal only — to perfect himself, to attain new heights in his art. Always, always. *(He turns, hoping to be embraced by Diagheliff, who stands back.)* What have I done? What have I done? She is not an artist. I've thrown my life away!

DIAGHELIFF: Good! Suffer! Die! I look at you and glass explodes in my heart. You want to puncture my heart and kill me? I can't endure this. I won't work with you. I can't work with you. I don't need you. There are stables full of young men. Academies! And, if they are not geniuses, they are beautiful and talented. The public will hardly know the difference. *(He exits.)*

Scene Four

Anna is standing in a hotel lobby. This can be designated by a potted palm and a chair. Dimitri joins her.

BARON: Am I late? Well, it's no wonder. I've just discovered the world's greatest work of fiction — our contract with the theater! Nothing is true. Nothing! They promised us twenty musicians and we have five who speak no distinguishable language I'm acquainted with. Yes, there are bathrooms, but none of them work and three dancers have diarrhea. I'm beginning to detest producing. It's debasing. Where is Romola and how are you, my dear?

ANNA: *(A little testy.)* I'm fine, Baron. Romola should be here any minute.

(A bellboy walks by rapidly with a suitcase that is far too heavy for him. The man with the pipe comes by arm in arm with an older, obviously wealthy woman who has a cane. They stop to confer together nearby. Both Dimitri and Anna stare at them. The man with a pipe and the woman then stroll by. Neither gives Anna and Dimitri a glance.)

ANNA: I hate the English.

BARON: Yes. Despicable.

ANNA: Do you know that man?

BARON: What man? Where? Which man?

ANNA: That man with the pipe.

BARON: Oh, no. Never met him.

ANNA: Don't bother. He's a sadist.

(Two maids pass. Romola comes in with the bellboy carrying suitcases. She is accompanied by the Madonna and Child, although no one sees them. The Madonna, however, is intrigued with everything that is going on around her.)

ROMOLA: We're to be in Room 234. *(She kisses Dimitri on both cheeks.)* I'm so glad you're here, Dimitri. I couldn't do this without you.

(They walk, but it is basically scenery that is moved on and off around them by the bellboy and maids. Romola lights a cigarette. They are standing at the edge of the hotel room. We can see Nijinsky directing Vassily where to put an armload of clothes. Romola smokes quickly and then puts out her cigarette with the toe of her shoe.)

ROMOLA: This will be my last cigarette.

ANNA: You sound like a condemned prisoner.

(Dimitri strides into the room and greets Nijinsky. Romola, Anna, and the Madonna follow carrying Romola's suitcases.)

BARON: Vaslav. So good to see you settled. This is lovely. What a view. It does remind me of that little section of Paris with all the strange shops. You know the one — where you can buy a new cranial saw or a wax model of a human nose complete with hair. You did know I was coming. *(Looking from Nijinsky to Romola, who looks distinctly uncomfortable.)* Ah, well. I think I'll have a shot of vodka. Vassily can get it for me. *(He follows Vassily.)*

(Romola and Nijinsky embrace briefly.)

NIJINSKY: Good morning.

ROMOLA: How was the theater?

NIJINSKY: Good. Very good. Big.

(They speak at the same time.)

ROMOLA: Where shall I put my things?

NIJINSKY: Tea?

ROMOLA: Yes. My things?

NIJINSKY: There.

ROMOLA: Anna, please take my suitcases in there for me.

BARON: Let me.

ROMOLA: Don't unpack them.

(*He takes the suitcases from Anna and the Madonna into one of the bedrooms. They both follow him offstage.*)

NIJINSKY: Vassily, would you get us some tea.

(*Vassily exits.*)

ROMOLA: I hope he won't poison it.

NIJINSKY: The Baron?

(*The Baron enters.*)

ROMOLA: Yes, well . . . there are some private things to say, but obviously, we must understand everything between us . . . so I've brought the Baron.

BARON: Yes, you see, she said that this is rather embarrassing, but . . .

NIJINSKY: Please, Dimitri. Don't insult me. I can look at her face and understand.

BARON: He says to continue.

ROMOLA: I'm nervous.

NIJINSKY: Tell her, she must talk without stopping. I am very nervous.

BARON: Vaslav asks that you speak freely.

ROMOLA: I can guess what he said. It's not so easy to speak as he supposes. (*She faces Nijinsky directly.*) What did you think of my dancing? Will I be able to dance like Pavolova, like Karsavina?

NIJINSKY: No, never.

BARON: Why not? She's very lithe and graceful.

NIJINSKY: You begin too late.

ROMOLA: I understand.

NIJINSKY: But, I compose little dances for you dance beautifully.

ROMOLA: Don't bother. I will never dance in public again.

NIJINSKY: But that's silly. I tell her an artist can never . . .

ROMOLA: An artist what? I'm not an artist. God, I'm so sick of hearing this!

BARON: You have to go slower. He'll never understand and he forbids me to translate. This is a disaster.

NIJINSKY: How can I love you if you are not an artist? An artist can traverse a whole world — by pacing from one wall of a room to the other. You see only four walls. A prison. I can't live like that! I asked you to learn to dance, because for me, dancing is the highest art in the world. I wanted to teach you, but you became frightened. You didn't trust me. At that moment, I felt death. I had put myself in the hands of someone who could never comprehend me.

BARON: Vaslav wants you to dance.

NIJINSKY: Baron, STOP!

ROMOLA: Then it's settled. We shall get an annulment!

BARON: This is impossible. I cannot be put in this situation! Vaslav, be reasonable. I must translate. These are very delicate matters. How will you understand each other?

(Nijinsky turns his back.)

BARON: Romuschka, what am I to do? Please I beg you — both of you — come to some agreement. Surely something can be done.

(Romola is silent.)

BARON: So what shall I do? What shall I tell Diagheliff? Oh, yes, Sergei — or had you forgotten. He must be told something. What?

NIJINSKY: Shall we tell him about our intimate little dance company, Baron?

BARON: No. I tell you — I am haunted by stupidity. I see it now. I scarcely have the character for my own relationships, let alone an entire company of them. I don't know how Sergei does it. *(He looks from one to the other. He shrugs.)* I suppose I'll have to ask him — if he's still speaking to me. *(He exits.)*

ANNA: Romola, would you like to see where I've placed your things?

ROMOLA: Not now, Anna. Please leave.

NIJINSKY: *(To Anna.)* — Tell Vassily not enter.

ANNA: *(Happily.)* Oh, he'll love that. *(She exits.)*

ROMOLA: Did you understand what I said? We haven't slept together. The Catholic Church will grant us an annulment.

NIJINSKY: Yes. I know this "annulment." I will do what God tells me. *(He closes his eyes.)*

ROMOLA: Do what your heart tells you.

(Three prostitutes steal quietly out of the other bedroom and slip around Nijinsky, rubbing sinuously against him. He opens his eyes and steps from them. He moves toward Romola and cups her cheek with his hand.)

NIJINSKY: Only God knows our heart.

ROMOLA: People don't love each other because of the love of God or the fear of God. We love someone because the world doesn't make sense if we don't.

NIJINSKY: Sense! *(He laughs softly.)* Roma, Romuschka, you are a dangerous girl for me. You have the willfulness of a rich girl. You live entitled, oblivious but you suffer. You would like money and jewels. I am not a prince. Only an artist, but I will give you all my money and jewels. You love me and I am drawn to you with iron straps. Who knows what it is. You are innocent and wicked and brave. And you're beautiful — that doesn't hurt. You are more beautiful than you are supposed to be. So beautiful that you should be stupid, but you're not stupid. I love you. *(He kisses her. She*

kisses him. The prostitutes put the arms of one around the other. They separate her legs and place his knee between them. Romola and Nijinsky become
more passionate. He holds her fiercely to him.)

ROMOLA: What is it, Vaslav?

NIJINSKY: You need words. I don't have them. I am a lullabyer. Rockabye, bye,
bye, bye. Rockabye, bye, bye.

(Romola disengages herself and goes to dress for an upcoming performance she
will attend. The Madonna brings out a simple wooden chair and places it
near the cross and exits. Nijinsky walks to the chair and sits down, staring
venomously at the audience. He remains there throughout the following scene.

Other characters enter with chairs and place them so they are facing the
audience — as if the audience is the performance. Romola enters. Others.
Emilia and Diagheliff enter together. Emilia has a pair of binoculars that
Diagheliff wants to borrow. We hear the opening of Petrouschka. The audience and Nijinsky watch.)

Scene Five

*Diagheliff bends toward Emilia and whispers. His voice, however, is a voice
projected over the music and dancing. Is should have a "microphone" sound
and be similar to the voices in the beginning of the play.*

DIAGHELIFF: This is his greatest role, ma chère . . . oh, and then end, exquisite. Petrouschka dies, of course. For love, what else is there? Watch him,
how he suffers, how he extends with a trembling arm his agony and sad-
ness to the only people who understand him — the gray common crowd
of Russia. Is it not extraordinary how he seems to be made of wood and
yet executes the most difficult steps? Look at those pirouettes and *toures
en l'air*. Perfect, perfect, but always in character. And you will see the suf-
fering of this doll, Petrouschka. In his last breath, even, Petrouschka's heart
is filled for love for the ballerina. He sends her his last tragic kiss. See
how he presses the palm of his hand to his pale lips and *(Petrouschka on
stage is doing these actions facing Romola.)* trembling, jerkings . . . see . . .
see how he does it! He extends his arm toward the vastness of space. Ah,
yes. *(He stands.)* Bravo, bravissimo. *(He stands and claps as the others. The
music stops but Nijinsky keeps dancing. Romola stands.)* But what's wrong?

ROMOLA: He is still dancing!

DIAGHELIFF: Stop, Vatza!

ROMOLA: Oh, Vaslav, stop!

Scene Six
Le Deuxième Mariage

Everyone but Romola and Nijinsky leave. Romola makes a slight costume change, which is brought to her by the Madonna who helps her dress and then exits with the clothes that Romola has discarded. The Madonna returns and waits and watches. The sky begins to fill with eyes again, although quite slowly.

Nijinsky is still staring at the audience with palpable anger. Uncomfortable pause.

ROMOLA: Please tell me what the pianist should play for you.

NIJINSKY: Quiet. Do not speak.

(Romola retreats. Silence. Suddenly, Nijinsky is on his feet.)

NIJINSKY: I used to deceive my wife because I had too much semen. I had to ejaculate. I liked whores, but I did not ejaculate into them. I have lots of semen and I keep it for another child. I hope I will be presented with the gift of a boy. God is a prick who breeds with one woman. I am a man who breeds children with one woman.

I used to give my wife roses that cost five francs a piece. I brought her roses every day, twenty, thirty at a time. I loved giving her white roses. Red roses frightened me. I loved her terribly. But I already felt death. My wife wept and wept. She suffered. I wanted a simple life. I loved Tolstoy. I loved the dance. I wanted to work. I worked hard. I was like a draft horse, whipped until it fell and all its guts dropped out its ass. I lost heart. I noticed I wasn't liked. I weep and I weep. I love Tolstoy. I love Russia although I am a Catholic Pole. I will work on a farm. I will practice masturbation and spiritualism. I will eat everyone I can get a hold of. I will stop at nothing. I will make love to my wife's mother and my child. I will weep, but I will do everything God commands me.

I do not love anyone. I am evil. I wish to harm everyone and be good to myself. I am an egoist. I am not God. I am beast and a predator.

(Romola walks over again and says sottovoce.)

ROMOLA: Please won't you begin. Dance *Sylphides*.

NIJINSKY: How dare you disturb me? I am not a machine. I will dance when I feel like it! You are stupid. You are beasts. You are meat. You are death. I feel God. I feel God. You came to be amused, but God wants to arouse you. I will dance frightening things. See? I can mimic a crazy person like my brother, Stassik. I can be a whore, an old Jew with peyes, a cripple, an aristocrat. Who says workmen are good? Workmen are as depraved as aristocrats. They have less money. They drink cheap wine. My stomach is clean. I do not like meat. I saw how a calf was killed. I saw how a pig was killed. I saw it and felt their tears. I could not bear it. See? I can dance like a dying pig, like a dying Czar, like a soldier creeping in the shadow of the gate and shot — "unh" — in the snow. Silence? *(He executes violent, angry movements. The Madonna goes over to him and starts to dance with him.)* Ay, I feel God. He loves me. I love him. Today . . . Today . . . Silence! *(The Madonna stops her dance and retreats.)*

NIJINSKY: Silence! Today is the day of my marriage with God! *(Nijinsky throws himself to the ground and makes fucking motions to the floor. The Madonna puts her arm around Romola.)*

END OF PLAY

T for 2

By Gina Barnett

THE AUTHOR

Gina Barnett has worked in the theater as an actress, writer, teacher, and director for over twenty-five years. She is a member of the Writers Guild of America, East; The Dramatists Guild, and Ensemble Studio Theater. Her work has been published by Applause Theatre Books, Smith and Kraus, and Klett Verlag in Germany. Her work has been produced off-Broadway, regionally, and in Canada.

AUTHOR'S NOTE

A probing look at a near-future society and four lone survivors, who—despite their differences and the soul-crushing atmosphere of their repressive society—cobble together a loving, raucous, underground family.

INTRODUCTORY STATEMENT

T for 2 is a five-character play, but there is a sixth and *equally* essential character: the "Above World." While the majority of *T for 2* takes place in Emmett's underground bunker, it is essential that the "Above World"—its stink, sounds, the fact that everyone is masked, that the tools and agents of terror are everywhere—be visually and *dramatically* presented as well. While there are no "dialogue scenes" in that world, its threatening and ever-present danger weaves throughout the play, building in dramatic intensity as the "search" for the bunker progresses. This state of increasing conflict between the "home" below and the "terror tactics" above can and *should* be dramatized by vivid, wordless scenes, sounds, and — when possible — actual *soldiers' actions*, in between the "dialogue" scenes in the bunker and — where indicated — *during* those scenes. *T for 2* should be performed without an intermission.

ORIGINAL PRODUCTION

T for 2 won the Theatrefest Regional Playwriting Contest and was produced by Geoffrey Newman on July 6, 2001. It was directed by Frits Ferres; scenic design was by Jehudi vanDijk; costume design was by Karen Ledger; lighting design was by Herrick Goldman; sound design was by Michael Wojchik; the production stage manager was Dale Smallwood; graphic design was done by The Lost Boys Consortium. *T for 2* was cast as follows:

EMMETT	Jerry Rockwood
FRANK	Brian Edwards
BRI	Gretchen Krich
LO	Barbara Haas

CHARACTERS

    EMMETT: An older gentleman, between 60 and 75 years of age
    FRANK: A young male soldier, between 18 and 22 years of age
    LO: An older woman, between 55 and 65 years of age
    BRI: A slightly younger woman, between 35 and 45 years of age
    A GUARD: Played by actress who plays Bri

SETTING

    New York. The majority of the action takes place in a bunker-like room underneath Manhattan's Metropolitan Museum of Art. There are two other "suggested" sets as well: a tunnel, and an exhibition or museum space. The production requirements are not elaborate and might be best served with suggestive props and lighting. There are, however, sound cues and effects that create an overall ambiance and are integral to the production.

TIME

    The future.

T FOR 2

ACT I
Scene One

Lights up on a man sitting in a chair reading to himself. His room is small and windowless, a bunker really, full of clutter: books in a locked-up bookcase, a worn armchair, a tattered landscape on the wall. A silver tea set, last vestige of better times, sits precariously on a decrepit sideboard. Clearly efforts have been made around the room, which feels more like a cell than a room, to brighten the inherent despair. The man Emmett is sharp-eyed and quick-witted. He wears a tattered sweater and worn-out pants. Delighting in his reading, he sings/mutters bits of a poem he's reading.

EMMETT: "O Blush not so! O blush not so!
　　Or I shall think you knowing;
　　And if you smile the blushing while . . . Then maidenheads are going . . ."

"There's a blush for won't, and a blush for shan't,
And a blush for having done it:"

"There's a blush for thought and a blush for naught,
And a blush for just begun it . . . "
(Abrupt and startling, the sound (or suggestion) of boots marching overhead. The sound grows closer, louder, more threatening, followed by rapid rhythmic knocking on a door. Emmett rises, tucking the book under his chair, quickly shutting the doors to his bookcase. He answers the knock with a single knock of his own, is answered by another signal, then unlocks the door. A soldier, wearing army fatigues and a full-face-covering oxygen mask, enters. He removes his mask and hangs it on a small hook by the door. He does this in a manner as unremarkable as if he were hanging up a hat. This is Frank. He is tense and rarely, if ever, makes eye contact. He struggles mightily with breathing in the first moments after removing his mask. But Emmett stands by, encouraging him, breathing with him, coaching. Then . . .)
EMMETT: What a surprise! I wasn't expecting you today, Frank.
FRANK: The statue is being unveiled later. There's so much going on I was able to slip away.

EMMETT: Well done. Come in, come in, my boy. Sit. Let me make a fresh pot. *(He picks up the teapot and starts to exit. Frank steps forward to intercept him.)*

FRANK: May I?

EMMETT: Absolutely! *(Emmett holds out the pot. Frank takes it, cradles it in his arms, and exits. Quickly, Emmett hides the mask and oxygen tank. He digs out the book of Keats. Frank re-enters a moment later without the pot.)*

EMMETT: I was just thumbing through this — poor Keats, died so young. Never outgrew his hormones . . . I remember the day I picked this volume up. Half price at a little country bookstore. After, I hiked up a mountain. A woman hiker rounded the bend. We chatted, shared a box of Sunmaid raisins. We could have . . . right there, on a cool thick moss, our bodies nursing kittens burrowing into the moist bosomy earth . . . We . . . could . . . have . . . BUT!

You know, I swore my whole life I'd never be one of those old people who do nothing but talk about the past. Terrible, the promises you break. Isn't it, Frankie?

FRANK: *Frank*, Emmett.

EMMETT: All right . . . So! What'll it be today, "Frank"? Got time to do it "all"? Splendid! Let me check on the tea *(Emmett exits through a small darkened upstage passage. Frank looks around.)*

EMMETT: *(Off.)* Surplus power's off, Frank. *(Emmett re-enters.)*

EMMETT: I left the pot on the plate in case it comes on early. It's good you came, I'm running low on supplies.

(Frank removes a small handheld device and holds it up to Emmett's neck, near his collar where there is embedded some sort of scanner. The device makes a sound. He pushes a button or two, then pockets it.)

EMMETT: How tall is the statue?

FRANK: Twenty stories. The only thing on the horizon.

EMMETT: Hasn't he had enough of himself already?

FRANK: He was the first, Emmett. The hope. You mustn't dishonor —

EMMETT: — Statues honoring men of ideas, okay. But just because this . . . this individual popped out of a silicon womb fertilized by a bunch of chemicals, why should he get to be Jesus?

FRANK: Get to be who?

EMMETT: Just an expression. Too much for today . . .

FRANK: Inside, at the base of the statue will be a New Memory Center. Persons will be able to go there to see evidence.

EMMETT: Of . . . what?

FRANK: Proof . . . of . . . "Attestation of . . . Excellence!" That's it.

EMMETT: Well! I'll be sure to get my ticket! Be first on line . . . So! Shall we start with dinner? Home-cooked or restaurant?

FRANK: How 'bout we have "hors d'oeuvres" at home and *then* go out?

EMMETT: You're inspired today, Frank! . . . Hors d'oeuvres . . . let's see . . . "Mozzarella!"

FRANK: " . . . Moz . . . arella."

EMMETT: A cheese. Mostly a texture really, because the flavor was so subtle, like chewy milk. Smoking it was quite popular.

FRANK: In a cigarette?

EMMETT: No, no! You'd smoke it over a fire imbuing it with a husky autumnal scent. The cheese would melt in your mouth, the smoke play about your senses like a dream. "Mozzarella" accompanied by thick slices of vine-ripened, beefsteak tomato. Juicy, drippy, ruby red. And . . . let's see, oh! fresh asparagus, like I've told you about —

FRANK: . . . Asparagus . . .

EMMETT: — thin, like twigs, in a light vinaigrette. Crunchy, crisp, greeeeen as a spring night.

FRANK: Spring — the warming one?

EMMETT: That's it, Frank! Spring, summer, fall, winter. Each with its own light, its own rhythm and soul. People tended to fall into two camps, spring or autumn lovers. I was an autumn, snapping October days, wind whisking around the corner.

FRANK: You'd button up!!

EMMETT: Yes! Right up to your chin, tuck your head down, just so. Pull your cap over your ears, stuff your hands in your pockets and scurry. Scurrying was invented for the fall. Winter . . . with early darkness and all, brought most everyone inside for several months . . .

FRANK: Sitting by the fire.

EMMETT: Yes! With . . . ?

FRANK: Hot . . . chocolate!

EMMETT: And . . . ?

FRANK: A book!!

EMMETT: Yes, yes! Good boy, Frankie! Good boy! Doing so well!

FRANK: Can we get to the restaurant?

EMMETT: Patience, Frank.

FRANK: Not a lot of time today.

EMMETT: I know. Still, mustn't rush . . . How's it going with the list?

FRANK: First the restaurant, Emmett.

EMMETT: All right. Ah . . . La . . . Grenouille! One of New York's finest. Fifty-second Street, I think. Lovely entrance, bar. Two enormous flower arrangements setting off bar from dining area. Lilies with birds of paradise, an archway of botanic sex organs severed for our visual gluttony. There was this period, Frank . . . all over town you couldn't sit down to a meal without some horticultural skyscraper threatening to dive into your soup. Ha!!

At Grenouille the arrangements were of the fountain sort, they'd loom over one's head during the essential Pause Before Entrance into the Food-shrine. Now, the Pause — the wait to be seated — was almost as important as the meal itself, Frank. For it was during this brief yet essential about-to-be-becoming that one got to take in the whole of the room: the glitter and smells, the pitch of voices and clinks of fine china, the buzz and hum of civilization at its dizzying peak . . . Are we drinking? We must have a drink.

FRANK: Just one.

EMMETT: Vodka. Absolut! Stolichnya. Served ice cold in a chilled martini glass. Shaped, comme ça, very like a lily. Its center glowing. Rolling down your insides like a puppy on the loose. Two of those and you'd have to squint for the shimmer it painted on the world. Liquor, you see, slowed things down just enough to allow infinite appreciation; understand, when biting into a crisp stalk of celery, let's say, why the jaw was placed in such perfect proximity to the ears. And the nose! So ingeniously perched above the mouth. Chewing . . . Swallowing . . . *Eye contact* . . . The tinkling of silverware. Mozart in the background, the perfect compliment to the drizzle of conversation fluttering about the room. And then . . . *she* would enter, all lips and eyelashes and blond silky hair.

FRANK: Blond silky . . .

EMMETT: Let's give her a name today, shall we? . . . Tanya!

FRANK: . . . Tanya . . .

EMMETT: Skin like peaches and cream. Cream . . . cream . . . came from cows, which gave us milk and, from that, came cheese and —

FRANK: *(Suddenly angry.)* Stay with Tanya!!

EMMETT: Oh, but cows were magnificent, Frank! Eyelashes you could paint with. They'd bellow and moan, Moooo. Mooooo . . .

FRANK: Enough cows, Emmett!

EMMETT: Easy, Frank. It's not good to rush this part.

FRANK: But —

EMMETT: Take it slow . . . Slow . . .

FRANK: Blond . . . silky, go *on.*

EMMETT: You know, women were real for me, Frank, not like knights in armor or dinosaurs — the things I just read about. I miss them more than fresh air and clear water. Wherever they are.

FRANK: . . . M sector.

EMMETT: Where?

FRANK: That's where they are. M sector.

EMMETT: M sector? Really . . . You ever been?

(Agitated by the direction their discussion is taking, Frank gets up and begins to pace.)

EMMETT: Might be worth a little trip. Might be just around the corner! We'll dig a tunnel!

FRANK: NOT just around — they must be kept far away. Far aw —

EMMETT: Of course . . . the temptation — *(Emmett opens a book and removes a small silk glove and puts it to his nose. He breathes in deeply and exhales luxuriously. Offers it to Frank.)* Come on. Breathe . . . *(Emmett places the glove under Frank's nose. Frank backs away. Emmett pursues, gingerly.)* Come, come, it's a piece of silk. What harm could it do?

(Slowly Frank approaches and sniffs the silk. Emmett holds it closer. Suddenly Frank gets a whiff of the scent. A queer look comes over his face.)

EMMETT: Sometimes, in an elevator, or walking down the street, a wisp of this would float by, tickling your brain. You'd spin around to see what could possibly have made the air so sweet. And there she'd be, curls bouncing, hips waving, "hello, hello, hello!" The clickity-click of her heels on the pavement.

FRANK: What is it?

EMMETT: Perfume. She'd place a splash here, and here, and sometimes just a drop . . . *(Emmett mimes a woman putting perfume on her neck and wrists. He takes one finger and stretches it out as if to put a drop on Frank, but Frank stiffens and moves away. Pause.)* Arpège, L'Air Du Temps, Joy . . . !

FRANK: Arpège . . .

(The teapot makes a whistling noise. Frank slowly becomes more aware. Emmett hears it too, but way back in his mind.)

EMMETT: Brought one perfume out near the end, Black Hole. Idiots! Cynical idiots!

(The whistle continues growing louder.)

FRANK: Emmett? EMMETT!!?

EMMETT: Eh?

FRANK: The tea!!

EMMETT: Oh. The . . . yes. Well . . . Well . . .

FRANK: I'll take care of it?

> (Emmett, distracted, nods. Frank exits. A moment later he marches back holding up a used and dried out tea bag.)

EMMETT: That's it, I'm afraid. The taste has long since gone, but the ritual remains.

FRANK: . . . Ritual remains . . .

EMMETT: You might perhaps try to dig me up another when you're putting in my requisition?

> (Frank exits and then re-enters a moment later carrying the tray to Emmett. Emmett watches as Frank sets the tray down, pours Emmett a cup, hands it to him. Emmett coaches him on how to do the ritual. This is all performed with the utmost care and attention by Frank.)

EMMETT: Well done, Frank!! Really, bravo, boy!

FRANK: I remembered to pour yours first.

EMMETT: Yes! And then one should say, "Milk? Sugar?"

FRANK: . . . Milk? Sugar?

EMMETT: Milk, please. Just a splash.

> (Frank pours imaginary milk into the cup.)

EMMETT: Just a splash . . . Good. From our beloved Elsie. The cow. And I'll just take a half-teaspoon of sugar.

> (Same imaginary action. They sip in silence.)

EMMETT: Mmmmmm.

FRANK: . . . Mmmmmm.

EMMETT: You never answered my question, Frank.

FRANK: Tanya . . .

EMMETT: It's nice the way you say her name. Could you . . . ?

FRANK: . . . *Tanya! Come on!*

EMMETT: All right, all right . . . Moving on . . . Soup! A bisque! I love a good bisq —

FRANK: Where is she?

EMMETT: Hmmm? Oh, she's at the next table . . . Hello!

FRANK: What's she look like? . . . Her hair and face! Her skin! Come on, hurry! Hurry —

EMMETT: Tick tock, tick tock, gotta keep running to Masta's clock.

FRANK: The unveiling is about to start —

EMMETT: An "orgasm" is a thing not to be rushed, Frank.

FRANK: A what?

EMMETT: An orgasm . . . Listen to me, Frank. There's a word for this thing I lead you toward — and for which you've so kindly allowed me to be spared — It's called an *orgasm*, Frank. That is the word for it.

FRANK: — No, no, no, no, no!!!

EMMETT: This sweeping feeling is a perfectly natural biological response —

FRANK: Can't hear you!

EMMETT: The frontal tail served *two* purposes once upon a —

FRANK: The frontal tail serves elimination ONLY.

EMMETT: No! Elimination AND *procreation*.

FRANK: Can't hear this word.

EMMETT: Well, I'm going to explain —

FRANK: No, no, no, what we do doesn't have a word!

EMMETT: Yes, it does. Used to be words for everything.

FRANK: Not THIS.

EMMETT: Language was as living as the trees.

FRANK: I'm forgetting that word, Emmett.

EMMETT: It can't hurt you, Frank.

FRANK: YES IT CAN. IT CAN.

EMMETT: Sticks and stones can break your bones, but words can nev —

FRANK: STOP IT. NOW!!

EMMETT: . . . It's just you and me, Frank. I'm a lone Diplodocus combing the earth for the smallest shreds of vegetation. And you're my pup. Don't let's lose what little we have.

FRANK: Why are you doing this?

EMMETT: Doing what?

FRANK: This. THIS.

EMMETT: What? What am I doing?

FRANK: Giving me words! Telling me to go to M sector. It's creed, Emmett. Language is the weaponry of fools! Do you want them to put a probe in me?

EMMETT: No, Frankie, no. I don't want any harm to come to you.

FRANK: THEN STOP GIVING ME THE WORDS.

EMMETT: But you being different should know that —

FRANK: This is exactly why your kind have to be shut up.

EMMETT: Everyone is shut up.

FRANK: Down here with your books full of words. You think you're better than everyone because you were spared and you can remember. Most pray not to remember.

EMMETT: Who'd want to? Everybody panicking — queasy dread —

FRANK: STOP! Get back to Tanya. Now . . . or . . .

EMMETT: Or what, Frank?

FRANK: Or . . . I'm taking you in, Emmett . . . I'm *taking* you *in.*

EMMETT: Now, there's . . . there's no need to take me in, Frank —

FRANK: We have an arrangement.

EMMETT: Yes, we do. And I'm . . . You're right. I'm sorry. Please . . . don't take . . .

FRANK: I have moved your name down the list! For the *fourth* time.

EMMETT: So, you did then.

FRANK: You were up at the very top. Next in line! And I moved it at great risk.

EMMETT: My gratitude knows no bounds, Frank.

FRANK: Then take away that word and get back to Tanya. NOW.

EMMETT: Of course . . . Well, but you can't *erase* a word, Frank. I mean, once it's —

(Frank's expression stops him.)

EMMETT: All right. The words "ORGASM" and "PROCREATION" are now officially erased —

FRANK: That's it. Let's go. Move! MOVE!! *(Frank stands and heads for his oxygen mask. It isn't there. He looks around, doesn't see it. Panics. His breathing becomes tight and labored, as though he's suffocating.)* The tank, the tank? I left it right there.

EMMETT: Beats me . . . Check the kitchen.

(Frank runs out in a panic, re-enters a moment later.)

FRANK: It's not in there!

EMMETT: What's the hurry? It'll turn up.

FRANK: I left it right there!

(Suddenly there are sounds of a procession, a rhythmic marching from above.)

FRANK: You took too long! You took too long! The unveiling!

EMMETT: Easy now, soldier . . .

FRANK: Today of all days. And I'm down here!! *(Frank runs around the room looking for the mask. The pounding from above increases.)*

EMMETT: Frank . . . Frank. Frank . . . Listen. FRANK! Nothing will happen to you.

(The procession sounds become very loud.)

FRANK: What have you done with it? I can't go up without it. There's no AIR! *(Emmett withdraws a dog-eared photograph of a woman from his sweater pocket. He holds it up to Frank. Frank pushes him away. Emmett tugs on him.)*

EMMETT: Look. LOOK, Frank.

FRANK: Today of all DAYS.

(Emmett grabs the boy's arm, pulling on him with all his might. Frank loses his balance and stumbles onto the floor.)

EMMETT: LOOK, damn it! LOOK! *(Emmett places the photo in front of Frank's face. Frank becomes transfixed. The two of them sit on the floor, the procession sounds fade. Both men, panting from their exertion, stare at the photo.)* Milk didn't just come from cows you know. No sir. In the beginning milk oozed from the pores of a woman's breasts.

FRANK: You've had this all along? All this time?

EMMETT: If I supply everything for you, how will you be able to picture things for yourself when I'm no longer around? . . . You'll be my memory, Frank . . . Look how her hair pours over her shoulder like maple syrup. Isn't she lovely? And there's a beauty mark on her neck, tear shaped, like a drop of milk chocolate, can you see it?

(Frank dives back into the photo. Emmett spots the perfumed silk on the floor. He picks it up and places it on Frank's lap. Frank noticing the silk picks it up and smells it as he eyes the photo.)

EMMETT: M sector can't be that far away, Frank . . . And she's there. You'll have to find her . . . *(Emmett moves away from the boy and picks up his teacup. The marching from above fades away entirely. Emmett stirs his tea with a spoon.)* What a sound, eh? *(He stirs some more.)* Silver against porcelain. The centuries of civilization it took to evolve such a sound . . . Listen.

(Frank closes his eyes. A smile begins to creep across his face for the first time. Emmett stirs.)

EMMETT: . . . Listen . . .

(The sound of the spoon against the porcelain grows louder and more beautiful as the lights fade.)

Scene Two

The tunnels: an underworld, corroded, drippy, a sewer. A lump of something or other lies in a heap. Out of the shadows two shapes emerge. It is very difficult at first to determine what these shapes are. They skitter like scared animals. The lump makes an odd groan, a strange gasping sound. The two shapes circle it, pull off its cloak, revealing a large oxygen tank. The lump awakens, sees the two shapes hovering over it like vultures, and screams in terror. The shapes scream back and run into the shadows. The lump sits up, it is Frank.

He grabs for the tank. It is empty. He tries to suck anything he can out of it, but there is no air. His breath is shallow, weak, and rasping. One of the shapes emerges out of the shadows.

LO: Fuck the tank.

(*Frank stares mutely back.*)

LO: Fuck it. Don't need it. Plenty to go around. (*And she takes in a deep breath through her nose, to demonstrate.*) Use your mouth. Your mouth.

(*Frank attempts to breath through his mouth, as he does the other woman appears.*)

FRANK: Wh . . . what . . . are . . . ?

LO: Speak up, soldier . . .

BRI: He doesn't know what we are . . .

LO: Is that . . . ? He doesn't — you want to know what we ARE? What do you think we are . . . ?

BRI: Don't cha know a couple a hot babes when you see 'em?

(*Lo and Bri laugh uproariously. Frank stares in wonderment.*)

LO: We're WOMEN, stupid.

(*Frank passes out. They approach his body, see what they can take. While Lo messes with his tank, scanner, pockets, etc., Bri goes for his boots, gets one off.*)

BRI: Now *this* is what you call good news.

LO: Gimme!

BRI: Finders keepers.

LO: One each then.

BRI: What's the good in that? We'll take turns.

LO: Ha! Like you'd ever.

BRI: I would, totally useless otherwise . . . He's kinda cute . . .

LO: Yeah, the girls'll be lining up.

BRI: That'd be us. Line starts here.

FRANK: T . . . t . . . aa . . . nnnn . . . kkkk?

(*Bri pulls a small wafer from her pocket.*)

LO: Bri! That's our supply!

BRI: Gotta fatten him up, so he's sweeter going down.

LO: He's eating. Air. The hard stuff. One thing at a time.

(*The sound of boots over gravel. Bri presses the tank mask tightly over Frank's mouth so he can't scream. They sit stiffly waiting for the soldiers to pass by overhead. They do. Pause.*)

LO: So . . . you a runaway or a dishonorable?

(*Bri digs in his pockets again and unearths the Tanya photo and the glove.*)

BRI: Ooooh, what have we here? Got yourself a girlfriend, ey?

LO: The picture's ancient.

BRI: A dream girl, then . . . huh?

LO: Yeah . . . I bet you want it back . . . Thought your breed transcended all that crap.

BRI: *(Sniffing the glove.)* Holy shit, Lo. *(She holds out the glove. Lo sniffs it.)*

LO: Where'd you get this? Huh?

BRI: We got nowhere to go.

LO: A little more time with tunnel stink on him and he won't either.

BRI: They'll know where you've been, boy. Sewer rat sniffing around for hot babes.

FRANK: . . . Give it back and I won't report you when I go up.

(Lo kicks him.)

LO: *That's* how you deal with this breed.

FRANK: They'll take you in. If I report you, they'll —

BRI: No wonder they discharged this one.

FRANK: Not discharged. Checker K14! Regiment 12R. Still on active duty.

(Lo swoops down and grabs his tank and mask. Frank freezes in terror.)

LO: Not anymore, boy. Now, let's begin again. Who is she? And where'd you get this?

(He clams up. Lo drops his mask on the floor and is just about to stomp on it when Frank blurts out.)

FRANK: 7D12 . . . I'm his checker. Bunker QR7.

LO: Liar! QR7 was eliminated.

FRANK: He's the one gave me her.

LO: Who "he"?

FRANK: To hold on to.

(Bri begins to crush the mask.)

FRANK: For . . . HOPE! She's . . . she's in M sector.

LO: Sorry to break the news, kid, but the only place this bitch is, is in a cold grave.

(Bri signals Lo, who, behind Frank's back, withdraws a rope from underneath her clothing. She slips behind him and quickly wraps him up. Weak from hunger, he can't put up much of a fight and they quickly get him down and tied up.)

BRI: You know . . . I'm thinking, why wait? There's more than enough to chew on right now.

LO: You got a point. He'll only get thinner. You want to do the honors?

BRI: Who went last time?

LO: I did.

BRI: Oh goodie! *(Bri runs into a dark corner, scrounges around, and returns with a large object. She stands over Frank.)* Don't worry. You won't feel a thing. I'm *very good.* Where is he?

FRANK: QR-

(She raises the object over Frank's head.)

FRANK: He's hidden!

BRI: Why?

FRANK: He's . . . He's . . . one from . . . before!

BRI: Liar!

FRANK: He is. He's old!

BRI: How old? *How old?*

FRANK: I'm . . . I'm his memory.

(Beat. Bri lowers the object.)

BRI: What are you talking about?

LO: Bri, you are not falling for this. It's a trick. Just another one of their sweeps.

BRI: Like we're such a threat, two stinking bags of bones.

LO: Hey, we are the carriers of free thought. Could start the next "pandemic!" The Thinking Influenza.

BRI: Can it, Lo.

LO: Come on, do him, Bri. We'll cook him up, be done with him.

BRI: What else does this old one have, checker? HUH?

FRANK: . . . Books!

LO: HA!

FRANK: . . . Tea . . .

LO: HA! HA!!

FRANK: Keats!

LO: KEATS! HA! Keats. That's good!!

BRI: How could he make up Keats? . . . Who's Keats?

LO: Keats! Keats! He was a poet. William Butler Keats.

FRANK: No . . .

LO: YES! See? He doesn't know SHIT!

FRANK: *John* Keats.

LO: Smart ass. Do him, Bri. Drop it!

BRI: Just hold on a sec —

LO: DO IT!

BRI: Tea, Lo! Earl Grey. Camomille, mint . . . *Soap*!! Oh God . . . Remember soap? Apricot and lemon.

LO: Those were fruits.

BRI: Scented soaps.

LO: I like stinking. Rats and I can't tell each other apart. You're gonna come back smelling like a rose and be eaten alive.

BRI: But maybe, Lo, we *don't* come back.

LO: You think for one second what this guy must've done to get himself a set-up? Some kiss-ass-snitch-pervert-freak with his checker, tea, and Keats!

BRI: There were days, Lo, when "deals" could still be made. You know whereof I speak.

LO: Shut it, Bri!

BRI: You and your great three minutes. Just long enough to cut the cord and give it a slap.

LO: MONTHS!

BRI: Enough! It was a million years ago.

LO: Three solid MONTHS!!

BRI: All right already!

LO: Well, stop bringing it up.

BRI: The guy got soap, checker? A bed?

LO: BRI!!

BRI: Clean water?

LO: Fine! You want to go, go. I got other plans.

BRI: What other plans?

LO: Two-thirty at Sassoon. Color, perm, the whole tamale.

BRI: We are down to our last box of bars, Lo. Yup. Our great supply. And you said we'd never live long enough!

LO: . . . Shit . . .

BRI: So, you know, after we're done feasting on bozo here. And then, you know, each other . . .
    (Beat.)

LO: What was the old man's part, boy?
    (Frank doesn't speak. Lo raises the object then drops it right beside Frank's head. She picks it up.)

LO: My aim's not as good as Bri's. Always takes me a lot of tries. *(She raises it again.)*

FRANK: When . . . when you say part, you mean the ones they take?

LO: I mean the one he played to get set up.

FRANK: Because when they need something. For study or . . . they . . . take his parts.

BRI: . . . Happy now?

LO: Oh yeah! Let's rush right over. I've got a spare foot I'd love to donate. Crazy fucking shit.

BRI: The guy isn't necessarily evil, Lo. Just because he got set up doesn't mean he's evil. He's just made his deal, like . . . you did yours . . . Tea, perfume, books . . . Keats!

LO: Keats . . . Now how'd that . . . ?

BRI: I think we gotta, Lo.

LO: Shush a minute, will you? . . . It's coming . . .

BRI: What's co — ?

LO: Keats. Wait a minute . . . *(Slowly Lo begins to recite the Keats poem.)*
"Here, where men sit and hear each other groan:
Where palsy shakes a few, sad, last gray hairs,
Where youth grows pale, and spectre-thin, and —

FRANK: . . . dies;
. . . Where but to think is to be full of sorrow."
(Both women stare at him, dumbfounded. Fade to black. End of scene.)

Scene Three

Emmett's bunker. A knocking is heard. It is the signal knock from Frank. Emmett enters, returns the signal knock, unlocks the door. Frank enters.

EMMETT: You're okay! You're okay!! Look at you!! Look at you!! My brave, brave boy! Not a lot to eat out there, huh? What'd'ya live on?

FRANK: Power bars.

EMMETT: Power bars?

FRANK: From before. Don't need the masks, Emmett! All life long they say you must refill every thirty-six hours. But there's plenty to breathe. Place is full of air! When my tank got on empty I passed out because I'd been trained, "no tank air, death." But I could've just kept breathing.

EMMETT: I told you, Frank, if you can breathe down here you can do so above. But they just slap that mask on you from day one, tell you it's essential, and nobody knows!

FRANK: The women know.

EMMETT: What?

FRANK: They taught me how to breathe the air. *(Frank takes in a deep breath.)*

EMMETT: What women? You found women? Are they far? Oh, good God!! Where? Where are they?

(Crossfade, down to half-light on the bunker and up on the women, who are waiting above.)

BRI: Been down there awhile. Could be a good sign! Tell you this, he's got real food and water, I ain't never leaving.

LO: Don't get your hopes up, Bri.

(Emmett and Frank talk excitedly for a few seconds and then Emmett shoos Frank out the door and begins straightening up the place.)

BRI: . . . A bit of cheese or jelly. Or . . . pickles! Oooh, all warty on the outside, sour juicy inside. Sliced thin . . . on rye . . . with mustard and a big tall glass of ice water . . . You know I remember the very last shower I ever took. I was in some stupid rush too, can't remember why. But I barely got wet before I had to race out the door. God . . . If I'd only . . . you know. Just been in it, for real. Leaned my face into the warm water.

LO: I was a bath person.

(Frank calls out from the darkness.)

FRANK: He's there.

BRI: Ohmigod, ohmigod, ohmigod!! *(Bri jumps up to go. Lo doesn't move.)*

BRI: LO!!

(She still doesn't move.)

BRI: LO!!

LO: . . . How do I look?

(Lights come up full on Emmett's bunker as he rushes around rearranging things like a finicky housewife. Frank enters with Lo and Bri behind him. It's as though he's brought in two monster aliens from another planet. Emmett is shocked speechless, but ever the gentleman — he tries to cover his shock. Bri meanwhile eyes the bunker as though she's just entered Versailles. Lo stands off to the side, as if trying to hide.)

EMMETT: Frank . . . ? Ah . . . what you do now is you introduce me to your friends. You say, Emmett, this is . . .

BRI: Look at this place. LO! LO, we struck GOLD!! Oh God, a CHAIR. A chair and . . . and . . . CARPET. YOU got CARPET? . . . Oh God, what a place, what a PLACE!!

FRANK: Women!

EMMETT: . . . Yes . . .

BRI: Where the hell are we anyway?

EMMETT: Hmmm?

BRI: This place? Where the hell . . . ?

EMMETT: Well, 81st and Fifth actually. Sub-basement of the Met. Only part that didn't cave in.

BRI: No shit? The MET! Lo, LO!!! I'm dead. Dead and gone to heaven. Dead and gone to heaven!!

EMMETT: You've . . . been living in the tunnels?

LO: Long time . . .

BRI: We still had faces when we found each other, right Lo?

EMMETT: Lo?

BRI: Yeah, short for Lolita! And me, I'm Bri, short for thirsty. You got water or what?

EMMETT: Frank . . . ? Why don't you bring our guests Bri and Lolita some water.

(Frank picks up a tea set and starts to exit.)

EMMETT: No, you don't need the tea set now, Frank.

FRANK: Yes. Time for tea.

EMMETT: No, Frank. I'm OUT.

FRANK: That's okay. Taste is gone. But the "ritual" remains.

EMMETT: Frank —

(But Frank is gone.)

EMMETT: So . . . Lolita. Unusual.

BRI: Her father's favorite book.

EMMETT: So, a literary background? And . . . Bri is it?

BRI: Like the cheese. Soft on the inside, RIPE on the outside!!

EMMETT: And I'm Emmett. You've met Frank, obviously. Frank's . . . my checker. He keeps an eye on me, regulates my food and water. He's not like the others. He's from a human mother.

LO: *What?*

(Frank enters with an old chalice filled with water.)

FRANK: Power's on. I put on the plate. *(He crosses to Bri holding out the water.)*

BRI: Oh, Lo . . . *Lo. (She can hardly bring herself to reach for it.)* Oh Lo . . . Look at it. Look! *(Bri puts her hand in the water and smells it, rubs it all over her face.)* Feel it!! Lo . . . Lo!! Feel it!! *(She's almost weeping she's so ecstatic. She puts water on Lo's face as well. Lo slowly succumbs to the pleasure of feeling water on her face. The two women douse themselves, drink, etc. etc. in a frenzy of delight. The men watch.)* Jesus, Lo!

FRANK: . . . Jesus?

EMMETT: Ah, in back there's an old filing cabinet. I can fill it with a few inches of warmed up water, if you'd . . . ?

(Bri looks up in shock.)

EMMETT: Come, Frank, let's . . . let's do that for our . . . guests.

(Frank and Emmett exit.)

LO: Did you hear what he said? Bri! BRI!!

BRI: I'm having a bath, Lo. A BATH!!

LO: About the boy?

BRI: A BATH!!

LO: He's from a hu —

BRI: — SOAP. WATER!!

LO: A HUMAN MOTHER, Bri!! The boy's from a human mother!!

BRI: I heard. I heard. You think you're the only one gave hers up?

LO: No. But if he's alive, mine could be too!

BRI: NO!

LO: YES!!

BRI: No. Now stop it.

(Lo turns as if to go, Bri grabs her.)

BRI: STOP IT! Look at me! Look at — he's gone. All grown up. We are not
    looking any more.

LO: Bri . . .

BRI: No! Stop it. It's over. Sssssh . . . *(Bri holds her tight. The men re-enter, the
    women hear them and instantly part. Beat. Frank is agitated.)*

FRANK: Now, Emmett.

EMMETT: . . . Later, Frank.

FRANK: Now. Tell me about her.

EMMETT: Not now. We've . . . got *company*, Frank.

FRANK: Tell me about Tanya.

BRI: Who's Tanya?

FRANK: She's a woman. Like you. Milk comes out of her.

EMMETT: Frank, that's rude —

FRANK: Go on. Go ON, Emmett.

EMMETT: Still got the picture I gave you, Frank? Why don't you go in back
    and look at —

FRANK: I want the words, Emmett. You gave me the words. Told me the words
    were special.

EMMETT: But Frank. It's . . .

(But Frank is already getting excited.)

EMMETT: Perhaps, if you'd excuse us just for a few moments? If you go through
    here, there's another space, not as grand but —

FRANK: No, no. Want them here.

(Lo heads out, Frank stops Lo from leaving.)

FRANK: YOU! Stay . . . Show me where the milk comes out.

EMMETT: FRANK!! That is not acceptable!

LO: *(To Bri.)* I told you!

FRANK: But they're women, Emmett.

EMMETT: Yes, I know.

FRANK: And I brought them, back . . . for the milk.

EMMETT: It doesn't work like that, Frank.

(The sound of boots approaching overhead begins, very quietly.)

FRANK: But you said —

EMMETT: I know what I said, but — . I've been trying to teach him about, well nature and suc —

BRI: Hold on. You want to see where the milk comes out, Frankie?

FRANK: It's Frank.

BRI: Auntie Bri'll show you —

LO: BRI!!

EMMETT: Bri, really. It's not . . .

BRI: Haven't seem 'em myself in I don't know how long. Should be quite a vision. *(Bri begins undoing her many layers of clothing. Lo rushes over to stop her. The boots grow louder.)*

LO: You WILL NOT!

BRI: I AM GETTING MY BATH, LO. I AM HAVING MY TEA AND I AM GETTING MY BATH. And if this is what I gotta do to get that — *(She continues shedding clothing. The boots get closer.)*

LO: You will NOT do any such thing!

BRI: Quit playing the prude. We've both done lots worse. Let me —

LO: NO! BRI! Put your —

(The soldiers are right overhead. Very loud and threatening.)

FRANK: STOP!

(Everyone freezes. The marching abruptly stops when it is right above the bunker. All four of them stare up as though praying or trying to see through the ceiling. BLACKOUT.)

END OF ACT I

ACT II
Scene One

Hours later. Emmett sits alone in his room, sleeping. After a few moments, Bri enters. She is looking remarkably better. Clean face, combed hair. She wears some of Emmett's old clothes. She is much younger than she'd appeared when first seen. While he sleeps, she snoops around a bit. She comes upon an old silver tray, picks it up, dusts it and looks at her face for the first time in years. She drops the tray, startling Emmett awake.

EMMETT: Well . . . !

BRI: Sat in it long enough to get my hands all wrinkly!! Looka that! Nearly froze to death, but damn it, I got 'em wrinkly!! You wouldn't believe what come off me. Like an old rotten tree with mushrooms and bugs and shit. Stuff was hanging off me, "No . . . no . . . no! Don't make us go!!" A whole ecosystem!! Just like me in the beginning, carting all my shit around, thinking "I'll be back home in no time!" Jeez, it's frigging cold in here. I need my layers.

EMMETT: Winter must be coming.

BRI: That sweater's all you got?

EMMETT: It gets so cold . . . I remember the day I almost burnt a Bosch to keep warm. I heard his voice leaping up from the flames. He was laughing. I was crying and he was laughing. I'm sorry, Hieronymous, I cried. I'm not, he said. What's to be sorry about? Matter is constantly rearranging itself. Stop taking it all so personally. I watched as this beautiful painting went up in flames, warming my fingers for an extra moment. All that exquisiteness extinguished for a few seconds of a mediocre man's comfort. I stomped it out, cold as I was. Couldn't let the Bosch burn.

BRI: *(Eyeing his sweater.)* Is that cashmere, or a blend, you think? Must be warm though, huh? I had a cashmere thing once. Lifted it from a store on Madison. Fucking snoots. Seven hundred and fifty bucks for a sweater no bigger than a napkin. Felt really shitty about it after. Just couldn't enjoy it. Finally, I wrapped the thing up, stuffed it into one of those envelopes with the padding inside, and mailed it back! I mailed it back, can you believe that?

EMMETT: Well, obviously, you're not the type to . . .

BRI: I have killed, you know. Two of 'em. Never given it a second thought . . . How we . . . de-volve.

(Emmett removes his sweater and slowly drapes it over her shoulders. Silence.)

BRI: . . . We should figure a way to pipe the warmed water direct from the pot to the tub. Could move the cabinet right into there.

EMMETT: Redecorating already?

BRI: It just makes more sense. Don't it?

EMMETT: It works for *me*.

BRI: Yeah, but, it ain't just you no more, is it?

EMMETT: . . . Lolita's still asleep?

BRI: Rats were so fierce, a bunch of uninterrupted hours, this is heaven for her. Where's the boy?

EMMETT: He went up.

BRI: Don't they notice he's gone all this time and then suddenly he's back?

EMMETT: Haven't yet. I think they're far less efficient than they'd have us think. Of course, convincing everyone the air was toxic.

BRI: You knew?

(Emmett nods.)

EMMETT: Maybe it's time you get Lolita up. She can have her bath and then —

BRI: Why did you tell him so much?

EMMETT: Hmm?

BRI: The boy.

EMMETT: He wanted to know. He came one day to bring supplies. Caught me reading. "What's that?" he asked. "I've got clearance for books," I told him. "Check." But he wasn't asking for that. He was curious. He's different from the others, coming from a human mother.

BRI: Yeah well, nine months hearing a human heart, maybe it's good for something.

EMMETT: Anyway, he started spending more and more time down here. To no ill effect. So far. But, you never know, the tunnels are probably *a lot* safer in the long run.

BRI: Oh, no, no, no no . . .

EMMETT: I'm just saying you'll be safer in the tunnels —

BRI: You're done saying! Sitting here in the lap of luxury. Giving the boy pictures, getting him all crazy with woman scent, sending him on a hunt. And he got lucky. Two for the price of one. What'd you expect? Lana Fucking Turner?

EMMETT: Look, I didn't —

BRI: You've no idea what it's like up there.

EMMETT: Yes, I do —

BRI: Well, then, how could you? A gentleman of culture such as yourself. How could you just boot us out? Like your friend Hieronymuck said about matter: Just think of Lo and me as two giant molecules just happened to drop into your orbit for a visit. Like permanently.

(Frank's secret knock. Emmett stares at Bri for a moment, as if to say, "I'm not through with this discussion," but then lets Frank in. Frank's behavior is slightly more natural. He's carrying a box of supplies.)

FRANK: Standing on line at the oxygen center, I'm wanting to yell to everyone, "You don't need the mask!! You don't need it. It's a trick!"

EMMETT: Well, it's a good thing you kept your head about you, Frank.

FRANK: I don't think they use the center as a way to track anymore. That's how they always did it, everyone going for a refill every thirty-six hours. But no one noticed I hadn't even been there.

BRI: Maybe they've come up with a newer system.

FRANK: No need. Everyone's so terrified of running out of air they bring themselves in. We're all in masks. Can't tell who's who. Women might be all around just like the air! Tanya could've been standing right next to me!

EMMETT: Well, it's good you kept your head.

FRANK: I'm going to make tea now, Emmett.

EMMETT: No, no, later, Frank . . .

FRANK: No, now, Emmett. I've got a fresh bag.

EMMETT: Well, let's just get these things put away first. Come on.

(Bri swipes a wafer from the box before Emmett takes it to the kitchen area. He and Frank exit. After a moment, Lo enters. She has yet to bathe and has been sleeping for a long while. She sees Bri all clean and dressed up.)

LO: Is that you!!?

BRI: Have a good sleep?

LO: Yeah. Okay . . . Let's hit it.

BRI: Lo . . . !

LO: You got your bath, Bri. Now let's go.

BRI: Didn't get my tea yet. It's coming now. Frank's just come back with a big box of supplies! Take a bath why don't you?

LO: Don't need a stinking BATH.

BRI: Beg to differ.

LO: Up yours.

BRI: Look, Lo. You'll have a wash. We'll eat. Chat. Emmett's got some extra clothes. Feel. Cashmere. There's food here, Lolita. Real food. And books. Look! You used to read, you told me so. You loved it. Remember? We can survive here.

LO: We survived in the tunnels. We stay here, we are sitting ducks. I just know it.

BRI: I'm not leaving! He tries to kick me out, I'll kill him.

LO: Bri!

BRI: I'm not going back out there. You want to go, you go alone.

LO: I can't do that! You know I wouldn't last an hour. Bri, we've been together all this time, I'd never make it alone.

BRI: And now you don't have to. Come on . . .

(The men's voices are heard approaching from off. Lo scurries off back to the other doorway.)

EMMETT: Remember, we are doing tea *differently* today, Frank, you understand? *(He and Frank enter with the tea set.)* All right then. Something new! A picnic perhaps!

FRANK: A what?

EMMETT: A picnic. A lunch or dinner outside on the grass, Frank. Big sheet or blanket spread out with all kinds of treats. *(Emmett spreads an imaginary picnic blanket on the ground and then sits. Bri looks at him amazed. He indicates for Frank to put the tea set on the floor.)* Let's see. We've got potato salad, and fried chicken, cheese and crackers —

BRI: What's this?

FRANK: It's tea time, Bri. Very delicious. Sit. *(Frank pats the floor beside him. She stands watching.)*

EMMETT: Lemonade . . .

FRANK: Where's she sitting?

EMMETT: Grapes!

FRANK: Next to me.

BRI: Who? Me?

FRANK: *Tanya.*

EMMETT: Frank, we discussed this in the kitchen —

FRANK: What's she wearing?

EMMETT: Frank. What did I tell you in the kitchen? While we have guests, we cannot —

FRANK: A picnic. Must be . . . summer! What do the women wear in summer, Bri?

BRI: Skirts, sandals . . . cut-offs!

FRANK: Cut-offs?

BRI: Short pants, like to here, Frank, that you'd trim at the bottom so these threads would sort of dangle . . .

FRANK: Cut-offs . . .

BRI: You can see their legs . . .

EMMETT: So! Fried chicken . . . hard-boiled eggs . . . and . . . pickles!

FRANK: See her feet too?

EMMETT: *(Passing an imaginary plate of pickles, he holds it up to Bri.)* Pickles?

BRI: Love . . . pickles! *(Slowly she sits and takes the imaginary pickles.)*

EMMETT: Sweet or garlic?

BRI: Oh, garlic.

FRANK: Does she have that paint on her toenails that Emmett told me about?

EMMETT: Frank, let's just stick to the menu, okay?

FRANK: Toenail Polish! That's it!

EMMETT: Bri, could you *please* pass the pickles?

BRI: All right . . . Passing the . . . pickles.

EMMETT: Peter Piper picked a peck of pickled peppers.

BRI: A peck of pickled peppers Peter Piper picked!!

BRI/EMMETT: *(They recite spontaneously together, going faster and faster and then breaking into laughter.)* If Peter Piper picked a peck of pickled peppers, how many pickled peppers did Peter Piper pick?

   (Lo pokes her head into the room. Frank instantly spots her.)

FRANK: You're up!!

   (Lo ducks back into the darkness. Frank gets up and follows, stands at the doorway talking to her.)

FRANK: We are having a picnic. Join us?

LO: No. I . . .

FRANK: We've got pickles!

LO: What . . . ? *(Lo pokes her head in and then takes a few tentative steps into the room.)*

BRI: It's a pretend picnic, Lo!

LO: Sorry. I'm not . . . presentable.

FRANK: Please . . . won't you? Sit by me.

BRI: Come on, Lo. There's tea. Real tea.

   (Lo steps into the room a bit more.)

FRANK: Sit by me and *Tanya.*

BRI: *Who the hell is Tanya?!!*

   (Lo comes farther in.)

EMMETT: Tanya can't stay, remember Frank? She has to go to work?

FRANK: Why?

EMMETT: She's late. Got to go. Good-bye, Tanya. Hurry now, don't be late!

FRANK: But I don't want her to go. That's not the arrangement —

EMMETT: Already gone! In a cab! Vanished!

FRANK: NO, Emmett!! Bring her back!

EMMETT: Not NOW, Frank.

FRANK: RIGHT NOW!! Bring her back, I say!

EMMETT: While we have company, Frank, we cannot do our usual, ah . . . routine — !

FRANK: THIS is NOT the arrangement. I brought you the tea. Now you —

EMMETT: It is *impossible* now, Frank.

BRI: What's with this friggin' arrangement?

FRANK: I waited long enough. I order you, you do it the way we always do —

LO: Order? ORDER?

FRANK: YES!

LO: You don't make the orders here, boy.

FRANK: WE HAVE AN ARRANGEMENT!

LO: You HAD an arrangement. And don't you speak to Emmett in that tone.

EMMETT: Things change, Frank.

BRI: Yeah, chill. Have a gherkin!

FRANK: *(Beat.)* All right. That's it. I'm taking you in! All of you. *(He pulls out his scanner and begins pushing buttons.)* Up, up. Let's go. MOVE! NOW! *(Beat. They don't.)*

BRI: . . . Ah . . . Fried chicken, Emmett? Extra crispy. *(She holds out the imaginary chicken.)*

EMMETT: . . . Yes, don't mind if I do.

BRI: You a breast or thigh man?

EMMETT: Thigh.

BRI: We should get on quite well then.

(Emmett holds up an imaginary platter to Lo. Lo slowly steps in. Frank stands, torn between leaving and staying.)

BRI: Pickle, Lo?

(Lo sits. Bri puts an imaginary pickle on Lo's imaginary plate.)

LO: Just one! I'll be up all night from the garlic . . .

BRI: Pickles . . . fried chicken . . . sun on your face . . . and grass under your toes! God . . . remember the Sheep's Meadow in the park?

EMMETT: Those gorgeous silvery buildings standing guard on the horizon.

BRI: Lying on your belly, the cool grass tickling your sides. Somebody's radio . . .

(Frank is agitated. Wants to join now, but can't. Emmett senses this.)

EMMETT: We've got *real* company and *real* conversation today, Frank. Things are different. Do you understand? It's a picnic with our new friends. *Your* friends who taught you how to breathe the air.

(Frank storms off into the kitchen.)

BRI: SHIT!

LO: *(Jumping up to leave.)* BRI!

BRI: SHIT!!
LO: Come ON.
BRI: Just . . . tea.
LO: Now! Forget it. Let's GO!
BRI: My first good sit down in I don't know how long. Well, it's been real.
   (They bolt for the door. Frank enters and blocks their way. They freeze. Slowly
   Frank withdraws an imaginary bottle from behind his back.)
FRANK: . . . Wine?
   (Blackout.)

Scene Two

   Days later. The bunker has been changed slightly to accommodate four people, but this has been done somewhat artfully, considering the little at hand
   to work with. Lo is reading to Frank.

LO: I had a dove and the sweet dove died;
   And I have thought it died of grieving:
   O, what could it grieve for? Its feet were tied,
   With a silken thread of my own hand's weaving;
   Sweet little red feet! why should you die —

   Why should you leave me, sweet bird?! why?
   You liv'd alone in the forest-tree,
   Why pretty thing! would you not live with me?
   I kiss'd you oft and gave you white peas;
   Why not live sweetly, as in the green trees?
FRANK: So . . . the bird . . . died?
LO: Yes. Because it was caged. Loved to death.
FRANK: Can that happen? I . . . love Emmett. Could that happen to him? Could
   I love him to death?
LO: No. You're keeping him alive here, bringing food supplies. You're loving
   him to life!
   (Pause.)
FRANK: In the tunnels . . . with the . . . rock? You wouldn't have, would you?
LO: Maybe . . . Yes, actually. Sure. But that was then, Frank. I couldn't now.
FRANK: Why?
LO: Well, for the same reasons you couldn't. Let's read another?

FRANK: Did you read to your baby?

LO: . . . No . . . Sang though.

FRANK: Sang?

LO: Um hmmm.

FRANK: What did you sing?

> *(We hear the secret knock. Frank answers and lets Bri and Emmett in. They're carrying things they've found — pieces of sculptures, scraps of artworks buried under the museum.)*

EMMETT: Thought I'd covered every nook and cranny of this place. But this is a woman who understands scavenging.

BRI: Never could resist a good bargain. And for my first artifact.

EMMETT: Me?

BRI: Absolutely. A real treasure. A relic, late . . . Crustacean period, I think,

EMMETT: Look! *(He holds up a vase, a painting.)* And . . . look!

BRI: Every little thing he sees, little piece of a broken something here, another there, he picks it up, rubs it, gives it a sniff says: Chinese, Ming Dynasty. Roman, fifth Century. Egyptian. How can a person know so much?

EMMETT: Ech, what good is it really?

BRI: Win friends and influence people. Bet you used to walk around the museum, picking up the girls . . . *(Bri holds up another vase, and a small gold necklace.)*

FRANK: What are those?

EMMETT: They're precious relics, from earlier times, earlier civilizations. There have been many epochs of human history, Frank, where cultures rose —

LO: — and fell —

EMMETT: — to great heights. Creating marvels! Objects of exquisite beauty —

LO: — On oceans of blood.

FRANK: Blood?

BRI: Give it a rest, will ya, Lo?

LO: Hey, just trying to give the kid the complete picture.

> *(Frank removes a marble hand from the bag of artifacts.)*

FRANK: What's this?

EMMETT: Oh, now that's ancient Greek marble, Frank. Now the Greeks were an amaz —

> *(Lo grabs the hand, interrupting Emmett's speech.)*

LO: Forget that, Frank. *(She extends the marble hand.)* This was a handshaker. Hello, pleased to meet you.

FRANK: *(Hesitantly reaching for it.)* . . . Hello.

> *(They shake, using the marble hand.)*

FRANK: . . . Sing to me, Lo.

LO: Wha . . . ?

FRANK: Please?

LO: Oh, um . . . "I'm a little teapot, short and stout, here is my handle, here is my spout. When I get all steamed up hear me shout: Tip me over and pour me out."

(Emmett and Bri clap. Lo laughs and bows. Frank suddenly and impulsively grabs Lo and embraces her. She stiffens.)

FRANK: I'm loving you to life, Lolita! Loving you to life!

(Fade to black.)

Scene Three

The bunker is now filled with all manner of artifacts Bri and Emmett have excavated: pieces of old paintings, potsherds, mirrors, vases. Emmett is off, Bri is dozing. Lo and Frank are sitting side by side while Frank is reading aloud to Lo.

FRANK: "I . . . do . . . not . . . like . . . them . . . Sam . . . I . . .

LO: "Am." I . . . do . . . ?

FRANK: Not . . . like . . . green . . .

LO: Yes!!

FRANK: Eggs . . . and . . . ham!!

LO: Very good, Frank.

EMMETT: *(Off.)* Frank!

FRANK: Just a minute. More. "I . . . do . . . not like them in a . . . tr . . . ain, I do not —"

EMMETT: *(Off.)* FRANK!

(Reluctantly Frank gets up. Lo puts the silk in the book as a bookmark.)

LO: Go ahead. I'll mark our place. You're doing really well. So smart.

FRANK: And there's all these others.

LO: Yes!

(Frank exits. A moment later he re-enters. He nudges Bri.)

FRANK: You seen my socks, Bri?

LO: I washed them out and hung them on that pipe on the back.

FRANK: Oh. Thank you. *(Frank exits quickly.)*

LO: Bri! He can't!

BRI: We have to Lo.

(Emmett enters.)

LO: EMMETT! You can't, Emmett.

EMMETT: Well, what do you propose?

LO: It's too dangerous. He's learning how to read! If they —

EMMETT: He'll be fine. He's been working the system for years.

LO: But they'll notice. He's been gone too long this time.

EMMETT: He's got to go. He is my checker. We're out of supplies. Four people are living on the rations of one.

LO: We've lived on lots less, we can again.

BRI: LO!! There is nothing left to eat.

EMMETT: He'll be back this afternoon with food. We need food. He's done this hundreds of times. It's what he does. He's a checker.

(Frank enters again, fiddles with his oxygen tank. They all look at him, like he's their long lost grandson.)

LO: Oh God . . .

EMMETT: So handsome. Such a fine boy. Aren't you Frank?

(Frank stops his activity, sensing them all looking at him.)

FRANK: Moz . . . arella . . . !

(Emmett and Bri laugh as they would for a toddler pronouncing a new word. Lo stands frozen. Frank exits again.)

LO: He's not going to fit in anywhere if you keep this up. Wrapping him in the past.

BRI: Lo!

LO: You don't care about him at all. Either of you.

EMMETT: How can you say that?

LO: OH! Supplies gone. Let's send up the barking seal!! Now, after all we've done —

BRI: You've no right, Lolita. Emmett's let us live here. You've no right!

LO: And you have no idea what it's like up there. Conning the boy with tales of women so he keeps you plied in fucking tea.

BRI: That's not what he's —

EMMETT: He's a *checker*, Lolita.

LO: He WAS a checker. He's NOT ANYMORE.

BRI: So we'll just sit down here and starve then?

LO: Fucking silver tea sets and —

BRI: — Watch each other just fade away —

LO: — Chinese porcelain, Japanese silk —

BRI: — Wonder who'll go first?

LO: The very shit that brought it all down. It's sickening.

BRI: LO!!

LO: It's garbage.

BRI: It isn't. Besides, we've got to eat.

LO: Ah, human hunger. There's no bottom to it.

BRI: Well, stop blaming Emmett. It's not his fault. He's kept us alive here —

LO: By using the boy. Why not? He's just another gadget for your comfort —

BRI: Oh, and you haven't been living off of what he's brought?

LO: There's got to be another way.

BRI: There is no other way. Frank goes up. He gets food. He comes back . . . Life . . . goes on.

LO: No, damn it! I won't let you —

BRI: We'll eat you then.

LO: FINE! Take a bite, THIGH man!

EMMETT: Oh, Lo, please!!

LO: Who *wouldn't* you sacrifice?

(*Frank re-enters all dressed up in his uniform, oxygen mask in his hand.*)

FRANK: Yelling.

EMMETT: Yes. Sorry, Frank.

FRANK: Over me.

EMMETT: No, no, Frank. Over me.

FRANK: Oh.

EMMETT: Lo doesn't think you should know about spring, and such, Frank.

LO: Emmett!

EMMETT: That it's wrong of me to share these things with you. To teach you about a long gone world.

LO: Stuffing you with dust. Then sending you up there on his errands, as though you're still one of them. Christ! He's learning to read, Emmett.

FRANK: Spring was the warming one, right? . . . Winter there was snow. Trees like skeletons reaching for the sun. Wind on your face like mint.

LO: God . . .

FRANK: Icicles weeping for spring . . . Tears watering the earth for pink blossoms.

LO: Who are you quoting, Frank?

FRANK: Quoting?

LO: Which poem that Emmett read you?

FRANK: No. I see it. Up here. And . . . I'm going up there to use it.

LO: You can't, Frank, they'll —

FRANK: Then what good is it?

LO: Just . . . stay down, Frank, we'll figure out another way. Please.

EMMETT: Now who's being greedy?

LO: This is different.

EMMETT: Is it?

LO: Yes! He's like a son —

EMMETT: That you won't let go.

LO: Because he fills my heart, not my stomach.

EMMETT: It's still greed.

LO: Fuck you!

FRANK: THIS!! Is not acceptable. Now, I am his checker and I'm going up.

LO: Just, just listen for one moment, Frank. You're very different now and if they find that out, about the reading and —

FRANK: Lo! *(He becomes very stiff and monotone, the old Frank.)* K 14! CREED: Desire is the shadow of perversity. Language the weaponry of fools . . . As there is neither reality nor unreality, all finite concepts are non-existent. Should I go on? Good . . . ain't I?

EMMETT: Atta boy, Frankie! You show 'em!

BRI: You look very handsome, Frank.

(They all stare silently at him. Emmett goes to embrace him. Frank awkwardly returns the embrace.)

EMMETT: Be careful, son.

(Frank starts to put on his mask.)

LO: Be careful. You know how they are . . . Just keep to yourself and don't . . .

(Frank does a comic gesture, zipping his lips shut or something of that nature. He turns and heads out. Stops.)

FRANK: What's this "fuck" I keep hearing?

EMMETT: Just an expression, Frank.

FRANK: Oh. Like . . . Jesus?

EMMETT: Yeah, like Jesus. See you later.

(Frank puts on his mask and exits. Long pause.)

EMMETT: He'll be back.

Scene Four

The bunker. Days later.

LO: Oh. Oh! So you're saying nothing was your fault?

BRI: Enough already!

EMMETT: No, no. I'm curious. Why has it got to be *my* fault?

LO: It was *everybody's* fault.

EMMETT: *Everybody's?*

LO: Yes!

BRI: What'd I do? I didn't do anything. Shit! I never even went to Saks.

EMMETT: Never went to Saks?

BRI: Not once.

EMMETT: Well, my dear, your conscience is clear!!

LO: Quit joking about it, you two!

BRI: Oh, lighten up. You did yours too, you know. Lo gave up her baby for steak.

LO: Bri!!

BRI: For fucking chuck meat.

LO: It was SIRLOIN!

BRI: Miss Holier-Than-Thou, never stops wailing about her great three minutes.

LO: They MADE me.

BRI: Shut up already!

EMMETT: STOP IT NOW! Nobody came out clean. Just . . . stop. Christ. Where is he? He's never taken this long!

BRI: Hold on, my friend. It's only been a couple of days, give or take a couple of days.

EMMETT: I never should've let him go up.

BRI: What's done is done.

LO: We never should've left the tunnels.

BRI: "We never should've left the tunnels."

EMMETT: I so much wanted him to get to M sector.

LO: Then what?

EMMETT: Let nature take its course.

LO: *What* nature?

(Frank's special knock.)

BRI: You see? YOU see?

(Emmett returns the signal knock. Then unlocks the door. Frank enters carrying a large box of supplies.)

EMMETT: They lost faith, but I knew, Frank. I KNEW!!

FRANK: Things are scarce. It took a lot longer than I'd expected.

BRI: Frank!!

LO: You're back!!

FRANK: Got MILK!!

(Bri dives into the carton.)

BRI: And some . . . ? *(She holds up a container.)*

FRANK: They're a new formula wafer. Builds strong bodies in twelve different ways! Like Wonderbread. Remember Wonderbread?

EMMETT: Did I tell you about Wonderbread?

FRANK: Had to get Skippy all over it, corner to corner.

EMMETT: Right you are, kid. What a memory, huh? Come let's get this stuff put away.

(They exit.)

BRI: See? *(Bri exits. Lo goes to the bookcase. Frank enters a moment later.)*

LO: You were gone a long time, Frank. We were worried sick.

FRANK: Things are scarce.

(Lo takes the book out from the case. As she does so, the perfumed glove falls out. She picks it up. Looks at it. Smells it. Frank watches her. She notices him watching.)

LO: Smells nice. Perfume . . . smell. *(She holds it out to Frank, he sniffs it.)*

FRANK: Promise her anything, but give her Arpège.

(Something in the tone of his voice unnerves Lo, but she says nothing. She opens the Green Eggs and Ham *book, and sits.)*

LO: Where were we? Here! Shall we? " . . . I do not like them in a . . . "?

(Frank looks at her blankly.)

LO: Can you read it, Frank? Here?   Tr   Tr . . .

(Still nothing from him. Bri enters. She carries a small plate with the wafers.)

BRI: These wafers are good. Much better than you'd think from looking at them. Lo?

LO: No. Thank you. Frank . . . ?

FRANK: Hmmm? Oh . . . um . . . Tr . . . ain! Train!!

LO: Good, keep going.

BRI: Oh, give the boy a chance to relax, Lo. Been above all these days. Must be tired, huh Frank? You go back the refill center? Just to have a look at all those poor folks who still don't realize?

FRANK: Realize what?

BRI: About the air, Frank. I swear I have half a mind to run up there myself, God damn monsters, making everybody so terrified of the friggin' AIR.

FRANK: They'd take you in.

BRI: Yeah, but somebody'd maybe see me first. See me breathing and laughing and shouting. And they'd know. And maybe, just maybe, they'd tell it!

FRANK: What would that do?

BRI: Get the bastards where they live, that's what. Ha!

LO: Bri . . . !

BRI: Well . . . it's good to have you back, Frank! We missed you. Awful quiet around here without you.

(Emmett enters carrying the tea set. Frank goes over and takes it from him.)

EMMETT: Except for all the carping. Thank you, Frank.

(Frank puts down the set, and then, as if he's suddenly short circuited, stops all movement. Only Lo notices, as Emmett and Bri are chatting.)

EMMETT: What a lot of stuff he brought. We'll be set for some time!

BRI: There's these things, Lo, taste like . . . apples!

FRANK: An apple a day keeps the doctor away!

EMMETT: That's it, Frankie.

FRANK: Frank, Emmett.

BRI: They look like crackers but taste just like apples! Juicy even.

LO: Need any help, Frank?

FRANK: With what?

LO: The tea?

FRANK: No. I'm fine, thanks. You forgot the spoons, Emmett.

EMMETT: Did I?

FRANK: Stay. I'll get them. *(Frank exits.)*

EMMETT: See? All that worrying for nothing.

LO: He's not right.

EMMETT: Hmmm?

LO: Frank. There's something not right.

EMMETT: He's fine. Just a little tired.

BRI: Must be so hard for him, going back and forth.

LO: I'm telling you, he's not right.

EMMETT: He's always a little stiff when he comes back. Happens every time.

(Frank enters with spoons. He returns to the tea set, begins the ritual.)

FRANK: I saw the statue. It's up. All the way.

LO: What statue?

EMMETT: They erected a twenty-story monstrosity of the first silicon whatever-they-call-it.

FRANK: Man. They call it a man.

EMMETT: Popped out of a silicon womb fertilized by a bunch of crazy chemicals. It's no man.

FRANK: Man is just chemicals, like everything else. Just chemicals. Right, Emmett? That's what you said. Don't take it personal, it's all just matter rearranging itself?

BRI: You did say that, Emmett. I heard that one myself.

EMMETT: Frank says it's the tallest thing on the horizon.

FRANK: It's the only thing on the horizon. There you go, Bri. *(He holds the cup out to her and she takes it.)*

BRI: Thank you, Frank.

EMMETT: And now you say . . . ?

FRANK: You know what it says on the statue? "Conquest of the lower self can only begin with nonattachment."

EMMETT: Frank, you forgot to offer Bri her milk and sugar.

FRANK: Oh. Sorry. What's a "lower self," Emmett?

EMMETT: I would presume it refers to a man's baser instincts, greed and cruelty. Things of that nature. Lo will take her tea now, Frank.

FRANK: And "nonattachment"?

EMMETT: That's a bit harder to explain.

BRI: Lo can. Right Lo? She's an expert!

EMMETT: *Please*, serve Lo now, Frank.

LO: So you were able to read all that then?

FRANK: It's spoken. Persons come from all over to listen. "The end of longing is the beginning of bliss."

LO: Why'd you go there, Frank? Did they make you?

FRANK: Who make me? I wanted to go. It was beautiful.

EMMETT: Really?

FRANK: Evidence on display. Attestations of excellence. Demonstrations of the new breed. Very entertaining. Not like the shit down here.

EMMETT: Frank. We don't like that kind of talk.

FRANK: Fuck, shit, you say it all the time.

EMMETT: Well those are remnants of our *lower selves*, Frank. But we expect better of you.

FRANK: Why?

EMMETT: Well . . . it's . . .

FRANK: Because I was evolved, Emmett. I didn't just happen. I was evolved.

EMMETT: . . . I suppose.

FRANK: Farther than you can understand. Or imagine.

LO: *(To Emmett, scared.)* You see what — ?

FRANK: *See what?*

LO: Just . . . I see what you're saying, Frank.

FRANK: It's not your fault.

LO: What isn't?

FRANK: You can't be expected to understand. Like apes reading. How could you?

BRI: Hey, Frank, I have a surprise for you!

LO: Give it later, Bri. We're having tea now.

BRI: No! I've been waiting for days to give it to him.

LO: But Emmett's not gotten his tea yet.

BRI: Pour Emmett's then, Frank. Hurry up.

> *(He does so at a slow pace. Bri gets up and picks up something from behind the chair and hides it behind her back.)*

EMMETT: Be right back. *(Emmett exits with the empty plate that held the biscuits. While Frank is focused on the tea, Lo signals Bri to put her gift down. Bri ignores her.)*

LO: And I'll have a little milk, please, Frank.

> *(Frank brings over the pitcher, but doesn't pour.)*

BRI: Ready?

LO: Wait until later, Bri, after tea.

BRI: Hey I risked life and limb digging this up, cleaning it off. It's his welcome home gift. *(She takes from behind her back a small piece of an oil portrait of a reclining nude, none of her face can be seen, most of her torso and a little leg. It's a piece of canvas, which she stretches out for him to see. Frank looks at it, but a strange expression comes over his face. Bri notices nothing.)* Isn't she gorgeous, Frank?

> *(Frank slowly approaches.)*

LO: Bri, we're trying to focus on the tea and now you've got him all distracted.

BRI: Plenty of time for tea.

> *(Frank approaches Bri, who is focused on the painting.)*

BRI: She's a stunner, huh? Oooh! And here's where the milk comes out!! A real orgasm for the eyes, ey Frankie?

> *(Frank hearing "orgasm," tenses up and snatches the canvas.)*

BRI: Oh, don't hurt her, she's very fragile.

> *(He stares at it, clearly wrestling with some horrible inner confusion, then tosses the canvas away and stares at Bri. She can tell he's struggling and tries to reach out to him. Suddenly he grabs her, forcing himself on her. Pumping into her and then throwing her on the floor. Bri screams. Emmett rushes in and he and Lo try to pull him off her. But Frank is very strong. He's fierce.)*

EMMETT: FRANK!! FRANK. STOP. Get off her. It's Bri, Frank, you mustn't.

LO: *(Same time.)* FRANK! FRANK. STOP.

BRI: *(Same time.)* GET OFF ME!! GET OFF!

> *(They struggle for several moments. Finally, Bri bites him hard on the ear or cheek and he pulls away, screaming and curling into the wound.)*

BRI: Jesus — fucking —

LO: Bri, are . . . ?

BRI: Christ! What'd they do to him?

(Emmett keeps hold of Frank.)

EMMETT: What did they do to you, Frank? FRANK?

LO: You did this! YOU!

BRI: Fucking monsters!

EMMETT: FRANK. Look at me. LOOK AT ME. They've done this to you Frank. *They've* done this. But we'll get you back. Just look at me, son. Look at me.

(Frank spits in Emmett's face.)

LO: Frank, look at me.

EMMETT: We'll just have to work harder to make him remember is all.

BRI: No way. Look at him. Why'd you come back, huh? Why not just let us starve?

FRANK: Came back so you won't starve.

EMMETT: That's right, son. You see? To keep us going.

LO: Yes, Frankie. There's my good boy.

FRANK: . . . Can't harvest your parts if you starve.

BRI: . . . WHAT??!!

EMMETT: Frank? You . . . You didn't turn us in . . . !

LO: NO, FRANK!

BRI: Holy fucking —

EMMETT: — You didn't come back just to turn us in. I know you didn't. You couldn't!

FRANK: Put your name at the top of the list.

LO: Nooooo . . .

BRI: How could you? HOW COULD YOU??

EMMETT: You'll stop them, Frank. I know you will. Look at me, Frank. LOOK AT ME. You've got to stop them.

(Bri runs in and out of the various rooms in a panic, grabbing clothes, food, etc.)

BRI: It's too late.

EMMETT: You'll stop them, Frank.

BRI: Forget it. It's too late.

EMMETT: Frank!

BRI: They're not taking one single piece of me. Not one single CELL. LO. Let's go. LO!! LOLITA!! Emmett! LO! Come on, grab some stuff. LO! EMMETT. *(Bri goes to grab Lo, who is in a pool of grief.)* Stop your weeping and MOVE IT. Come ON.

LO: NOOOO!

BRI: We can't stay here. They'll be here any minute.

EMMETT: Not if he stops them.

BRI: He's not going to stop anyone. Your boy! Let's GO.

EMMETT: Bri, wait — we'll get him back.

BRI: Then what? What about next time? They'll just do him worse the next time. I'm going.

LO: BRI you can't!!

BRI: They'll be here any minute.

EMMETT: You can't go back to the tunnels.

BRI: Fuck the tunnels. I'm going UP.

EMMETT: WHAT?

BRI: LO! Come —

LO: Wait —

BRI: I'm sick of waiting. It's me or him . . . Fine!

LO: BRI!!

BRI: Let those monsters see me running around, gulping the air. Someone'll see. Better than this. Better than this. LET THEM FUCKING SEE. *(She pushes Emmett out of her way and runs out. He stumbles against the wall, terrified and broken. Beat.)*

LO: . . . Frank . . .

(He won't look at her.)

LO: Look at me, Frank.

(He can't. She crosses to Frank, slowly kneels and gently reaches out for his face. He turns his face away.)

LO: Why can't you look at me, Frank?

FRANK: Hate you.

LO: No. I don't believe that, Frank.

FRANK: Hate you to death.

LO: Don't say such things, Frank. They hurt. *(Very slowly she touches him. He stiffens but doesn't move away from her. She puts her arm around him, he doesn't relax, but he doesn't fight.)* . . . Frank . . . Emmett told you so so much. But did he ever tell you about the heavens, Frank? The stars and galaxy's and such . . . ? Hmmm? *(She looks at Emmett as if to ask him to speak. He looks away from her.)* Emmett . . . ? EMMETT!

EMMETT: He's right. It is ROT. All of it.

LO: Stop. We need you — Frank needs —

EMMETT: I'm done.

LO: *Emmett* —

EMMETT: He wants it, he can dig it up for himself, shit that it is.

LO: *(Beat.)* The . . . stars, Frank. Such a gift . . . and the night sky . . . so vast . . . and far, telling us every single night.

FRANK: . . . Telling what?

LO: . . . To see . . .

(Frank who was tense and scared, begins ever so slightly to soften and listen. But it's a battle. Lo still holds him and, as he begins to relax, his head rests on Lo's chest.)

LO: To remember. To be grateful . . . It was a great kindness, Frank, that the stars let us see their light.

FRANK: . . . I hear something.

LO: What, Frank?

FRANK: Inside you. I hear beating . . .

LO: That's my heart, Frank . . .

FRANK: I can hear it . . . *(And Frank turns over and weeping embraces Lo. Emmett stands behind them watching as Lo rocks Frank back and forth.)* I'm sorry.

LO: It's okay. You're back now, Frankie, we've got you back . . . I've got you . . .

FRANK: . . . Too late. Too late . . .

(A loud crash. Bright light. The soldiers have broken through and found the hideout, Frank pulls away, as if to pull Lo and Emmett up so they can escape, but she holds him back, clutching him to her breast.)

LO: No, Frank. Let them see.

(Blackout.)

Scene Five

Lights up on a glass case in the New Memory Center. On a platform inside the case is Emmett, his back to the audience. He is a museum exhibit. His tea set is beside him. Frank is looking at him. A guard approaches.

GUARD: The museum is closing now, sir . . . *(The guard moves on, then stops.)* You were his checker, right? They told me you come here most every day . . . Heard you got a lot of points turning him in. Must be very proud.

FRANK: You're new?

GUARD: Just started today, sir. K 22. It's an honor to meet you, sir.

(There's an alarm sound, but from outside.)

GUARD: Not again! Guess you've heard about the person keeps popping up without a mask screaming "Breathe the air, take big gulps." They haven't been able to catch the person. Course others are starting to wonder, how can they go all these weeks without a tank?

FRANK: Because . . . you don't need it.

GUARD: . . . Sir?

(The siren fades. Pause. The Guard looks up at Emmett.)

FRANK: Everyone has gone?

GUARD: We're the last.

FRANK: You know what that is next to his chair?

GUARD: It's a teapot, sir.

FRANK: Yes . . . and do you know how they drank tea?

GUARD: Sir?

FRANK: With milk and sugar . . . *(Frank slowly removes his mask. The Guard is visibly stunned.)* You'd stir like this . . . *(He mimes stirring an invisible cup.)* The spoon . . . would touch the side of the cup. . . . The taste is gone, but . . . the ritual. . . . It took centuries. Centuries of . . . civ . . . il . . . i . . . zation.

(Quietly we hear the sound of a spoon lightly stirring in a tea cup. Frank keeps up the mime as the sound grows ever so lightly louder. Frank offers the Guard the imaginary cup. After a brief hesitation, the Guard takes it. Frank shows the Guard how to mime stirring. The Guard does so.)

FRANK: Silver against . . . porcelain . . .

(They stir, and listen as the sound grows louder and the lights fade.)

FRANK: There's plenty to breathe. . . try.

(The Guard begins to reach for his mask as the lights go to black.)

END OF PLAY

The Syringa Tree

By Pamela Gien

To my father and mother, with my love and gratitude.

THE AUTHOR

A principal member of The American Repertory Theatre, Cambridge for four seasons, Pamela played Estrella in *Life's a Dream* with Cherry Jones, Annabella in *'Tis Pity She's a Whore* opposite Derek Smith, and Sonya in the premiere of David Mamet's adaptation of *Uncle Vanya* opposite Christopher Walken. She played Gabriella in Ronald Ribman's *Sweet Table at the Richelieau* and Angela in *The King Stag,* both directed by Andrei Serban. She also appeared in several productions directed by David Wheeler, including *Gillette* by William Hauptman and *The Day Room* by Don de Eillo. She played Stella/Ann in *The End of the World with Symposium to Follow* directed by Richard Foreman. She played Lavinia in *Titus Andronicus* for the Public Theatre's New York Shakespeare Festival, Alicia in *Piano* by Anna Deavere Smith, and starred opposite David Selby as Hannah Jelkes in *Night of the Iguana* at the LATC, for which she won a Drama-Logue Award for Oustanding Achievement in the Theatre. She has also performed in the New Works Festival at The Mark Taper Forum in Los Angeles opposite J.T. Walsh, The Humana Festival at Actors Theatre of Louisville and at South Coast Repertory. Her TV appearances include guest starring roles in "Tales From the Crypt," "Reasonable Doubts," "Hunter," "Secret Lives," and "Into Thin Air." She recently began working in film, appearing in *Men Seeking Women* with Will Ferrell, directed by Jim Milio and *The Last Supper* starring Bill Paxton, Jason Alexander, Charles Durning, and Ron Perlman. *The Syringa Tree* premiered at ACT in Seattle last February. Pamela has also completed a new screenplay, *The Lily Field.*

ACKNOWLEDGMENTS

It is my great privilege to thank the many artists and friends who have gathered around this play with their generosity and love.

In many respects, *The Syringa Tree* has been a solitary journey, but I never once stood there without the seemingly infinite wisdom of Larry Moss. There are no words to thank him enough for the magnificence of his commitment to me, for his unyielding faith in this play, for teaching me that it was all right to give voice to that quiet whisper within, in all its joy, fear, and grief, and for "loving" that voice, so passionately, so skillfully, out into the world. I thank him for his vision, his fierce heart, his gentle spirit, his artistry, his excellence. My brilliant teacher, director, and friend. I love and thank him forever.

And standing with me also, Matt Salinger, my heaven-sent producer, who tells me constantly to stop thanking him! He graces my life beyond measure. He has labored tirelessly and proudly, given the very best of himself, and has taught me so much. I thank him for his great courage, his innate goodness, his artistry, skill, and most of all, his profound love. I dreamed once that I was carried high in the air on his strong hands, and as in dreams, some rare people come into our lives like angels, allowing us to flourish. I love and thank him with all my heart.

The Syringa Tree has in some magical way gathered a family of extraordinary people around it, generous artists and friends who have helped us with their time, inspiration, their very smart notes, and their passionate speaking about this piece. My profound thanks to the few I can name here:

Jason Alexander; Ron Orbach; Howard Sherman; Julie Harris; Paul McCrane; ACT Seattle; Twyla Tharp; Matthew Broderick; Rosie O'Donnell; Paul Bogave; Barbara Shottenfeld; Juliette Binoche; Diane Sawyer; Mike Nichols; Mali Finn; Lillian Ross; Oprah Winfrey and Oprah Magazine; Cherry Jones; Andrei Serban; Aldon O. James, Jr. and The National Arts Club New York; Sandy Bresler and Bresler, Kelly and Assoc; Joel Gretcsh; Carolyn Mignini; Jane Brooke; John Cirigliano, Jeff McCracken; Karla Blake; Jimi Kaufer; Amy Handelsman; Frank Dwyer; Fred Orner; Leonard Soloway and Steven Levy; Kate Blumberg; all at Playhouse 91 New York; Jim Randolph; Bill Evans; Robert Brustein; Cheryl Dooley; Ashley Osler; Steve Spiro; Jamie Donovan; Bjorn Johnson; David and Chip Selby; Lisa Rinna; Rick Olson; Sunra Currie; Jennifer Butler; Tish Goldberg Hill; Heather Schroder; Jonathon Karp; Lynnette Luyt Tulkoff, Nick Starr and Vida Ulemek; Pam Shaw; Gerri Pope Bidwell; Susan Brandis Slavin; Marishb Hargitay; Joan and John Alperin, Victor Tomasino, Sharon Budge; all at Larry Moss Studio; Rev. Steve Chindlund; Ilona Maister; Rod Menzies; Catherine leOrisa; Ginny and Rory O'Farrell; Leora Rosenberg; Jason St. Johns; Bobby Pearce; David Valdes; Frank Darabont; Anna Garduño; Michelle Danner, Maarten Kooij; Penny Charteris; Pamela Rahube; Caroline Kgobane; Sally Rahube; Sr. M. Imelda; Rosebank Convent, Johannesburg; Tsidii Le Loka; Alan Ralphs; Ralphs family; Walter family; Thosama Theko, Paul Suzman and Janet Suzman.

Thank you to all those I cannot mention here. Your words, letters, and deep feeling have meant the world to me.

My heartfelt thanks to very, very special friends Gannon, Avery, and Betsy Salinger. Your kindness made so much possible.

My thanks forever to true angels Dan Levitan and Howard Schultz for their vision, unsolicited generosity and their love in bringing *The Syringa Tree* to New York.

Thank you to all those who honored us with the 2001 Obie and other awards and acknowledgements in New York. We are profoundly grateful.

Thanks always to John Kelly for his tears and so much more, including bringing Matt Salinger to me. My thanks always to Howard Rosenstone for his early faith, kindness, and care.

My deepest thanks to Sam Cohn, with whom it is a joy and honor to work.

My love and thanks to Jim Milio for his generosity, faith, and friendship.

To Gordon Edelstein for his courage and great passion, and to Mame Hunt, Dramaturg at ACT, for her superb and compassionate work.

My thanks to William Ivey Long, and a huge debt of gratitude to Tony Suraci for his beautiful sound design, and for working with so much love; to Jason Kantrowitz for his evocative, poetic lighting; and Kenneth Foy for his understanding and for the exquisite simplicity of his design for New York and London. These have all been gifts of true artistry.

My thanks and love to Jean-Louis Rodrigue for his deep passion, skill, and care.

Thank you to Jeremy Taylor for the kind, generous use of his lovely, lovely song.

Thank you to Miriam Makeba with deepest respect and love.

My thanks to Michael Q. Fellmeth at Dramatists Play Service for his patience, kindness, humor, and wisdom.

Joyful thanks to Trevor Nunn, Padraig Cusack, and all at The Royal National Theatre in London. Thank you for the gift of being at your beautiful space in your gracious company.

And in memoriam to my lost friends, J.T. Walsh, Jane Spuehler, and Inez Mendez. Thank you for your love and support in the earliest days. I feel it even today, and I miss you terribly.

To all my family, with my deepest love. My thanks most especially to Elizabeth Claire Snelgar for whom I named Elizabeth, and Megan Duncan who was always Monkey. They are a wellspring of love; to Pete and Lol with love and hope. And to my Aunt Grace for whom I named the family in this play, and with whom I jumped on a train to a beloved place, my love and thanks always.

My most profound thanks to my parents, Shirley and Dr. Isaac Gien, for their unbounded love and support. To my mother, who allowed me to reawaken a painful time, thank you for your courage. And to my father, for the wisdom, compassion, and beauty of his words to me throughout my life. I'm always on that walk with you. I carry you in my heart forever.

To my husband, Kevin Ralphs, my thanks always for his love, support, and understanding. Thank you for being the soundest of sounding boards.

My thanks to the memory of my grandparents, George and Elizabeth

Walter, the only truly "real" characters in this play, who let me run wild at Clova those many years ago, and who came into my mind so unexpectedly to bring me this story. Thank you for the smell of fires, the red polished floor so cold under bare feet, the sweetest of memories.

And finally, my thanks to the children of South Africa, one and all, whose journeys haunt and inspire me still. I'm grateful every moment. This story goes out into the world for you.

AUTHOR'S NOTE

I never imagined I would write *The Syringa Tree*, and I never imagined I would write about South Africa, the paradise lost into which I was born. The play began in an acting class taught by Larry Moss when he said, "Turn to the person next to you and tell them a story." Without warning, the image of an attack on my grandparents' farm, Clova, came roaring into my mind. I had not thought about it for decades. We never discussed it. Clova was lost to us, and I was never taken back to what had been the simple but idyllic place of my childhood holidays. I quickly tried to think of something else to tell when he said to the class, "Don't censor whatever it is that came into your minds. Tell *that* story. It will choose you." I tried to make sense of the murky images and began to mouth the words. The second part of the exercise was to stage the story we had just told. I stood there trembling as though I had an earthquake in my body. I felt terribly vulnerable dealing with my own life. At the end of it, Larry said to me, "You have to write this."

I had no idea at first what I was writing. I wrote with fear, grief, and shame but also with love, joy, and a well of remembrance. At first I wrote autobiographically. And then I began to love the freedom of combining those events with the poetry of language and imagery. It developed as a more fictional story, deeply invested with aspects of my life. I chose names of people I loved and who inspired me, but with the exception of the grandparents — whom I have depicted with the most accuracy my young memory at the time allows — all the other characters are built out of inspiration and imagination. The family who lived next door to us, for example, was indeed that of a Dominee, but a man very different than the one depicted here, a man I remember as humane and kind, and his daughters were my sweet and first friends. The families depicted here are fictional, and because the play is so personal, I want to make that distinction clear. Another example is the character of Salamina who was inspired by several women who took care of me. They were of different origins, some Sotho, some Xhosa or Zulu, and I've tried as much as possible to accurately reflect tribal differences in the language, but some of the sounds were so strong and poetic in my memory that I wanted to include them. The coming together of it is the mystery. I wrote it, never imagining the journey I was embarking on.

The Syringa Tree was originally performed by one actor, but it will be exciting to see it performed by any variation, from just two or several actors doubling roles, to as many actors as there are characters in the play. It provides opportunities for unique and inventive staging in that it is performed on a bare stage, with a swing, and an *imaginary tree*. This is enormously important, as it allows the tree, and the journey of the play, to exist powerfully in the imagination of the audience. The audience becomes an imperative and active participant when their imagination is called upon in this way.

Similarly, there should be no props. In the original workshops we experienced the excitement of creating vivid, evocative images through the use of lighting, sound and language on a bare stage. A testament to the gift of this decision, by director Larry Moss, is the multitude of letters we receive from audiences saying they "went" there, they "saw, felt and heard South Africa." The bare stage may seem daunting at first, but trusting the imagination of the audience has been deeply gratifying, and many say they create their own inner pictures, the way one does in reading a novel. Of course, we were immensely indebted to our gifted lighting, set, and sound designers for their contributions to this idea.

When performed by a single actor, certain principles are useful. The illusion of the tree is simply created by the actor standing at, or on, the swing, creating its height and expanse visually. Whenever Elizabeth disappears up into her tree, scrambling up onto the swing will create that illusion, especially when it is quickly followed by the next character standing at the side of the swing speaking up to her. Elizabeth comes down from the tree by simply scrambling over the swing from upstage to the downstage side, as if that were her last rung in climbing down from its branches.

The actor in a solo performance of the play *never* leaves the stage. Stage directions like *"Elizabeth races off"* or *"Eugenie wanders away toward the house"* *never* mean that the actor physically leaves the stage but are simply there for the creation of the staging. The play should be performed in a continuous flow, like a dance, each scene melting into the next, but each with its own dynamic. One character leaving at the end of a scene transforms seamlessly into the next character in the following scene.

Attention to dialects is imperative. The many different South African dialects include a standard "English South African" for the Grace family, with Eugenie slightly more British; various black dialects for Salamina, Iris, Zephyr,

Peter, Dubike, Pietros, and Moliseng, particularly Sotho, Xhosa, and Zulu and a heavy Afrikaans accent for Loeska and the Dominee. Sergeant Potgieter and the police might be heavier accents, while Matron Lanning and the doctor might be softer. Father Montford might have a slightly Irish sound.

Vocal delineation among characters, through variations in pitch and tone, give each a distinct voice. These are further assisted by chosen psychological gestures for each character. These choices become crucial in the audience's ability to quickly identify one from the other. As there are no costume changes, and no props, the actor has to convey each character with speed and depth, and the psychological gesture functions as an invaluable shorthand. Offered purely as a guide, some examples of psychological gesture in the original production are:

Elizabeth as a child, physically hyperactive; her feet never stop in the dance of inner distress; her legs and body stiffen with fear, her arms stretched out, with hands patting down the air methodically as if to keep everything in place. It is the physical manifestation of her inner fear, trying to keep everyone safe.

Eugenie's gesture was the right hand delicately playing with her right earring, while the left was held across her waist, containing or protecting her body. The gentle fingering of the earring has to do with her position in the house, her social standing, her ladylike quality and her anxiety, while the arm crossed around herself is the beginning of her closing herself away from the world.

Salamina's physicality is robust, her warm body seemingly part of the rich earth around her. She is weighted, powerful, sensual, and strong, in contrast to the Salamina at the end, more vulnerable after a life of physical labor and loss. Her voice should be full and resonant. Salamina and Zephyr embody a powerful expression of the rhythms of Africa. A common gesture is the quick double clapping of hands, both palms up, in a traditional sign of gratitude. Another is the reference to any child. This is never done with palm down but the palm up, hand at the height of the child. The palm is left open and up to allow for the child to grow and flourish.

Sergeant Potgieter is created instantly by the removal of his cap and the wiping of his brow in the heat.

Loeska points in bossy authority, fingers covered in red trumpet flowers. Moliseng, because of her very young age, refers to herself by pointing to herself, and when ordered to hide away, instantly stands dead still and covers her eyes and forehead with both hands, as if to disappear.

One aspect I believe to be enormously important to the telling of this story is the tone of Elizabeth's narration. Elizabeth never "comments" or brings *any political awareness* to her narration. She is the voice of an innocent, telling us simply what she *sees*. She is a witness, and her words are her simple way of trying to make sense of what she sees. There is *never* a value judgment, only fear, matter-of-fact observation, excitement, curiosity, joy, the simple feelings of a child. For example, the line "To get me ready for the Dominee, all my brown runs down in rivers, into the ground again, to make me nice and shiny and clean and white again..." is a simple laundry list of what is required when the Dominee comes to visit. If it has any spin on it, good or bad, her innocence is lost. Another example is, "Pietros is much blacker than Iris, but not as black as Salamina..." This is the simple curiosity of the child. There should be no loading it emotionally, politically, good, bad or any other way. It's a curious and interesting fact. This note is not intended to impose on any desired line reading but given in the hope that the audience will supply their own thoughts and feelings. It was arrived at through years of process and, because of the nature of the material, is crucial for the successful delivery of the play. Elizabeth's beating of her closed fists against her chest, in the rhythm of the heartbeat, is a powerful sound that can be made by the actor's own body. It can change in rhythm, according to the moments in the play, and is an emotional, primitive sound, evocative of so much — our own memories of the womb, the racing beat of fear, the pounding in excitement and the haunting sound of the African drums, beating from time immemorial.

The Syringa Tree has been the most profound and surprising gift of my life. It has called me to be the best of myself as a person and as an artist. Carried in this story are my deepest feelings about a hauntingly beautiful place caught in sorrow. It is also a story filled with joy and wishes. Some might come true.

DIRECTOR'S NOTE

The Syringa Tree was developed over a period of three years, including four workshop productions and a premiere engagement at Seattle ACT before it opened in New York. I tell you this to convey how diligently Pamela and I worked to develop the staging. The passion and excitement we felt as *The Syringa Tree* grew and flowered is indescribable. After seeing the play as a solo performance many people have said that they thought they saw many other actors on the stage. These brief notes are to help you as you begin your journey with the play.

When you find the intention, you will find the character. Examples: Salamina's quieting of Elizabeth at the top of the play for fear of waking up the mistress and thereby endangering her job is the "you be quiet the madam she has got a big headache" intention *to fiercely warn*. Elizabeth's demand and appeal to Salamina for attention, understanding, and love throughout her childhood is the "look what I learned in school today Scottish dancing" intention *to excitedly impress*. Moliseng's monologue of birth and independence is the "your bullet cannot kill me" intention *to celebrate, to exalt*. Eugenie's enormous need for control, which she tries to maintain throughout the play with elegance and kindness, is the "Elizabeth if I told you once I have told you a hundred and fifty times" intention *to impatiently educate*. These active verbs/intentions are what drive the play forward.

When you talk of smelling, seeing, tasting, touching, or hearing, your sensory work will bring Africa to life. Be specific in all your sensory choices. However, one of the pitfalls to avoid when performing this piece is indulging in emotions and taking pauses that stop the action. An example of where this can occur is when Elizabeth leaves South Africa ("As I walk out onto the runway I smell the air…"). You must see it and smell it, of course, but you must also move through it without indulgence.

The lighting in *The Syringa Tree* can be very minimal. I had six lights to work with in two years of workshops that brought slight gradation of shadow and light, up and down in subtle degrees, on a small dimmer. For New York I had all I ever dreamed of, and as I am mad for the magic of light, we had 102 light cues. In both instances, I saw *Syringa* as a dream. Prior to the murder we used vivid golds, roses, blues, and pinks — the world of childhood fantasy. Within these colors we changed to starker choices for moments of violence. After Moliseng's final speech we bled the stage of pastel color and went to sepia tones. Whatever you decide, the light should lead Elizabeth through the play, coming up before each scene. The lighting should be lyrical and gentle, except for the obvious moments where violence and terror call for abrupt change. Pamela Gien's *The Syringa Tree* will reward you and the audience with an indelible journey to South Africa and an understanding of the power of hate and the even more powerful healing of love.

NOTE ON COSTUME DESIGN
For a single performer: a simple, straight sleeveless shift, rounded neckline, a few inches above the ankle in length, with a simple, soft short-sleeved fitted T-shirt underneath. The color of the shift is important and must be an earth tone, the rose brown that is used in the set, particularly for the mud floor, so that it seems that the actor rises up to tell the story from and as part of the earth. Only the sleeves of the underneath piece will show and should be toned with the shift, either a soft gray or earthy rose brown. The simplicity of style in the shift is to create a neutral column that can function for men, women,

and children and also have the feel of a uniform or tribal dress. It should be a simple shape that says nothing but that can be anything. These principles should be adapted for use by multiple actors, always using simplicity of shape for neutrality and the earth tones used in the set.

ORIGINAL PRODUCTION

The Syringa Tree was first produced by A Contemporary Theatre (Gordon Edelstein, Artistic Director Susan B. Trapnell, Managing Director) and Matt Salinger in Seattle, Washington, on February 18, 1999. It was directed by Larry Moss; the set design was by Peggy McDonald; the lighting design was by Ann Ciecko; the sound design was by Tony Surac;i the dramaturg was Mame Hunt; and the stage manager was Angela T. Vokolek. All roles were performed by Pamela Gien.

The Syringa Tree was produced by Matt Salinger at Playhouse 91 (Patricia Greenwald, Steven M. Levy, Leonard Soloway, Managers) in New York City on September 14, 2000. It was directed by Larry Moss the set design was by Kenneth Foy; the lighting design was by Jason Kantrowitz; the sound design was by Tony Suraci; the costume design was by William Ivey Long; and the production stage manager was Fredric H. Orner. All roles were originally performed by Pamela Gien and then, after one year, by Kate Blumberg.

The Syringa Tree was subsequently produced by Matt Salinger, in association with Us Productions, at the Royal National Theatre in the Cottesloe in London, England, on February 14, 2002. It was directed by Larry Moss; the set design was by Kenneth Foy; the lighting design was by Jason Kantrowitz; the sound design was by Tony Suraci; and the production stage managers were Fiona Bardsley and Angela Fairclough. All roles were performed by Pamela Gien.

CHARACTERS

ELIZABETH GRACE: 6 to adulthood, white, English South African
LOESKA (LUCIA) HATTINGH: 8, Elizabeth's friend next door, Afrikaans
SALAMINA MASHLOPE: 39, Xhosa, Grace family maid, nanny to Elizabeth
EUGENIE GRACE: early 30s, Elizabeth's mother
DR. ISAAC GRACE: late 30s to 70, Elizabeth's father
MOLISENG ELESSEBETT (ELIZABETH) MASHLOPE: Salamina's child, birth to 14

IRIS KGOBANE: 19, Sotho, nanny to Elizabeth's new baby brother, John
PETER MOMBADI: 40s, Grace family driver
ZEPHYR: late 60s, Zulu, Hattingh family gardener
JOHN GRACE: infant to adult, Elizabeth's baby brother
DOMINEE HATTINGH: 52, Dutch Reformed Minister, father of
    Loeska
PIETROS: Sotho, Grace family help
MABALEL: tiny black girl
MABALEL: Dr. Grace's skeleton
DUBIKE: Salamina's very old cousin
MATRON LANNING: Baragwanath hospital matron
YOUNG DOCTOR: at Baragwanath hospital
GRANNY ELIZABETH: early 70s
GRANDPA GEORGE: 82
SERGEANT POTGIETER: a police officer
FATHER MONTFORD: a Catholic priest
ANDREW: Elizabeth's American husband
MRS. BIGGS: spry for her 70s

SETTING

A bare stage, with a smooth mud floor. The effects of day and night, interior, exterior, shuttered windows, open countryside, vast skies, or deep African night should be created through lighting on a simple, very slightly textured earthy backdrop. This backdrop can be shaped according to the best use of any particular stage and in the original New York production created a half moon, semicircular enclosing space. The colors used should all be of the earth, the deep brown colors of mud for the floor, and soft earth, rose dust colors in the background. Off center left, a child's old wooden swing hangs down on long, long ropes attached invisibly to the ceiling, as if it were hanging from an immense tree. No attempt at a realistic tree should be made. The tree should always exist only in the imagination of the audience. *No props* are to be used. They are imaginary, created by the actor(s) on this bare stage.

THE SYRINGA TREE

The Graces' backyard. Johannesburg, 1963. Late afternoon, the Syringa tree against a clear blue sky. In the soft, lazy buzz of early crickets, six-year-old Elizabeth swings upside down by her knees.

ELIZABETH: You not allowed to go in there. You have to have a special paper to go in there. *(She climbs upright, perching on her swing.)* Did you know . . . you can tell how lucky you going to be . . . if you look at those little white spots on your nails. If you've got a little white spot on the nail of your thumb here, it means that you going to get a present! If it's just a little white spot, it's just a little present, but if it's a big white spot, you're a very, very lucky fish because you going to get a very nice BIG present! Gifts, friends, foes, lovers to come . . . journeys to go! Then on this first finger's nails here . . . if you've got a spot, it means that you've got a friend. Sometimes it's just a little not-so-sure friend . . . I think this one here is Loeska, my friend from next door. She has different dresses every Sunday, with petticoats. Loeska . . . Loeska! Then on this middle finger's nails here, if you've got a spot, it means that you've got a foe. My grandpa George says a foe is someone who doesn't like you, and they want to hurt you, and sometimes you don't even know why . . . I am a very, very lucky fish because I don't have *any* on that finger's nails. *(Looking away, trying to wipe it off on her dress.)* Gifts, friends, foes . . . *(Leaping down out of the tree.)* Did you know, Loeska stamps her foot and shouts *Rah, Rah, Rah!* when she sings her new song! She sings . . .
> "Ag, please Daddy won't you take us to the drive-in,
> All six, seven of us, eight, nine, ten!
> We wanna see a flick about Tarzan and the Ape man . . .
> And when the show is over you can take us home again!"

And then she lets *me* sing with her . . .
> "Popcorn, chewing gum, peanuts, and bubble gum,
> Ice cream, candy floss, and Eskimo Pie,
> Ag, Daddy how we miss tiggerballs and licorice,
> Pepsi Cola, Ginger Beer and Canada Dry!"

(Racing off toward the house.) "Popcorn, chewing gum . . . "

SALAMINA: *(Rushing out of the kitchen door.)* Houw, houw, houw, Miss Lizzy . . . what are you doing?! You be quiet, be quiet, yhe! The Madam she is sleeping, she's got a big headache. Yjo, Batho ba Modimo! . . . Miss Lizzy? What are you doing in the Madam's dress? Yhe! You be quiet yhe? If you wake her up, the Master he's going to give you a big, big hiding! Come, help me to iron. *(Elizabeth follows the heavily pregnant Salamina to the ironing room.)*

ELIZABETH: *(Singing.)* "Popcorn, chewing gum . . . " See, Salamina, I've got *my* baby on my back!

SALAMINA: Oh, very good, Miss Lizzy! Very, very good!

ELIZABETH: *(Trumpeting.)* Danteraaan! See what I learned in my school today . . . Scottish! Dancing! *(Jumping, her version of sword dancing.)* Toon-derroonderoonderooo! *(Like bagpipes.)*

SALAMINA: Yjo, Lizzy! You are jumping like a monkey!

ELIZABETH: *(Still jumping, arms stiff in front of her.)* I know! I'm hyperactive! I've had too much sugar! Pas de chat, pas de chat, and a change and change and change . . . *(Repeat.)* . . . that's ballet! Loeska showed me next door! *(Twisting.)* We can do the Twist and we don't get dizzy! I bet *you* can't do that!

SALAMINA: Yhe, not with my big stomach, Miss Lizzy! *(Salamina begins her work, ironing an enormous pile of snowy sheets.)*

ELIZABETH: *(Impatiently.)* When is your baby going to be *born*, Salamina?

SALAMINA: Very soon. The Master he say, yhe he say, the baby . . . it's coming any day.

ELIZABETH: *(In wonder and sweetness to the new baby.)* Haah, I will say hello to the baby! I will say to him, "Dumela! Dumela aghe!" *("Hello! Hello how are you!")*

SALAMINA: Dumela aghhee! Oh! You are my little picaninni, Miss Lizzy!

ELIZABETH: I'm not a picaninni. *(High on her toes.)* I'm big! Sing me my wedding song!

SALAMINA: Oh, you are getting married, Miss Lizzy!?

ELIZABETH: *(Setting off on a wedding march.)* Yes, I am a bride! *(Grand order.)* And you are my maid of honor! Sing to me, O maid of honor!

SALAMINA: Yjo, Lizzy . . . I am too tired yhe! I've got a big, big ironing to do.

ELIZABETH: Aah, sing to me Sally, I'm a bride!

SALAMINA: *(Gives in, sings.)* "Iquira lendlela, nguqongqo . . . " Yhe! *(Corrects her.)* You move your hips, Miss Lizzy, you are a bride! *(Interspersed with the words of her song, as she irons.)* " . . . Kutwa nguqonqothwane . . . " You don't tell anybody about the baby, Miss Lizzy? The baby it's not supposed to be here. The baby's got no pass, no paper . . . to be here. *(Singing again.)* "Iquira lendlela, nguqongqothwane . . . " You don't tell Loeska next door yhe? She will tell her father . . . the police will come and take the baby to live in the township . . . too, too far away. He will have to live with my mother . . . and she is too, too old!

ELIZABETH: Why can't he live with his dad?

SALAMINA: Mathias? Yjo, Lizzy . . . Mathias is no good yhe? . . . no good. Mmmph . . . *(Continuing to iron.)* So you don't tell anybody about the baby yhe? The Master, he will get a big fine from the police, a lot of money . . . Yjo, yjo, yjo . . . he will be very, very cross with you! He will give you a big, big hiding!

ELIZABETH: I'm not going to get a hiding! Because I am the Tokolosh! . . . *(Crouching on her haunches, making horns and advancing on Salamina.)* and I'm coming to get you . . .

SALAMINA: *(Terrified, jumping back, shielding her belly from the words.)* Jyeh Miss Lizzy! You don't talk about the Tokolosh yhe? The Tokolosh is a very, *very* bad spirit!

ELIZABETH: *(Creeping, down on her haunches.)* Yhaaa! *(Stops.)* Why's he so short? *(Resumes creeping.)* Haaaaaah!

SALAMINA: Yhe, Lizzy! You don't talk about the Tokolosh, yhe!

ELIZABETH: Yes, you so scared of him you put your bed up on bricks so he can't come in the night and steal your spirit! *(Frightening herself and Salamina with the sound of the Tokolosh sucking out the spirit.)* . . . thslooooo . . .

SALAMINA: *(Fleeing.)* Yjo Lizzy! Yhe!

• • •

Elizabeth's room. Dark, three o'clock A.M.

ELIZABETH: *(Waking suddenly, big fright, peering over the edge of her bed.)* Maaah! Ma?

EUGENIE: *(Urgent whispering.)* Yes, silly billy, it's only me! Come on, quickly, wake up!

ELIZABETH: Ha? Is it school?

EUGENIE: *(Hunting under the bed in the dark.)* No, silly, it's still dark outside. Come on, quickly, where are your slippers? Good Lord! What on earth are you doing sleeping in my dress! Honestly . . . come on . . . quickly . . . *(Throwing the blanket over Elizabeth's shoulders.)* Salamina wants you to come, she's having her baby.

ELIZABETH: *(Sudden burst of excitement.)* Her baby!?

EUGENIE: *(Herding her through the dark.)* Shhhhh! Quickly. Quietly!

· · ·

The servants' quarters, Salamina's room, dead of night. Elizabeth stands at the door in the flickering dark. Dr. Grace is delivering the baby.

ELIZABETH: They don't put the light on in Salamina's room, only a small candle. Salamina has her legs up in the air, and there's blood on the bed and all kinds of other yucky stuff also. She's all covered in sweat, and my mother is holding her face on the pillow, like *that* . . . and she's holding on to my mom's arms like *that* . . . and my dad is pushing on her knees, like *that* . . . and he says . . .

DR. GRACE: Push, Salamina, push Goddamn you! Don't get lazy on me now, Sally . . . Push!

ELIZABETH: And my mom says . . .

EUGENIE: Come on my girl, it's one more, Salamina, one more . . . he's got the head, come along, one more!

DR. GRACE: Push, Salamina!

SALAMINA: *(Screaming in one final push.)* Aaaarhhg . . .

ELIZABETH: And then the baby . . . eoouyew! It's also covered in all yucky stuff! And my dad picks it up in the air like that . . .

DR. GRACE: *(Out of breath, holding up the child.)* Oh God . . . Oh God! Look at that, Eugenie!

EUGENIE: Oh God, Isaac! It's a little girl!

DR. GRACE: A little girl . . . a little girl, Salamina . . . you and Mathias have a little baby daughter! *(He places the baby on Salamina's chest.)*

SALAMINA: *(Gently smells her, staring into the infant's face.)* Yjo . . . Oh jho yhe? . . . Yhe . . . *(She sinks back into the pillow, exhausted, a sudden well of tears.)*

· · ·

Elizabeth out in the yard, bright daylight.

ELIZABETH: Salamina called her baby after *me!* Well, actually, she gave her my name as her middle name . . . but her *real* name is Moliseng . . . Moliseng *(Pointing to herself)* Elessebett . . . *(Proudly delighted.)* that's Elizabeth! . . . Mashlope! Moliseng . . . *(Pointing to herself.)* Elessebett! . . . Mashlope!

SALAMINA: *(Her child in her arms, Salamina joins Elizabeth in a Celebration Dance naming Moliseng.)* Moliseng! Moliseng! Come, dance with Salamina,

Miss Lizzy! Yhe! *(Lifting her eyes and her right hand to the high, bright sky.)* Moliseng! Moliseng! Moliseng yhe!

• • •

Night. Salamina shrinks behind the garden wall, dogs barking, flashlights, police van patrolling the dark streets of the white suburb.

SALAMINA: *(Running, crouching in the dark, quieting the crying infant on her back.)* Thula baba yhe, thula Moliseng . . . sshhhh, sh sh sh shhh . . . you don't cry Moliseng . . . you don't cry jhe? . . . shhh shhh . . . (*When all is clear, she takes the baby from the blanket on her back, into her arms and kneels to light the fire outside the servants' quarters.)*

• • •

Elizabeth's room, night. Elizabeth wide-awake in her snowy sheets.

ELIZABETH: In my clean white sheets, ironed by Salamina, after my bath at five o'clock, with my hair slicked back, smelling of Vinolia Sandalwood soap . . . *(Listening intently for sounds in the darkened house.)* Loeska says we don't belong to the Queen anymore . . . and maybe the Queen should take all the blacks to go and live in England with her. Loeska says, the Queen should mind her own blerrie business, and go and live in her own blerrie country! I hope Salamina doesn't go and live with the Queen . . . in England. Did you know, sometimes you can't hear if someone comes into your house . . . even if you listen very . . . very carefully . . . *(Suddenly grasping at an imaginary speck floating away above her bed.)* Did you know, there's fairy dust in the air in my room . . . *(Frustrated.)* Nobody believes me! *(Jumps out of bed.)* When the fairies get dressed in the morning . . . they brush their teeth . . . they brush their hair, and then they put on their fairy dust powder . . . *(A soft tinkling sound in the wind as the speck floats away.)* Salamina said she *thought she* could see some . . . And Francesco the Clown has blue glitter ears! Sometimes the glitter gets stuck inside his ears, and then he has to come to my dad's consulting rooms to get them syringed. My dad takes a *big* syringe, and sucks out all the glitter *out* of his ears . . . And then when he leaves, there's blue glitter all along Jan Smuts Avenue, all the way back to the circus . . . *(Hearing someone enter the house, panicking . . .*) Dad?! *(Relief)* Dad? . . . Boy or girl?

DR. GRACE: *(Coming in from a night call, whispering.)* Shhh . . . boy. Go to sleep now, Elizabeth.

ELIZABETH: *(Calling out to him in passage.)* What was the name?

DR. GRACE: Shhh . . . you go to sleep now . . .

ELIZABETH: *(Listening to his footsteps growing faint on the stone floor.)* Sometimes he knows the name and sometimes he doesn't . . . *(Listening for him to enter his room.)* A newborn mouse should be safely in his bed after dark! *(She is beginning to drift off into sleep.)* But the drum, the drum, the drum . . . *(Her hands softly beat the rhythm of the drum on her chest, half sleeping, half awake, her bare feet patter down the dark passage.)* And like a newborn mouse, eyes barely open . . . *(Pulled by the beating of the drum, she finds herself outside the kitchen door.)*

• • •

Night. The path down to the granadilla vines. Elizabeth feels her way through the pitch dark, frightened, lured by the beating drum.

ELIZABETH: . . . Down the kitchen step . . . Outside! *(Calling defiantly into the dark.)* It's jolly dark out here!   But the drum, the drum, the drum *(Mesmerized, beating her hands on her body to join the rhythm of the drum.)* The drum, the drum . . . *(She is suddenly lit up by the glow of their fire, concealing herself in the granadilla vines, watching.)* . . . The fire! They stand around the fire, underneath the Syringa tree . . . Iris . . . Iris is new for my baby brother John . . . and Isaac . . . he's our garden man, and *he* has the same name as my dad! Isaac! And Peter Mombadi, my driver . . . and Zephyr! from next door . . . he's Loeska's garden boy . . . he's very, *very* old and somebody cut his fingers off!

• • •

The fire, outside the servants' rooms, dark but for the firelight. Elizabeth hidden, shining eyes peering out from the granadilla vines.

ZEPHYR: *(Drumming, sniffing the air and without turning his head, as if he has magical powers.)* Ii, fie, fo, fumm . . . I smell the blood of an Englishman . . . Haaah! Salamina! I think we've got a visitor, hiding in the granadilla bushes!

SALAMINA: Oh, Zephyr! Could it be Miss Lizzy again? Monkey . . . ? *(Tired,*

laughing to herself) Oh yho jhe! Oh yho! *(Pretending to hunt for Elizabeth.)*
Monkey? . . . *(Big surprise.)* Oh, Monkey! Come, sit with us, Miss Lizzy . . .
(Elizabeth crouches very still staring cautiously through the vines at Zephyr.)
Oh, you are shy!? *(Elizabeth scrambles out of the granadilla vine.)*

ELIZABETH: Ask Zephyr to sing me "Shoshaloza."

SALAMINA: "Shoshaloza," Miss Lizzy? Yhe Zephyr! "Shoshaloza . . . "?

ELIZABETH: Yes, "Shoshaloza!" . . . Driving in my car with Peter Mombadi . . .
we leave the windows *down* in the back seat, and all the dust comes in
on my white Panama hat! And I can hear the road gangs digging up the
road . . . Why are they singing it, Peter Mombadi!?

PETER: *(Taking off his cap.)* Oh, that one, it's the working song, Miss Lizzy . . .
it makes the work go faster.

ELIZABETH: *(Running back to Salamina, shows her.)* They stand in a big long
line to dig! And the ones in the back . . .

ZEPHYR: *(Looms over her.)* Haaaah! The ones in the back, Miss Lizzy . . . *(Zephyr
starts to sing, imitating the road gang. His voice rings out like the voices of
forty men slaving in the dust. Singing.)* "Stimela, siphum' eRhodesia . . . "

ELIZABETH: And then the ones in the front . . . ?!

ZEPHYR: *(Singing out.)* SHOSHALOZA . . .

ELIZABETH: And then all together . . . ! *(Zephyr reaches down and takes Elizabeth's hand with his mutilated fingers.)*

ZEPHYR: *(Singing.)* "Shoshaloza! kule zontaba stimela, siphum' eRhodesia . . .
Shoshaloza!"

ELIZABETH: Zephyr says . . . If ever you need to move a mountain that will
be a good song to remember!

ZEPHYR: *(Towering over her.)* Haaah! We are not working now, Miss Lizzy, we
are *eating* now! Come! *(A huge pot of steaming suurpap cooks on the fire.)*

ELIZABETH: *(On her toes to peer into the pot.)* Sour porridge, made with sour
milk, in the big pot on the fire outside their servants' rooms, because it
stinks up their whole rooms with that sour smell. And the gravy my mom
gives them, in the big house, left over from *(Delighted surprise.)* . . . *my*
supper . . . !

• • •

*The dining room, after dinner early evening. The first phrases of the second
movement of Beethoven's* Fifth Piano Concerto *play quietly. Salamina and
Iris, in pristine, neatly ironed uniforms, clear the table for the Grace family.*

EUGENIE: *(Gently fingering the pearl earring on her right ear.)* Thank you, Salamina . . . thank you, Iris . . . That will be all for tonight. *(Kindly.)* Oh, you can take what's left over as usual, but please, do leave a little bit of the meat for the children's lunch tomorrow.

SALAMINA: *(Two small, quick claps of cupped hands in the gesture of thanks.)* Thank you, Madam.

EUGENIE: Oh, and Iris . . . Iris? *(Iris has raced off.)* Iris wait! . . . Iris, don't forget to lock the kitchen door behind you, and take the key out with you! The Master found it still *in the door* this morning! *(Distractedly running her fingers along her throat.)* Good night . . . good night . . . thank you . . .

· · ·

The fire.

ELIZABETH: Zephyr just takes that porridge like that, in his hand, *(Imitating his mutilated fingers.)* and he goes like *that,* around and around in the gravy. But if you're a very lucky fish, after supper . . . Zephyr might sing you the prayer song . . . *(Imitating the slicing off of Zephyrs fingers.)* the forbidden song! . . . Loeska said it's forbidden!

· · ·

Loeska's garden, next door, bright daylight.

LOESKA: You are gunna get in terrible, terrible trouble singing that song hey!

ELIZABETH: Loeska picks off the red, trumpet flowers of the Bignonia Cherera . . . and makes herself into a big lady with long red nails.

LOESKA: *(Wagging pointed red fingers cloaked in the blood-vine trumpet flowers, at Elizabeth.)* You are gunna get in *terrible, terrible* trouble singing that song hey! You English, you born here just like us Afrikaners, but you've got no blerrie respect for yourselves. That's what my father says. *(She looks knowingly up at the skies.)* And he knows. God tells him everything! And that's why we've got no rain you know. It's because of *you* people making trouble with the blacks . . . *(Sliding her finger across her throat.)* They gunna come and *kill* you in your bed, hey!

ELIZABETH: *(Aside.)* Loeska is my friend from next door! She has snow white hair that sticks straight out like a thatched roof. And she was a *blue* baby. She had to have a blood transfusion to make her go pink again, and all her milk teeth are rotted out . . . to little black stumps, because she drank too much sweet Fortris when she was small to make her grow strong again. *(Looking over the fence.)* Her father is the Dominee of the Afrikaans church next door. We don't go to that church because . . . *(Pause.)* we too busy!

LOESKA: That is *not* our National Anthem! Our National Anthem is written by the great Afrikaans poet C.J. Langenhoven! . . . and you better stand up straight if you want to sing it with me! *(Saluting, singing heroically.)* "Uit die blou van onse Hemel, uit die diepte van ons see . . . *(Stamps her feet in time with an imaginary accompanying trumpet.)* Puhm puhm puhm!"

ELIZABETH: "Out of the deepest part of the sea, to the highest part of the sky . . . We will live, we will die . . . we for you South Africa!" *(Imitating Loeska, marching and saluting.)*

· · ·

The fire. Zephyr, an enormous black man, very old now, several fingers missing, stands slowly in ragged shoes, and with ceremony, wraps an old blanket around his shoulders.

ELIZABETH: Zephyr says, if we very lucky fish, the prayer song might bring God's blessings on Africa. *(Zephyr sings, his old voice deep and powerful in the dark night. His prayer is respectful, angry, imploring.)*

ZEPHYR:
"Nkosi sikelel' iAfrika.
Maluphakamis'u phondo Iwayo.
Yizwa imithandazo yethu.
Nkosi sikelela
Thina lusapho lwayo . . . "

ELIZABETH: And sometimes, like magic, everyone disappears . . . *(Suddenly Elizabeth is alone at the fire, dogs barking, flashlights searching. She stares into the dark as people vanish like ghosts.)* . . . into the granadilla bushes, up into the Syringa tree, under Salamina's bed.

MALE VOICE IN THE DARK. Polies, polies . . . *(Demanding papers.)* Pass, pass . . . !

ELIZABETH: Looking for people who've got no paper, looking for people who not supposed to be here! *(She smothers the fire embers with her hands, trying to see into the darkness. Then, stiff arms stretched out, hands warning everyone to stay hidden, to the soft strains of the same Beethoven filtering from the house, she vanishes up into her tree.)*

• • •

The Graces' backyard. Bright morning. Elizabeth stands on her swing, facing upstage, peering out over her shoulder.

ELIZABETH: Some things are allowed, and some things are not. *(With the same Beethoven wafting across the lawn from the house, Eugenie stands under the Syringa tree, staring up through the dense leaves, hunting for Elizabeth. In a strangely authoritative but dream-like state, Eugenie times her phrases to the music.)*

EUGENIE: Elizabeth! If I've told you once, I've told you a hundred and fifty times. But God gave you ears that don't *listen.* Now, you will come down and eat that egg! And if you do not . . . It will be on your plate . . . for lunch . . . ! And then for supper . . . ! And you will not go to ballet!

ELIZABETH: *(Gagging at the mention of egg, dreaming of ballet.)* Ballet . . . *(Gag.)* . . . ballet . . . *(Gag.)* . . . ballet! *(Elizabeth extends her arm from the swing like a mad dying Ondine.)*

EUGENIE: I can see exactly why Mrs. Strick strangled her five children. She was driven to distraction by children who *will not listen!* She went quite mad, you know . . . *(Quietly.)* . . . quite mad! *(Eugenie wanders into the house in despair. Elizabeth jumps down, dancing under the branches, magically transformed into a ballerina. Music suddenly stops.)*

ELIZABETH: *(Jolted to stillness.)* Some things are allowed . . . and some things are not.

• • •

The Graces' backyard. Late afternoon. Salamina hunts for Elizabeth who is high in the tree, on her usual perch.

SALAMINA: Miss Lizzy? Miss Lizzy Monkey? Eh Monkey, come down! The Master he is looking for you . . . *(Jokes with Dr. Grace.)* The monkey, she's *in* the tree, Master!

DR. GRACE: Thank you, Salamina.

ELIZABETH: *(Leaping down from her swing.)* Hi Dad! Do you *need* me?

DR. GRACE: Yes, my Lizzy, I need you! I need you very, very much! Come! Do you want to go for a walk?

ELIZABETH: Very *much!* *(They follow the path from the Syringa tree into the orchard.)*

DR. GRACE: *(Distracted, reflective.)* How many times have we walked on this path, Elizabeth?

ELIZABETH: Umm . . . fifty . . . um, *million* . . . and . . . um . . . sixty . . . times.

DR. GRACE: And how many times have I told you that I love you?

ELIZABETH: Um . . . Fifty million and . . . um . . . seventy-eighty-five . . . times?

DR. GRACE: I thought about you today.

ELIZABETH: *(Astonished, thrilled.)* Ha! What did you think about me?

DR. GRACE: I saw a little picaninni at my consulting rooms who reminded me of you. He had big eyes like you . . . soft little ears like you . . . and big, *long* feet like you!

ELIZABETH: *(Highly delighted.)* Big long feet like me! What was his name?

DR. GRACE: Oh uh . . . Matanzi.

ELIZABETH: Matanzi? *(Jumping like a Zulu warrior waving big, long feet in the air.)* Ha! Matanzi! Matanzi! Yhaaah!

DR. GRACE: His mom brought him. She carried him a long, long way on her back to see me. And then all hell broke loose. Mrs. Bezuidenhout got very angry and stormed out because we were seeing him in the same room as her little boy . . . *(To himself.)* threatened to phone the police . . .

ELIZABETH: *(Panicking.)* Did the police come there!? Are the police going to come and fetch Moliseng?

DR. GRACE: No, Lizzy, Moliseng will be safe here with us . . . we won't *let* anyone take Moliseng. *(Quietly, walking away from Elizabeth toward the house.)* Don't ever make this place your home, Elizabeth.

• • •

The Graces' backyard. Salamina, with Moliseng, almost three, close on her heels, hurrying out of the kitchen, in search of Elizabeth.

SALAMINA: *(Calling up into the tree.)* Miss Lizzy! Miss Lizzy Monkey? . . . *(Spots her.)* Yhe Monkey, come down! I've got a very, very bad news for you!

ELIZABETH: *(Climbing down off her swing.)* What happened Sally . . . what happened?

SALAMINA: Monkey . . . Moliseng . . . she was playing with your dollies. She took the dress of the bride dolly . . . she washed it. It shrank very, very much!

ELIZABETH: *(Stunned.)* Aah no! That is my most special dolly . . .

SALAMINA: We are so sorry Miss Lizzy eh? We will try to make a new one.

ELIZABETH: *(Close to tears.)* Ah no! . . . That is my *most* special dolly . . . *(Marching off in tears.)* I'm going to tell my mother what you've done . . . !

SALAMINA: *(Running after her.)* We are *so* sorry, Miss Lizzy jhe?

MOLISENG: *(Thrilled with herself, holding up the tattered remains of the shrunken dress.)* Nice and clean Miss Lizzy . . . Nice and clean! . . . Miss Lizzy Monkey help Moliseng to iron!

SALAMINA: *(Indicates Moliseng's height, palm up.)* She's a baby, Miss Lizzy . . . she doesn't know . . .

ELIZABETH: Mollie! You so naughty! *(To Salamina.)* If we make a new one, could we make it *with petticoats?*

SALAMINA: We can try, Miss Lizzy.

ELIZABETH: Mollie! Haah! She's laughing at me . . . *(Bending down to pull Moliseng's ears.)* Moliseng! Come here! You are very extremely naughty! Ow! She's pulling my hair . . . Ow! Let go! Eeeu! She's covering me with kisses! Moliseng let go! I'm going to tickle you . . . *(Starts to tickle her.)* kielie, kielie kielie . . . Run for your life . . . *(Moliseng darts off laughing, Elizabeth trying to catch and tickle her.)* kielie kielie kielie . . . run for your life . . . Haah! *(Sharply, horrified.)* Moliseng! . . . Don't run by the fence . . .

SALAMINA: *(Ordering the child to her side.)* Jo! Moliseng eh! *(Salamina's command stops Moliseng dead in her tracks, covering her eyes with her hands, as if to hide herself away.)*

MOLISENG: Moliseng . . . hide away . . . hide away! Moliseng! Hide away! . . . *(Now it's a game.)* Hide away!

ELIZABETH: *(Urgently.)* Yes, hide away, Mollie! The police are going to come and fetch you, and send you away!

MOLISENG: Poliesie, Miss Lizzy? . . . *(Wide-eyed, not quite sure.)* Miss Lizzy Monkey . . . hide . . . *(Pointing to herself very serious now.)* Moliseng . . . away!

ELIZABETH: Yes! It's White by Night here! You are not *allowed!* You've got no paper!

MOLISENG: *(Big game again, she darts off.)* No paper, Miss Lizzy!

ELIZABETH: Salamina's got a paper, but you've got no paper. *(Exasperated, runs off singing.)* Hide away . . . hide away . . . !

• • •

The Graces' living room. Sunday afternoon. Dr. Grace rushes out, his black bag in hand Eugenie looks up, surprised.

EUGENIE: Isaac? Where are you going?

DR. GRACE: *(Pause.)* . . . Emergency.

EUGENIE: Oh . . . I didn't hear the phone ring . . . ?

DR. GRACE: *(Looking out of the window at the approaching Dominee.)* It didn't . . . Oh God! Oh God oh God! Eugenie, you tell him . . . uh, tell him . . . Labushagne got bitten by a snake!

EUGENIE: *(Panicking as he flees.)* Ahg no man darling . . . I'm not *lying* to the Dominee *again!*

DR. GRACE: Sorry, love! Be careful, *(Humorously making horns on his head.)* the devil's coming! Bye! *(He rushes out. Elizabeth, covered in mud, runs up onto the verandah.)*

ELIZABETH: What did Daddy say?

EUGENIE: *(Looking down the drive.)* He said the devil's coming to get us! Good Lord . . . look at you! You're covered in mud from head to toe. Under the water this minute! *(Elizabeth aims for the front door.)* No! You go around the back and get Iris to *wash* you! Tell her to hose you down outside the kitchen door . . . and hurry up. They'll be here any minute.

ELIZABETH: *(Exhilarated, proud.)* Iris says when I get covered in mud I look like a little brown picaninni! *(Stops suddenly, looking up at Eugenie.)* Sometimes my mother leans her head against the jasmine of the verandah and she says . . .

EUGENIE: *(Closing her eyes and leaning her head in quiet, tearful despair.)* Oh God . . . !

ELIZABETH: *(Quietly staring up at Eugenie.)* Emergency, emergency . . . *(Elizabeth tears off around the garden to find Iris. Calling out.)* Irissy! . . . Come and wash me . . . Emergency . . . *(Sees the Dominee and his daughters now marching up the driveway.)* Emergency! *(She runs, starting to pull off her mud-soaked clothes, starting with her top.)* Iris can balance water in a bucket on her head, *(Imitating them.)* like the ladies who walk in the long, hot, dusty veld without spilling one single drop! I'm very, very lucky because I've *got* water at my house *(Pulls off her muddy top over her head.)* so I don't have to carry my bath on my head, but you have to be very careful *(Pulling off her shorts caked with mud.)* to only spray the flowers with the hosepipe . . . *(Sitting now in the struggle to get them off.)* . . . after half-past *five* because of the drought! *(She stands, stark naked now, smeared with mud, trying to cover herself with her hands.)* But this is an emergency *(Gleefully careening forward.)* because of being covered in mud! So Iris is allowed to *wash* me clean . . . to hose me down outside the kitchen door . . . And because it's such a hot day . . . *(Jumping in anticipation.)* . . . the water comes out nice and warm . . . ! *(Beethoven's* Kyrie Eleison *rings out as the warm water hits her naked body, sending her reeling back in its force, as Iris hoses her down . . . Elizabeth furiously washes herself soaring through the water . . . a kind of joyous backyard baptism . . .)* To get me ready for the Dominee, all my brown runs down in rivers into the ground again, to make me nice and shiny and clean and white again. *(Soft knocking.)* They knocking at the door! *(Big, loud banging.)* That same bossy knocking!

• • •

The living room. Persistent knocking. Eugenie hurries to the front door.

EUGENIE: *(Flustered.)* Elizabeth, where is Moliseng? You go and tell her to hide away . . . *hide away! (Going to the door, trapped)* Oh God! Oh God, oh God, oh *God* . . . *(Opens it, utterly charming.)* Hello, Dominee . . . *(The Dominee pushes past her into the hallway.)* Hello, Roelien . . . hello, Elsabe . . . hello, Loeska . . . *(As they file in without waiting to be asked.)* Please . . . do come in . . . *(The Dominee smiles, flushed, his Sunday suit bursting at the seams, Bible in hand.)*

DOMINEE: How kind of you, Mrs. Grace! And will we have the *pleasure* of the good doctor's company today?

EUGENIE: Please, have a seat, Dominee.

ELIZABETH: He always sits in my dad's chair. My mom says he *wedges* himself *in.*

EUGENIE: Unfortunately, Dr. Grace had to rush out on an emergency.

DOMINEE: My goodness, again! But the poor doctor never has a moment's rest. But when these babies come . . . they *come!* There's no stopping them! Whose turn is it today?

EUGENIE: Well, actually, I think he said something about a *snakebite* as he ran out . . . Labuschagne I think he said.

DOMINEE: Labuschagne . . . Labuschagne? Nee, nee . . . O ja, ja, Labuschagne! That's that huge family that lives on that farm *there* by Fourways. Ag shame man! I'll have to get Marie to send them a basket of dried figs. Was it one of the children, do you know?

EUGENIE: *(Now beet-red.)* Uh, no actually, I um . . . I think he said it was the *old* man.

DOMINEE: Good lord no . . . no . . . he passed on . . . with a heart attack . . . *last year! (Her lie revealed . . . Eugenie stares at him in silence, her cheeks burning.)* Ja! We have to be *very* careful of these snakes you know? The serpent of hell can creep up and nip you at any moment. We all know what happened to Eve, now don't we, Mrs. Grace?

ELIZABETH: They each have their very own Bible, with a white, silky ribbon in the middle. And you mustn't tell them any jokes! . . . because they only come to *pray* . . . for rain. *(To the Dominee, deciding to make serious conversation.)* "Africa . . . has no fucking water." *(A gasping silence.)*

EUGENIE: Eeelizabeth! Oh. Oh . . . OH! *(Realizing where it came from, bowing her head.)* OH! *(Pause.)* Can I offer you some tea, Dominee?

DOMINEE: Let us bow our heads and pray! *(Suddenly, Moliseng careens into the room.)*

ELIZABETH: *(Terrified.)* Ha! Moliseng didn't think!

MOLISENG: *(Singing, showing off.)* "Imithi goba kahle, ithi! ithi! Imithi goba kahle . . . " *(She stops.)*

DOMINEE: *(Pause.)* And whose child is this, Mrs. Grace?

EUGENIE: Oh she's . . . this one is uh . . . *visiting* us for the day. Just . . . just for today.

DOMINEE: I see . . . *(Smiling down at her.)* Just for today! Let us bow our heads and pray! *(A cavernous, rumbling sound accompanies his prayer, his voice thundering down into the bowels of the earth.)* Pray for the rain that will soothe our spirits, gladden our hearts, and soak our soil with the goodness of the Almighty Father . . . the rain that will ease our worries and answer our prayers. We pray that those among us who tempt the serpent *(Directed at Eugenie.)* in lipstick! *(Eyeing Eugenie's legs.)* and short skirts! . . . will see the plague of *drought* that their *sinful* ways have brought upon us . . . ! *(Suddenly, Loeska's gaze is diverted, along with everyone else's, through the window to the garden, where, among the brightly colored rhenunculus flowers, Salamina and Iris have elicited the help of Zephyr in carrying a mattress out onto the lawn.)*

ELIZABETH: Every time they come to pray for rain is the *same time* Salamina and Iris carry out my mattress to air in the sun. *(Mortified.)* Everyone turns to look at the big . . . wet . . . patch . . . in the middle. *(Looking out of the window at the endless sky, in a panicked, silent plea.)* Only the sun can dry it *out!* *(Taking their cue from the soaked mattress, the prayer brigade gather up their Bibles and leave. Elizabeth and Eugenie on the verandah, watch them go.)*

• • •

The passage. Elizabeth lies awake in the dark in her snowy sheets, listening to Dr. and Mrs. Grace argue outside her door.

EUGENIE: I am not having that man in my home again!

DR. GRACE: *(Joking at her expense.)* Well don't open the door then, Eugenie.

EUGENIE: That's not funny. He saw Moliseng today! God knows what he'll do now. Phone the police, I suppose!

DR. GRACE: Oh God, I don't think he'll do that, Eugenie!

EUGENIE: It's the same thing every Sunday. You take your little black bag and disappear. Why don't *you* sit here like an imbecile and pray for rain? Do you know what he called me? The Roman Danger! Catholics, even those poor souls among us who've lapsed! . . . are the Roman danger! Oh I can't wait for him to start on *you!* A Jewish Atheist! I mean, that'll just give him *endless* fodder.

DR. GRACE: Just be patient, Eugenie, just put up with it.

EUGENIE: Last week he wanted to know why we have Elizabeth "at a *Catholic* school . . . ?" *(Brightly.)* Oh! It's because we're hoping she'll go to hell! I said simply it's because the nuns are renowned for their educative skills, and frankly we don't care if she grows up to be a bloody Hindu in a loin-cloth! . . . as long as she's happy and brings joy into the world!

DR. GRACE: Good God, he must have fallen off his chair . . .

ELIZABETH: *(Listening.)* She didn't say the bloody Hindu thing . . .

EUGENIE: Well . . . I didn't *say* the bloody Hindu thing . . . but I mean, at least if you were *here,* I could escape to make tea or something . . . Oh I've a good mind to go and buy the ugliest hat ever *seen* and sit there in it next week!

DR. GRACE: I know. I'm sorry I run away Eugenie . . . I've had those bastards calling me a Fokken Jood since my first day of school when I was five years old. And they all had their polished black shoes and Bibles and my feet were bare. I just can't sit here and listen to it anymore . . .

EUGENIE: Where is this coming from, Isaac? One of your grandfathers is Afrikaans . . . he's a . . . he's a remarkable, compassionate man. You know, I hope to God I never go to heaven . . . all those bloody holy Joes up there. I'd much rather make myself useful and stoke the fires in hell!

ELIZABETH: *(Elizabeth is drifting off. Suddenly, startled, she scrambles up to the window next to her bed, trying to see out into the dark night.)* Something's happening outside! If you look under the shutter, where it touches the window sill . . . you can see the police van is coming back again. It drives up and down the road all night long, looking for people who've got no paper, and in the lights, shining on the road, they've got somebody down, and they shouting at him . . . " *Fokking kaffir!*" . . . *(Outside, over the garden wall in the street, the shadows of men, policemen caught in the headlights of their van, hold a black man down on his knees in the road. Shouting "Pass!" and "Jou fokken Kaffir!" muffled by the closed window. Dogs bark incessantly.) Heee* didn't think! . . . He's supposed to be at his home! If they catch you, without your special paper . . . and you don't have time to *(Trying somehow to tell the man.)* climb up into the Syringa tree, under Salamina's bed . . . If they catch you, they put you *down,* on the road . . . and they beat you . . . very much. *(Elizabeth is motionless, staring out. The van engine starts, the man thrown in the back. She retreats into her bed, her eyes following a stream of imagined blue glitter in the air.)*

• • •

The Grace kitchen. Elizabeth, sits on the red, white, and blue kitchen floor in the bright morning sun, licking her finger. On the outside of the window, facing in to the kitchen sink. Pietros is on a ladder washing the window, looking directly in at Eugenie.

ELIZABETH: If it's Wednesday, you can sit on the kitchen floor licking clean the empty tin of sweet condensed milk. And you can see *Pietros* on his ladder outside, washing the kitchen windows clean. Pietros is much blacker than Iris, but not as black as Salamina. Iris says because he's Sotho. *(Confused.)* But I think Iris is also Sotho. Salamina is Xhosa. You mustn't talk to my mom right now because she's *counting* how many spoons of flour and brown sugar . . .

PIETROS: *(Suddenly, quietly opening the window as he works.)* Hello, Madam.

EUGENIE: *(Jumping out of her skin.)* . . . I'm sorry! You gave me such a fright! Hello, Pietros.

PIETROS: How is the Madam?

EUGENIE: *(A little surprised that he would start a conversation.)* Oh, I'm fine . . . *(Flustered but kind.)* Thank you, Pietros . . . How are you?

PIETROS: Very good, Madam.

EUGENIE: *(Turning to leave.)* Well, good.

PIETROS: Madam?

EUGENIE: *(Turning back.)* Yes, Pietros?

PIETROS: *(With burning intensity.)* When the Madam she is going back to her own country?

EUGENIE: I'm sorry?

PIETROS: When the Madam she is going back to her own country?

EUGENIE: *(Confused, polite.)* This *is* my country, Pietros.

PIETROS: No, the Madam she has got her *own* country . . . *over* the sea?

EUGENIE: *(Kindly.)* Oh no . . . This is my country, Pietros, I was *born* here. And my mother was born here. And Miss Lizzy and Baby John . . . *(Offering them in a suddenly solicitous reasoning.)*

PIETROS: *(Almost prayerful, forceful insistence.)* No, Madam, this one it's my country. The madam she *must* go back to her own country over the sea . . . ?

EUGENIE: *(Rooted to the ground, staring up at him, quietly.)* Elizabeth, go and tell Salamina to get Daddy on the phone please. *(Suddenly shouting at her:)* NOW, ELIZABETH! *(Elizabeth tears outside in a big fright, shouting for Salamina.)*

· · ·

The Graces' garden.

ELIZABETH: Salamina?! . . . Salamina!? *(Salamina comes running, but frantically looking for Moliseng.)*

SALAMINA: Monkey! . . . Monkey! . . . Where it's Moliseng? *(Spotting her up at the fence.)* Jho Moliseng! You get *inside* the house!

MOLISENG: *(Running away, its a joyful game.)* Moliseng play *outside!*

SALAMINA: *(Furious, threatening her.)* The Dominee he's going to see you and phone the police!

MOLISENG: *(Jumping away, defiant.)* OUTSIDE!
(Salamina grabs her hard by the arm. Moliseng shrieks, dangling in her grip.)

SALAMINA: Hey!
(Moliseng starts to cry.)

ELIZABETH: *(Quickly.)* He's already seen her!

SALAMINA: *(Turns to her.)* What, Monkey?

ELIZABETH: On Sunday . . . *and* this morning. I was riding Loeska's bicycles, and Moliseng didn't think . . . she just ran right out! But I told him, *she* . . . *(Pointing at Moliseng.)* this one . . . is *visiting* us . . . for the day . . . just for today!

MOLISENG: *(Still crying, hanging from Salamina's hold.)* Just for today jhe!

SALAMINA: *(Impatient.)* Ssht! Moliseng eh! *(She bends to pick up Moliseng. Moliseng is still crying.)* Sh sh sh . . . *(Rocking Moliseng quiet on her hip.)* What did he say, Monkey?

ELIZABETH: Nothing. He just told Loeska to get inside the house and take her bicycles with her.

SALAMINA: *(Staring out over the fence.)* Oh . . . thank you, Monkey. *(She draws Moliseng close, and smells the skin on the back of her neck. She carries Moliseng away.)* Come, Moliseng jhe . . .

ELIZABETH: *(Pensive.)* Sometimes my dad stays very late at his consulting rooms. But if it's Friday . . . *(Sudden burst of excited relief.)* I can go with my mom to the drive-in! We have to wait until after it's dark.

• • •

The drive-in. Night. Crickets and frogs thrum. Elizabeth transfixed by the flickering screen.

ELIZABETH: My *most* special part in my *most* special film is Pollyanna. She sings "from sea to shining sea" . . . I wonder if they have glitter in America . . . My dad said America is the home of the brave . . . and the free, and free and brave live inside your heart . . . and if you listen very, very carefully you can hear . . . *(Beating the rhythm of the heartbeat with her fists on her chest, listening.)* free . . . and brave . . . free . . . and brave . . . like the drum that beats in the night . . . free and brave . . . *(Imitating the drum.)* boom boom, boom boom . . . *(Imitating Loeska, castigating.)* Rah rah rah! . . . boom boom, boom boom . . . rah rah rah!

• • •

The Graces backyard. Elizabeth rushes to the fence, looking for Loeska.

ELIZABETH: Loeska? *(Loeska doesn't come.)* My mom is sleeping because she's very, very tired . . . And Salamina's gone! . . . to visit her mom for her day off, to Soweto . . . Loeskaaa? *(No one comes.)* Loeska's not allowed to come to the fence anymore. She's forbidden. *(Elizabeth checks the little white spots on her nails.)* Gifts . . . friends . . . *(Holding it up in Loeska's direction, an invitation.)* friends . . . ? *(Nothing.)* Friends right here . . . *(Sudden relief.)* hah! . . . You can come and talk to Mabalel! *(She hurries off around the garden in the direction of the consulting rooms adjoining the house.)* Mabalel lives in my dad's consulting rooms. She stands by his desk and keeps him *(Standing like an old bag of bones hanging from a stick.)* companeeeey. She's his skeleton! She's all real bones, you know, and the medical students call her Mabalel, after the long poem of the picaninni who ran down to the water and got eaten by a crocodile! The whole village told her, "Don't go near the water!" But she waited . . . till they were lighting the fires at nighttime, and then she *ran* down the path with the bells on her ankles . . . ching ching ching! chi chi chi ching ching ching . . . She just put her foot like *that* . . . *(Crack.)* crocodile *snapped* her up! And she was gone forever. Mabalel . . . Mabalel. And because she's got no skin on her cheeks now, this piece here *(Indicates her own lower jaw.)* doesn't stick onto this piece here *(Indicates her own skull.)* . . . but now she's got special hooks . . . *(Elizabeth's jaw creaks open in a horrifying croak, imitating the tall skeleton leaning down to devour her.)* Yeaaaawh, yeeaaaaawh! *(Beating her chest in a frantic, fast heartbeat.)* Boom boom, boom boom . . .

• • •

Elizabeth in her father's empty consulting room. Heart pounding, his stethoscope in her ears, she listens gingerly to the heart of an old skeleton model.

ELIZABETH: Boom boom, boom boom, boom boom. Well, Mabalel, it must have been very sore to be eaten by that crocodile. But God gave you ears that don't listen! And now they've been *chewn off!* But *luckily,* I think your heart is still beating! So I think we can save you . . . Boomboom, boom boom . . . *(She screams in a huge fright.)*

EUGENIE: *(Suddenly at the door.)* You little devil, I've been hunting high and low for you! Put Daddy's stethoscope down this minute! Have you no ears? Get into the house! Salamina's putting supper on the table already . . . and you haven't even had your *bath* yet . . . I don't know, if I don't do it myself it just doesn't get done.

SALAMINA: *(Running in, extremely distressed.)* Madam, Madam . . .

EUGENIE: What is it Salamina? What's happened . . . ? *(Rushing out to the garden.)* Where's baby John? You haven't left him at the pool have you?

SALAMINA: *(Stops Eugenie.)* Madam, Baby John it's fine Madam . . . he's with Iris Madam . . . Madam, my cousin Dubike, he's by the gate Madam . . . *(Pointing at the gate, on the verge of tears.)* . . . he say . . . Oh Madam he say Moliseng she's gone! . . . jo, jojo . . .

EUGENIE: What do you mean Moliseng's gone . . . ? Moliseng's here . . .

SALAMINA: No, Madam, she is not here . . . I took her, Thursday, on my day off to my mother in Soweto . . . and she's *gone* Madam! . . . my cousin he say she's gone . . . !

EUGENIE: Gone where, Salamina?

SALAMINA: She's gone, Madam, ohhh jo . . . jo, jojojo! *(Slapping her body with both hands, she falls to the floor covering her face.)*

EUGENIE: *(Kneeling down to her, firmly.)* Sally you're not making any sense . . . I can't help you if I don't know what's happened . . .

ELIZABETH: Then Irissy comes running *(Indicates the baby moved from the back to the hip.)* with baby John . . . on her hips.

EUGENIE: Elizabeth, go and fetch Salamina's cousin at the gate, and hurry up. Iris what has happened?

IRIS: *(Flurried shock.)* Madam, Salamina she took Moliseng to her mother and now she is gone.

EUGENIE: Well where is her mother?

IRIS: Her mother she is at home.

EUGENIE: Well, then . . . Moliseng must be there also . . .

IRIS: No, Madam, nobody can *find* Moliseng!

SALAMINA: *(Rocking and wailing.)* Ohh Jo, oh jojo . . . jhe.

EUGENIE: Well what does her mother say happened?

IRIS: No, nothing Madam, *(Eyes wide as saucers, shaking her head.)* mm mm, she doesn't know *what* happened to Moliseng.

EUGENIE: Well that doesn't make any sense!

• • •

At the gate. Elizabeth rushes down to the gate, to find Dubike, Salamina's cousin. He is about fifty but looks a lot older, very thin and wearing a borrowed, ragged suit, several sizes too big for him. He holds a dusty brown felt hat in his hand and bows his head submissively as he speaks.

ELIZABETH: Dubike? . . . Dumela . . . *(Mesmerized by his appearance.)* . . . you must come into the big house to talk to my mother. *(As they walk up the drive together to the house.)* Dubike has to pick up the legs of his suit to walk because they're so long, and when he takes off his hat to say "Dumela" to me, a big puff of dust comes off him, and his sleeves are also very, very long . . .

EUGENIE: Hello . . . *(She does not extend her hand and he does not offer his.)*

DUBIKE: *(His voice gravelly, thirsty; he clears his throat.)* Good evening, Madam.

EUGENIE: I'm sorry, what is your name?

DUBIKE: Dubike, Madam . . . I am Dubike.

EUGENIE: Dubike, what has happened?

DUBIKE: Madam, Moliseng she is gone. She was very, very sick, and now . . . she is gone.

ELIZABETH: *(Loud shock.)* Is she *dead?*

EUGENIE: Elizabeth be quiet!

ELIZABETH: Irissy kneels down to hold Sally's shoulders.

EUGENIE: When was she sick, Dubike?

DUBIKE: She drank a bad, sour milk, Madam . . . She got very, very sick.

EUGENIE: When, yesterday? . . . Thursday?

DUBIKE: Ja, Thursday, Madam . . . We took her to the hospital, they told us to *go!*

EUGENIE: Well, then she's . . . *(Hugely relieved.)* Salamina she's in the hospital, she's in the hospital, Dubike!

DUBIKE: No, Madam . . . we went there again. Moliseng she is not there Madam. She's gone, Madam.

EUGENIE: *(Stunned pause, then quietly to him.)* What did they tell you, at the hospital, Dubike, what did they tell you?

DUBIKE: No, nothing, Madam. We went there *again.* We walk the whole day, a *long* way . . . Moliseng she is not there, Madam. She's gone, Madam.

EUGENIE: *(Taking stock of him.)* Oh my God. Which hospital, Dubike? Baragwanath?

DUBIKE: *(Angry resignation.)* Yes, Madam, Baragwanath.

EUGENIE: Oh my God *(Looking at her watch, then at Salamina crumpled on the floor.)* . . . Iris . . . Iris, is Peter Mombadi here tonight?

IRIS: Yes, Madam, it's Friday . . . he's here.

EUGENIE: Iris, I want you to go and put baby John in his cot and then would you please tell Peter to warm up the car, *(To Iris but looking over at Dubike.)* and I don't want him in his uniform please . . . and then if you could . . . *(Iris has raced off.)* Iris, Iris wait!!! . . . Iris, if you could you please lock up the house and give Miss Elizabeth and baby John their supper. And if you can, stay with them please . . . the master will be very late tonight, he's operating. *(Kneels down to Salamina.)* Sally . . . Salamina . . . go to your room and lie down. Irissy will bring you some supper. *(Getting up.)* Dubike, would you go with me?

DUBIKE: *(Fearful, polite.)* No, Madam, I will stay with Salamina.

ELIZABETH: *I'll* go with you!

EUGENIE: Don't be silly, Elizabeth. Go with Iris and be a good girl please.

ELIZABETH: My brother John starts to cry very much, because it's already dark and he doesn't like my mom to leave because . . . *(Very anxious, pointing at him.) heee* is frightened of the night!

EUGENIE: Iris, you can go now! Just take him please.

ELIZABETH: *(Covering her ears.)* He screams blue bloody murdaaah . . . I'm not going to stay here!

EUGENIE: Elizabeth, this is no time to be impossible. Go with Iris and be a good girl please. Now!

ELIZABETH: When Dubike comes nearer to help Salamina get up, I say, *(To her mother.)* you not allowed to go *in* there! *(Dubike shrinks back.)* And he jumps back in a puff of dust! He thinks I'm talking to *him*, but I'm telling my mother . . .

EUGENIE: Elizabeth, what are you talking about? *(Elizabeth is about to wet herself, increasingly distressed, her body getting stiffer and stiffer.)*

ELIZABETH: The police will *catch* you if you go in there! You have to have a special paper to go in there . . .

EUGENIE: *(Hurrying, kneeling down to her.)* Elizabeth, I need you to be a brave girl and stay home with Irissy. Now off you go. Go along . . . go on . . .

ELIZABETH: *(Frantic, races off, trying to shout but in a whimper.)* You not allowed to go *in* there!

· · ·

The driveway, a chilly highveld night. Peter Mombadi reverses the Mercedes out of the garage.

ELIZABETH: *(Whimpering, and then suddenly definite.)* Peter Mombadi is reversing the car out of the garage, and my mom is hurrying along the driveway pulling her jersey over her shoulders . . . so she doesn't get chilly . . . And when she gets to the car, I'm already *in* the back seat! I brought *my* jersey so I don't catch a cold, and my blanket for Moliseng and some of my sweets for her!

EUGENIE: Elizabeth, *get* out of the car this minute! Have you no ears! *Get* into the house! This minute I said! *(Elizabeth sits immovable, staring up at Eugenie.)* Elizabeth, I'm warning you . . . you're going to get the hiding of your life young lady . . . now move!

ELIZABETH: Peter Mombadi sits in the front seat without his cap on.

EUGENIE: Move, Elizabeth!

ELIZABETH: *(Tearful panic.)* Well if I go in, I have to phone Daddy because you need a special paper to go *in* there!

EUGENIE: *(Exasperated.)* Oh God, Peter, let's just *go!*

PETER: Yes, Madam. *(The car moves slowly down the driveway in the dark.)*

EUGENIE: He said . . . he said Baragwanath?

PETER: Yes, Madam.

EUGENIE: Peter . . . Peter would you mind . . . ? *(Curt.)* I mean, do you think you could please roll up the back windows . . . ? *(Pleasantly surprised, they're already closing.)*

PETER: Yes, Madam. *(The car moves out of the electric gates.)*

• • •

Seven o'clock P.M. Already dark night streets of Johannesburg. The car leaves the residential streets, making its way through the cold, deserted night.

ELIZABETH: It's already after half-past seven o'clock and we drive all the way down the driveway, out of the electric gate, onto Jan Smuts Avenue, *(Suddenly imaginary blue fairy dust glittering above her in the car.)* which is the *same way* Francesco goes back to the circus! . . . Then onto Eloff Street, which is the biggest road of all, *(Fairy dust disappears again.)* and goes *straight* to the airport . . . And then *after* the airport you can turn on that dusty little road where there's no lights . . . *(Relieved discovery.)* which is the same way Salamina and Zephyr go to their home for their day off, to Soweto. Usually we don't go on this road . . . *(Pitch dark, deserted now.)* My heart goes *(Fists on her chest again, imitating Peter Sellers.)* "boom, pooty poom, pooty poom pootyboompoom."

(Eugenie stares out at the moonless night, nervous, strained.)

EUGENIE: Which way are we going, Peter?

PETER: We are going on the main road, Madam.

EUGENIE: Good. That's a very good idea. And I think we'll just stay on this main road. I don't want to take any little side streets. Please, don't take any little side streets. Do we have enough petrol?

PETER: Yes, Madam.

(Elizabeth's face is plastered against the window, staring out into the dark.)

ELIZABETH: Loeska says if you go in here you'll be killed. They don't want you in here. They kill anyone who tries to help them. But I've already *been* in here with my choir with Sister Josepha . . . but Loeska says, *(Fingers wagging.)* "That was during the day and you didn't go all the way *in* there because the police never *let* you!" And she said some of those nuns are stupid and they got hacked to death because they wouldn't listen. And my grandpa's brother, Francis, went to the Congo to teach everyone the Bible and did you know . . . *heeee* disappeared! Loeska said, "They must have put him in a pot and *eaten* him!" But my dad said that is utter nonsense. *(Imitating fingers being cut off.)* And my other uncle, Walter, helped Mr. Marconi *(Sudden relief.)* to make the radio . . . *(Jolly singing.)* "Oh dear, what can the matter be, oh dear . . . " *(The car now deep in the township on a main road that is no more than a winding, dirt path deep with potholes. Were it not for the stillness of the night, the Mercedes Benz would be attracting a crowd of curious onlookers. There is no electricity here, and the dark streets are deserted except for the mangy dog that runs suddenly into the headlights causing Mombadi to slam on the brakes. They screech in the silence as the car skids to sudden stop.)*

EUGENIE: *(Jolted out of her seat, her hand flying out to restrain Elizabeth.)* My God! What *was* that? Did we hit it? What *was* that?

PETER: *(Shaken, both hands on the wheel.)* No, Madam, we are lucky!

ELIZABETH: It's a dog! . . . a dog! . . . you can see his bones!

EUGENIE: Good God! . . . *(Trying to see into the darkness.)* . . . running on the road as bold as brass . . . I hope we are lucky, Peter. I hope we are . . . *(The car continues.)*

ELIZABETH: *(Quickly to Eugenie.)* Grandpa George says you can *tell* how lucky you're going to be, if you look at those little white spots on your nails . . . gifts . . . friends . . . *(The headlights pick up the first electric lights for miles around. Its Baragwanath Hospital for Blacks on the outskirts of Soweto. The only road sign reads: Baragwanath Airport-Left. Trying to read the sign as they go by.)* Ba . . . ra . . . Bara . . . *(Frantic, to Eugenie.)* Baragwanath Hospital!

EUGENIE: Peter, please wait with the car right at the front door. Yes, I think if you just wait right here at the front door . . .

• • •

Baragwanath Hospital. Eugenie and Elizabeth, with her blanket and sweets for Moliseng, enter the hospital. In the trauma ward a white matron and medical students, shocked to see this woman and her child.

ELIZABETH: First we found the big fat Matron . . .

MATRON LANNING: Good Lord, Mrs. Grace, what on earth are you doing here, at this time of night?

ELIZABETH: And she sent us down the *long* corridor . . . it smells funny in here! . . . to the doctor's office. And he said he will look through all the

(Confused.) drawers of papers. *(Enunciates carefully for the doctor.)* Moliseng . . . Moliseng Elessebett . . . *(Pointing to herself.)* that's Elizabeth! . . . Mashlope. *(This is a state-subsidized hospital with no frills. Many of the children are here for tuberculosis, diarrhea, or malnutrition. It is gloomy and overcrowded.)* We looked in every room, in every bed, in every room . . . in every bed . . . in every room, in every bed . . . *(Extending her arms in anticipation.)* until we came to the very last bed . . . it's not Moliseng! *(Looking up to the doctor.)*

DOCTOR: *(Pause.)* . . . Perhaps we missed something in the records, Mrs. Grace. Come . . . come, let's . . . well, let's go and take another look.

• • •

Grace home. The dark passage, early morning hours.

DR. GRACE: *(Enraged.)* It was an *idiotic* decision! . . . You jeopardized Elizabeth's life, and your own!

EUGENIE: Would you just *listen* for a second?

DR. GRACE: Eugenie! I understand your concern for Salamina's child, believe me, but to make a stupid decision like that . . . an absolutely dangerous, stupid thing to do, driving through the township in the middle of the bloody night . . . with our *child* in the car! Why didn't you phone me?

EUGENIE: You were operating . . . it's impossible ever to *find* you . . .

DR. GRACE: Why the hell didn't you phone Baragwanath?

EUGENIE: You know as well as I do I had to go there myself. It's impossible ever to make any sense of anything on the phone, and if Dubike and the mother had already been *told* there was *no* such child there, how on earth would that have helped? She's just disappeared!

DR. GRACE: It was rash! And stupid, Eugenie!

EUGENIE: *(Raising her voice again.)* All right, it was stupid! I'm stupid! Is that what you want to hear? I'm *stupid, stupid, stupid!* This whole bloody *place* is stupid! *(Exhausted, she starts sobbing.)* I did . . . *(Controlling herself.)* I did all I could think of to do . . . and she's missing . . . vanished into thin bloody air . . . calling me stupid isn't going to *find* her . . . she's gone!

DR. GRACE: I'll call Johnston in the morning.

EUGENIE: We looked through Johnston's records, Isaac, there's nothing in there . . . not a bloody thing. How is this possible? How can this have happened . . . ?

DR. GRACE: God only knows . . . *(Early morning light now creeping in.)*

· · ·

Early morning, the backyard. The berries of the old Syringa tree strewn on the grass. Elizabeth finds Salamina sitting alone under the tree, silently rocking back and forth, an ancient, grieving motion. Elizabeth climbs quietly on to her swing, watching Salamina.

ELIZABETH: For two days my mom stays sleeping in her bed, sleeping and sleeping. The house is very, very quiet and Salamina won't come inside. She just stays underneath the Syringa tree, rocking and rocking, the way she always rocks Moliseng to sleep. I tried to sing to her . . . *(Sweetly.)* "Thula baba . . . thula baba . . . " but I don't think she can hear me. Haa! Iris left some soft pumpkin with some butter, and some hot tea for her . . . but I don't think she knows that it's there. She never stops rocking, even when the Syringa berries fall down on her. *(She sits in silence on the swing, watching the berries drop. Suddenly, leaping out of the tree.)* After two days, a man phoned and I told him sshh! My mom is sleeping! And he said, could I please tell my dad an urgent message regarding the child of our servant. When I phoned my dad at his consulting rooms, 46-7620 Rebecca, his nurse . . . she's black and she speaks Queen's English and always jokes she's "more white than white!" . . . Rebecca said my dad told her, if I phone, to put me right through. When I told him the man's name, Dr. Zwicker, he said, "Thank you, my love, I'll be home in ten minutes, and you must not tell Salamina . . . " You mustn't tell Salamina!

· · ·

The Graces' bedroom door, four o'clock in the afternoon. The same Beethoven plays quietly through the house as Elizabeth moves down the passage toward Eugenie's room, in a ghost-like little dance trying to keep everything quiet.

ELIZABETH: You can't see into my mom's room when she's sleeping because she closes the shutters to make it very, very dark. *(Peering in.)* And when my dad comes home and opens them up, the long shadows of the almond trees come creeping in *(Trying not to let them touch her.)* . . . to all the fairy dust . . . *(Grasping at it, trying to find it in the air above her. Dr. Grace opens the shutters. Afternoon light streams into the room.)*
DR. GRACE: *(Hurrying, anxious.)* Eugenie . . . Eugenie . . . come on, wake up . . . get dressed, Zwicker has an unidentified child at Tembisa.

EUGENIE: *(Rousing herself.)* Oh God, Isaac . . . what time is it? Where is Tembisa?

DR. GRACE: It's a brand-new state-of-the art hospital they're building for blacks out past Edenvale.

EUGENIE: Oh God, Isaac, it's not her. *(Suddenly tears.)* Did you tell him . . . *Baragwanath?*

DR. GRACE: Zwicker says this child is about three. He says on a bad night they send the overload from Bara to Tembisa, even though it's not officially open, and they're already behind on the paperwork. Where is your cardigan, Eugenie? *(He buttons up her coat over the nightdress. He is tender with her as one might be with a confused child that has just woken from a long sleep. Elizabeth still peering in at the door.)* I've told Elizabeth *not* to tell Salamina. Zwicker says they had three infant deaths at Bara on Thursday night . . . two from dehydration. You know, sometimes they don't know to bring the child to the hospital until it's half dead. I don't want to get her hopes up. Button your top button, Eugenie, it's nippy out there.

• • •

The kitchen door: Late sun streaming, Elizabeth runs out to the gate, the car already driving off.

ELIZABETH: When I got to the kitchen door with my blanket, and my sweets for Moliseng, the lights of the car are going, going . . . going . . . and the gate closed! *(Highly distressed.)* . . . I hope my dad has that special paper . . . ! *(She runs around the house, frantic, and inside, climbs onto her bed, trying not to cry.)*

• • •

Elizabeth's bedroom, dark now. Iris comes in quietly to check on Elizabeth.

IRIS: Miss Lizzy? . . . Miss Lizzy Monkey? . . . *(Terrified screaming, rushes out thinking the Tokolosh has stolen Elizabeth too.)* . . . JO! . . . JO . . . Miss Lizzy! Monkey!?

ELIZABETH: Iris said when she went to check on me, my bed was empty. She said she got such a fright, her heart jumped *(Illustrates graphically.)* right out of her throat!

Outside, the kitchen step. Cold, dark night, incessant frogs and crickets.

ELIZABETH: And then she *found* me! . . . sleeping, outside, on the kitchen step . . . *(Stiff and cold, waking slowly.)* I don't know how it happened, but all around me are empty sweet papers. Hah! Somebody ate all Moliseng's sweets! I think somebody ate them in their sleep maybe . . . When Iris kneels down to carry me to my bed, she's suddenly all lit up *(Staring at this vision.)* like a shining, brown candle in the night! *(Pointing to the gate.)* It's the lights, the lights of the car at the gate! *(Pointing back at Iris. The car engine throbs at the gates as they open, and then the tires crunch slowly up the gravel drive.)* The big black car, waiting for the gate to open. *(Furiously waving the car up the drive.)* And then it drives up the drive, and the lights go out. *(Rushing to the car.)*

IRIS: *(Grabbing Elizabeth's shoulders.)* Wait, Monkey! You wait here with Irissy, jhe? *(Elizabeth stops still, and silent, restrained by Iris, and listening with all her might.)*

ELIZABETH: You can only hear the frogs and the crickets now . . . *(Keeps listening intently in the dark, and then suddenly, footsteps in the gravel.)* And my dad's shoes . . . you can hear my dad's shiny brown shoes going around the back of the car in the dark, and then he opens the door and the light shines on my mom's hair! They walk slowly, slowly up the path . . . *(Rushing to them.)*

IRIS: *(Restraining her again.)* Wait, Monkey! . . . you wait here with Irissy . . . jhe?

ELIZABETH: *(Peering into the dark to see. Hands prayerful.)* Past the white frangipani flowers . . . all the way up to the Syringa tree. *(Sudden, quiet as she reaches the tree.)* Hah! Salamina has fallen asleep, like me. She's got Zephyr's blanket on her, *(Imitating Zephyr laying the blanket over her.)* . . . the one that he always wears at the fire, *(Imitates Zephyr's gestures at the fire.)* to sing the prayer song. Zephyr says . . . the spirits of our ancestors *fly* into the trees when they die . . . into the leaves and the berries and the bark. *(Imitates Zephyr again, creating a tree in the air with mutilated fingers.)* And that's why when you carve your mask out of a piece of wood, you can't choose the face *you* want, because the face is already there, and you just open . . . it . . . out . . . *(Like carving with Zephyr's hand, no fingers.)* into the world to see *who it is* . . . like being born. I think she was wondering if Moliseng might be *in* the tree. You can hardly see her now because she's been all covered with berries.

(Eugenie and Isaac kneel down in the dark next to the mound of berries that is Salamina.)

ELIZABETH: When Salamina opens her eyes, Moliseng is there! She stares at her through her big, fat, swollen eyes as if she might be dreaming . . . and then all of a sudden, the berries lift up into the air like *(Joyful explosion.)* confetti . . .

SALAMINA: *(Scooping Moliseng into her arms, smelling every inch of her.)* Jo, jojo . . . Moliseng, Moliseng, Moliseng! *(Moliseng, still very ill, begins to cry.)*

ELIZABETH: *(Jumping up to touch her.)* Dumela Moliseng, Dumela!

DR. GRACE: Be very gentle with her, Elizabeth, she's been quite ill . . . She's still not eating properly, and I promised Zwicker I'd watch her.

EUGENIE: Let's go inside, it's freezing out here.

SALAMINA: *(Watching them go in, she lags behind, smelling Moliseng, inspecting her.)* Oh jo jhe . . . oh jho Moliseng . . . ? Moliseng jhe? . . . *(Salamina goes down on her knees to let Elizabeth kiss Moliseng's cheeks.)* Jo . . . Elcssc-bett jhe?!

ELIZABETH: *(Jumping with joy.)* Dumela Moliseng! . . . Dumela!

(Jubilant, impassioned connected to the earth in a momentary, powerful, primitive dance of unbounded gratitude, Salamina takes ownership of her child.)

SALAMINA: Yhe! *(Feet stamping proudly into the earth, uncompromising.)* Dumela, Moliseng, Dumela!

ELIZABETH: Irissy helped me to pick out all the Syringa berries which got stuck! in Salamina's hair . . . Luckily, Moliseng is still too sick to eat her sweets . . . *(Hiding one hand behind her back.)* She stays with us in the big house! And my mom makes her special porridge, with NO sour milk! *(Elizabeth scampers up into her Syringa tree, standing on her swing.)* Moliseng! If you don't eat your spaghetti, you can get *so* thin that the wind will come, and pick you up and carry you far, far away . . . through the purple flowers of the jacaranda trees . . . into the yellow clouds of dust over the gold mines, out over the white sandy beaches of the Indian Ocean . . . all the way up past the moon! And you will never be seen again, like a little piece of glitter that just . . . *(She makes a gentle, unpredictable, whispering whistle.)* . . . blew away . . . *(The same soft tinkling sound on the wind as it vanishes. Jumping down from the swing.)* My dad gives her very sore injections and she screams blue bloody murdaaah! . . . And I'm at the window to check, and see, if the wind is coming to blow her away *again*! And after a few nights she's going back to Salameeny's room and after not too long . . . she is fat! and round! and shiny! and brown again . . . !

• • •

The fire outside the servants' quarters. In the firelight a celebration dance, Zephyr's powerful drumming as Salamina, Iris, and Pietros dance in the night. Moliseng sits in her blanket next to the fire. Elizabeth concealed in the granadilla vine.

SALAMINA: Moliseng! Moliseng! Come, dance with Salamina, Moliseng yhe? *(Holding Moliseng's hands, Moliseng still too weak to stay on her feet.)* Oh! *(Picking her up.)* Uppy Moliseng . . . jhe? *(She dances gently with Moliseng in her arms.)*

ELIZABETH: *(Leaping out of the vines.)* And me too! Uppy, uppy!

SALAMINA: Oh yjo! Uppy Monkey? Okay! Come! You climb up jhe? *(Salamina, arms filled with Moliseng, bends down to let Elizabeth clamber up onto her back.)* Jo! You are too fat Monkey jhe?! *(Heaving Elizabeth up on her back.)* Jhe! Jhe! . . . Moliseng! *(To Moliseng.)* Moliseng! *(To Elizabeth.)* Elessebett, *(Out to the sky.)* Mashlope!

• • •

The living room, Sunday afternoon. Moliseng, still recovering, and Elizabeth, playing.

ELIZABETH: *(Jovial, sweet.)* I'm not fat, Moliseng! You are fat!

MOLISENG: Monkey too fat! Monkey too fat!

ELIZABETH: *(Exasperated.)* She thinks I'm fat! We all jolly lucky fish because my dad is home today! Usually he's out, saving everybody's life. Everybody's life has to be saved NOW! Everybody's baby has to be born NOW! Everybody got bitten by a snake NOW! Take a Disprin and go to bed! And leave us in pieces and quiet! *(The phone rings and Dr. Grace gets up to answer. Chanting, fingers in her ears.)* Pieces and Quiet! Pieces and Quiet!

DR. GRACE: Sshh! Ssh! Good Lord . . . honestly! *(Answering.)* Hello? . . . Hello, yes, this is Dr. Grace.

ELIZABETH: *(Slow motion as she imitates him.)* And then his hand went up in the air like that, and down over his face, like that . . .

DR. GRACE: *(Covering his face.)* Oh God . . . Oh God.

• • •

Elizabeth's room, darkened quiet. Salamina sits beside Elizabeth, wide awake, in her bed.

ELIZABETH: Salamina has to put me to bed. What happened, Sally? What happened?

SALAMINA: Go to sleep, Miss Lizzy. Salamina it's here . . . you go to sleep!

ELIZABETH: But what happened, Sally, what happened?

SALAMINA: It's a very bad *accident*, Miss Lizzy, a terrible *accident. (She can hardly look at Elizabeth.)* Now you go to sleep! *(Trying to sing to her.)* Thula baba, thula . . . *(Salamina covers her face with her hand, and turns away.)*

ELIZABETH: All night long I can hear my mother running in and out of the house, looking for the car keys . . . I think my dad has them . . . and then she's looking for the gun . . . why does she need the gun? *(She starts to grasp at imaginary specks of fairy dust glittering in the darkness over her bed.)*

• • •

A hot, dusty road in the Northern Transvaal. First light. The white car is traveling fast, Elizabeth glued to the window, watching small groups of women walking in the veld some with babies strapped on their backs, most barefoot balancing parcels of food or buckets of water on their heads. Raggedy children chase an old tire or drag a stick through the hot sand as they walk.

ELIZABETH: Very early in the morning, we drive for four hours in the big white car to the foot of the Magaliesberg mountains . . . *(Hanging out of the open car window to see.)* We don't stop at Warmbaths to swim in the hot pools because we in a rush! . . . *on* to the red sandy road where the rabbits run across at nighttime, *(Excited anticipation.)* to the big wire gate of Clover. Clover is my grandpa's farm! It's called Clover because it is . . . ? Surprisingly *green!* He's got huge yellow buttercups that you can wrap your whole face up in . . . like a hat! One time, my grandpa George came to *me* for a holiday, and when he's on the train, going back home to Clover, the train moved and his hands are going . . . going . . . going to Clover and I jumped up to them and my big feet climbed all the way up the side of the train into the window and I'm going to Clover! And my mom can't get me! *(Big fright.)* . . . I forgot to put on my undies.

• • •

Grandpa George and Elizabeth in the train compartment. He stoops down to this unexpected traveling companion.

GRANDPA GEORGE: Oh Lord! Well, if you're a *very* lucky fish, maybe Grandpa George will open the shop on the farm for you, and give you some picaninni undies.

ELIZABETH: Haaa! Picaninni undies! I not wearing picaninni undies! I have *Princess* undies . . . from *Marks and Spencer!*

• • •

The farm, Clover. Elizabeth runs like a wild monkey, barefoot and free on the farm.

ELIZABETH: My grandpa has a lovely, lovely shop on the farm with a thatched roof that smells of burning fires, and a smooth mud floor . . . it's mud, but it's very, very clean and smooth. Everybody loves my grandpa's shop because everything is free. He can't take *any* money because the till is broken! He's got a huge paraffin pump for the little silver tins that light up the whole farm at nighttime . . . and shirts and undies for the picaninnies . . . He has teary eyes from the sun. He's eighty-two years old so he's a little bit deaf . . . but my granny says, "None so deaf as those who do not wish to hear!" *(Mystified horror.)* Haaa! He can make his self deaf!

GRANDPA GEORGE: Come along! Picaninni undies are good enough for picaninns, they are good enough for *you,* my girl! Come on!

• • •

Elizabeth and Grandpa George in his farm shop. Elizabeth hunts through piles of underpants.

ELIZABETH: Unfortunately, there are no small ones left in his shop . . . only size *large,* and they jolly stretchy! So we took them back to the farmhouse and we told my Granny, "We've got an underpants emergency!" And so she sewed *Eeeelastics! (Indicates from the back of the shoulder over the front of the shoulder straps joining the back armpit-high undy waistband, to the front armpit-high waistband.)* from here to here . . . *(Indicates again.)* and here to here . . . and now . . . *(Delighted shimmy.)* they don't fall down anymore . . . ! Actually, picaninni undies are jolly nice . . . soft and comfy! And roomy!

• • •

Clover. The Grace family car stops at the big wire gate. A brutally hot, dusty day.

ELIZABETH: We've arrived! Open the gate! *(Calling him out of the house.)* Grandpa? . . . *(Jumping excitement.)* *I* want to open the gate! *(Shrinking back.)* The police are here . . .

SERGEANT POTGIETER: Is it just the four of you?

EUGENIE: Yes, Sergeant, we're all here.

SERGEANT POTGIETER: *(Removing his cap, wipes his brow.)* Please have a seat, Eugenie. We regret to inform you that we have not, as of yet, caught the perpetrator. We believe him to be a freedom fighter from Rhodesia who slipped across the border at nighttime. It appears that he randomly attacked your parents. Now, as you well know, there is not a single door on this farmhouse that has a lock on it!

• • •

The bathroom in the farmhouse, lit only by one paraffin lamp. Elizabeth's grandmother, in her sixties, still pretty and plump, running the bath water.

ELIZABETH: My granny was in the bathroom, running the water for her bath, when she thought she heard a noise in the bedroom. So she picked up her paraffin lamp and when she got to the bathroom door, there was a big man with blood all down his shirt . . . and a knife in his hand . . . and she got such a fright she pushed the lamp at him and he pushed it back at her and the glass broke and cut her eye all down here . . . like that, and the paraffin burned her skin all down here . . . like that. She has very, very blue eyes. Some people make her shy when they say her eyes are as blue as English violets, like Elizabeth Taylor's eyes . . . and did you know . . . her name is also . . . Eee . . . lizabeth!

• • •

The doctor's waiting room at Bandelierkop, the nearest town. The town consists of eight houses, a general store with a petrol pump, a very small hotel. Granny Elizabeth having her eye stitched and burns bandaged

GRANNY ELIZABETH: What did they want, Dr. Winston? He's a farmer, he doesn't have anything . . . he gave everything away. Did you know, they took his medals, his war medals from the trunk under our bed . . . his medals for courage and bravery . . . they *took* them . . .

• • •

Clover, outside the farmhouse. Eugenie and Isaac Grace filing a police report.

SERGEANT POTGIETER: There's a murderer running around out there, with medals for courage and bravery on his jacket . . . Please, sit, Eugenie. It was dusk. He simply walked right into the open front door of the farmhouse. We found your father kneeling over his bed . . . twenty-two stab wounds in the back. Your mother managed to crawl to the phone in the passage. Now luckily, with the party lines we have for the farms around here, there was a conversation already in progress, when she . . .

• • •

Clover the previous night. In the dark passage, broken glass. Sounds of the conversation in progress . . . two voices "yes, well we all went in the bakkie to Ramagoepa" . . . "Oh, really?" . . . "Ag, yes, you know we . . . " Intermittent sounds of interruption on the line.

GRANNY ELIZABETH: *(Burned bleeding, trying to identify who is on the line.)* Dawn? Tom? Beth . . . Elizabeth, quickly . . . attacked . . . we've been attacked . . . George needs help! . . . Quickly, quickly *come! (They respond in V. O. as she listens.)*
V.O.: *(A stunned silence, then quietly.)* Oh God . . . Oh God, there's been an attack . . . there's been an attack at Clover . . .
GRANNY ELIZABETH: At Clover . . .
V.O.: Oh my God . . . *(They click off the line.)*

• • •

The porch, Clover.

SERGEANT POTGIETER: Now those farms are twenty miles away at least, and by the time they got here, the bath water, still running, had turned this farmhouse into a river of blood.

• • •

The gravesite, a small cemetery in the veld near Ramagoepa. The wind swirls the dust over a newly dug grave. It is a hot, dry day.

ELIZABETH: When we buried my grandpa, my granny sat very still and quiet. All the workers came, from all the farms around, and they brought . . . *(Straining to see who's coming.)* all the picaninnies! . . . all wearing white shirts from my grandpa's shop! And he went down, down . . . down . . . into the ground . . .

FATHER MONTFORD: "Hail our life, our sweetness and our hope . . . " *(The coffin is gently lowered.)*

ELIZABETH: And he went down . . . down . . . down . . . *(Touching the spots on each nail . . . resting at "foe." Flat stiff hands now, patting the air as if to stow him safely in the earth. Sweetly to him.)* Hide away . . . hide away . . . !

• • •

The Graces' backyard. Elizabeth sits in the Syringa tree. Her hands rest, in silence, on the third finger . . . little white spots . . . "foe." She tries to wipe that spot off on her dress, looking away.

ELIZABETH: When we came home from burying my grandpa, Salamina *left* us! But that's all right, because she doesn't want to look at me anymore. She just keeps turning her face . . . *away!* . . . like that! When she didn't bring the tea in the morning, we thought she was sick . . . *(Racing off to comfort her.)* so we *ran* down to her room, and . . . *(Stops dead.)* everything is *gone!* Just the bed up on bricks.

• • •

THE SYRINGA TREE 🌸 139

Salamina's room. The room is completely bare, just the bed, two red bricks under each leg, raising it about eight inches. Eugenie, still grieving, and Elizabeth stand in the doorway.

EUGENIE: *(Quietly.)* Work for you for years and years . . . you take them in, treat them as one of your own, and they disappear, without a word . . . in the middle of the night! *(Suddenly tears.)* With Moliseng!?

• • •

The Graces' backyard. Elizabeth, at the fence, frantically shouting to Zephyr working in the Dominees garden.

ELIZABETH: Zephyr! Zephyr! Zephyr! Salamina's gone!
ZEPHYR: She's gone, Miss Lizzy.
ELIZABETH: Where did she go? *(Suddenly . . . a prank?)* Haa! Where is she hiding?
ZEPHYR: We are going to find a new somebody for you, Miss Lizzy.
ELIZABETH: I don't want a new somebody! I want Salamina! I want Sally . . . You must go and fetch her and tell her to come home! *(Indicates herself.)*
ZEPHYR: She's gone, Miss Lizzy.
ELIZABETH: Zephyr, why? . . . why?
ZEPHYR: Your grandfather, Miss Lizzy . . . She was ashamed! *(Bending down to her.)* We all of us, yhe . . . ? We carry the sin of our brother. Ashamed! She was ashamed.
ELIZABETH: *(Tears.)* Why, Zephyr?! Why, why, why!
ZEPHYR: *(To the sky.)* We've got no answer for this place, Miss Lizzy. *(Defiant.)* Come, no more tears, yhe! No more tears. *(Towering over her, he wipes her face with his mutilated hand, and turns to go. He stops to look back at Elizabeth. He beckons for her to follow.)* You . . . come . . .

• • •

Elizabeth's bedroom at home, five years later. Elizabeth bounds in. Granny Elizabeth is staring out of the window at the front garden.

ELIZABETH: Hi, Gran . . . Gran? What are you doing in my room? Gran? What are you looking at out there? Gran?
GRANNY ELIZABETH: *(Startled.)* Oh! Elizabeth, I'm so sorry! *(Gasps.)* Oh look

at you today! All dressed up in your high school uniform! Well, I was really just looking at that old loquat tree out there, actually. It's almost ripe for picking, I think. *(Slowly.)* I could just see him, walking out with the sun on his shoulders, to pick that first loquat . . . Do you know, after all these years . . . I still miss him, so very, very much. Oh, don't wake your Mum, Elizabeth . . . She was his favorite you know, and he was hers . . . Oh my! He was hers.

ELIZABETH: *(Softly, turning away, shutting her out.)* Lovers-to come . . . journeys-to-go.

• • •

Eugenie's dressing room. Elizabeth plays in an old bridal veil. It is Granny Elizabeth's.

ELIZABETH: Lovers-to-come . . . *(Looking for a spot on the fourth nail.)* I don't know when I'll find him, but when I do, I want it to be a glittering night . . . Hundreds of wedding candles everywhere . . . The sweet soft smell of the night . . . White frangipani in full bloom . . . And in the firelight . . . the candlelight . . . The fire . . . ! Zephyr! Salamina . . . *(Forceful.)* Where *are* you Sal? You promised me my wedding song, and now when I find him, you're not even going to be with me. *(In the wedding song, Elizabeth conjures Salamina.)*

SALAMINA: Yhe! . . . You move your hips, Miss Lizzy . . . *(Laughing at Elizabeth's efforts.)* You are a bride! "Iquira . . . lendlela . . . !" Yeh Lizzy! Oh yeeeh jhe Lizzy! *(Laughing. She continues singing, fading further and further away, just a haunting memory now.)*

• • •

University of Witwatersrand, 1976. Elizabeth, twenty, on a campus pay phone. She has to shout to be heard over the sounds of a student march protesting apartheid

ELIZABETH: John, John? Can you hear me? It's Elizabeth. Listen, I'm at the University. Is Mom sleeping? Where's Dad? Well, promise me you won't say anything . . . don't tell either of them . . . promise me? I just saw a notice alongside my graduating class list, that thing the student union puts up, *(Reads.)* NEWS THAT WILL NOT APPEAR IN YOUR DAILY

NEWSPAPER . . . FATALITIES: I said *Fatalities . . .* Christopher Mzuma, sixteen. Peggy Ditwe, eighteen. Pietros Mseddi, twenty-four. Dora Mtwetwe, fourteen. Moliseng Mashlope . . . fourteen . . . Moliseng. I don't know, I don't know if it's her, Can you get here? *No!* You don't tell them, John, just get here. Because the police are going to close the road into Soweto but we can try to get in there if you get here quickly . . . I don't know, they said the kids have gone mad, burning their schools and buses and anything they can get their hands on. All right, I'll wait for you at the phones, and be careful! At the phones . . . *(Waiting for John, trying to remember.)* They kill you if you go in there . . . they don't want you in there . . . *(In the highveld wind, Elizabeth hears Moliseng's song, tiny, playful.)*

• • •

The Graces' backyard, 1963. Seven-year-old Elizabeth high in the Syringa tree. With Moliseng in tow, Salamina searches up through the leaves for Elizabeth.

MOLISENG: *(Joyful sweet singing, soft, as if born out of another time.)* "Imithi goba kahle . . . ithi! . . . ithi! . . . "

SALAMINA: *(Haunting, but growing full and present.)* Miss Lizzy? Miss Lizzy Monkey? Hey Monkey? Come down . . . Moliseng she wants to say good-bye to you!

ELIZABETH: *(Leaping down.)* Aah but it's not Friday yet?

SALAMINA: Yes, Miss Lizzy, it's Friday! *(To Moliseng.)* Come, good-bye to Miss Lizzy, Monkey.

MOLISENG: Good-bye, Miss Lizzy. *(Feet dancing.)* Moliseng going to big school in Soweto!

ELIZABETH: Haah! *(Dancing with her.)* Big school in Soweto, Mollie! Um . . . wait! . . . um, wait!

SALAMINA: No, Miss Lizzy, we are late yhe? My mother she is waiting for Moliseng on the train. Come, good-bye to Miss Lizzy.

MOLISENG: Good-bye, Miss Lizzy Monkey! I love you . . . *(Dodging, challenging her.)* Cover me with kisses! *(She grabs Elizabeth's ears and begins kissing her all over her cheeks.)*

ELIZABETH: *(Kisses.)* Bye Mollie, bye . . . Bye! And don't pull anybody's hair there! Bye! Bye!

• • •

A police barricade outside Johannesburg. 1976: Elizabeth, twenty years old, with John, trying to get to Soweto.

ELIZABETH: *(Thoughts racing.)* Moliseng, fourteen, running, running, to the street corner . . . What is she thinking, leading her fiery, raggedy band to the front lines of riot police? . . . What is she thinking standing face to face with them? . . . Turn back, Moliseng, run for your life! . . . Climb up into the Syringa tree, under Salamina's bed, hide away, Moliseng, hide away! What is she thinking, with a brick in her hand . . . ?

• • •

Soweto, in intensifying scorching, white daylight. Moliseng, fourteen, in a ragged school uniform, runs defiantly in the dust toward the police line. She leads a tattered band of children, armed with rocks and sticks. She is exhilarated, impassioned, young.

MOLISENG: Your bullet cannot kill me! I am Moliseng! Moliseng *(Pointing to her heart, as Elizabeth did in naming her.)* Eleseebett Mashlope! I stand with you on this street. This it's my street. My corner. My country. This it's my place. I am *in my place.* I am part of this earth, but I will not lie down like mud to disappear. I am the mountain that rises up to spit in your face! I am Moliseng! I will not walk down the road of my mother, bow my shoulders, hide my head in shame. I will stand up . . . *I* stand up! Your bullet cannot kill me . . . You will see me forever in your dreams, running in the fire of freedom. You will not sleep, you will hear my heart beating, beating, beating, speaking in my own tongue . . . Amandla! *(Moliseng's body lifts up, feet flying in the dust as gunshots ring out, a bullet through her heart, a massive exit wound in her back.)*

ELIZABETH: Hide away, Moliseng, hide away! . . . Moliseng, free and brave, free and brave . . . like the drum that beat's in the night, free . . . and brave, and dead . . . dead at fourteen.

MOLISENG: *(Dying, trying to suck her life back out of the air.)* . . . Cover . . . me . . . with kisses . . . ?

• • •

The Syringa tree. Elizabeth, twenty, motionless, silent, under the tree. The berries fall.

ELIZABETH: I'll never tell you. I'll never tell either of you. You brought Moliseng into the world, caught her in your own hands . . . *(Hands like Dr. Grace's lifting the newborn Moliseng.)* I'll never come back here. I vow never to need anything from this place. I'll say . . . I'll say I'm leaving because . . . because nothing changes. And you'll say . . . my old dad, you'll say . . .

DR. GRACE: But *we* change things, Lizzy, each of us in our own way . . . *we change* them.

ELIZABETH: No, we don't . . . *no* we *don't!* We tried to find Salamina, but in the chaos, you know, and you're not allowed in there . . . and anyway it's years since she left us! Eight, nine years . . . and Moliseng . . . I have no words to tell you. I'll sit underneath the Syringa tree and promise I'll never tell either of you. And the berries fall, and I wonder if Moliseng might be *in* the tree. No words, no water, no baptism . . . no Irissy to hose me down, no warm water washing rivers of shame back into the earth to cleanse you. Running . . . running . . . I'm leaving this place . . . *(She stops, looks at the swing for a long moment. Goes.)* I'm leaving . . .

• • •

Jan Smuts Airport, Johannesburg. Early evening, the last streak of sun across the sky.

ELIZABETH: And as I walk out on to the runway, I can see you at that big glass wall that runs all the way along, with all the fingerprints on it . . . and kisses on the glass, everyone saying good-bye through the glass, because of terrorism . . . so you can't hold anyone up till the last minute, you have to leave them at that big glass wall that runs all the way along . . . and kiss them through the glass, and try to tell them stuff . . . *(Brave, cheerful.)* I love you . . . don't forget me! And you can still smell their hair on your cheeks, and feel the shoulders of their jacket, that nice brown wool . . . I love you . . . ! And as I walk out onto the runway I smell the air and I try to *remember* it . . . I'm never coming back here again. And the sun is setting over this extraordinary sky, our huge big blue sky from when we were little . . . And I can hear your voice, walking with you under the lilac flowers of the Syringa tree, *and* I can see your face through the window . . . *(Reading his words through the glass.)* "Missing me already" you're saying . . . "I love you, my Lizzy . . . I love you, my love" . . . *(Pointing to herself.)* my love!

• • •

America, the present.

ELIZABETH: And here I am, in the land of the free, and the home of the brave . . . *(Softly banging her fist on her chest, trying to hear the words in her heartbeat.)* Free and brave? . . . free . . . and brave . . . ? *(She hears nothing.)* I have no medals for courage or bravery on my jacket, stolen or deserved . . . I have none. Nothing changes, no matter how we dream of how it could be . . . that's the voice I hear, running, running . . . *(Trying to block her ears.)* And you write to me, my old dad . . .

• • •

Cape, South Africa. The present. Dr. Grace, in his seventies, retired, in the Cape.

DR. GRACE: My dearest Elizabeth! Look! Things *do* change . . . Front page! *VOTE THE BELOVED COUNTRY* . . . Lizzy! Did you ever think this day would dawn? All of us, voting . . . together! Much of the life you knew here will now be lost, but so much more, for so many more, will now be gained. You can come home now, Elizabeth! You can come *home* now my love! Love to John . . . if you hear from him . . . ? I miss you both, Dad.

• • •

Pasadena. Elizabeth, grown-up, on a swing in her own tree now. It is starting to rain. As she swings, the V.O. of Elizabeth, seven years old.

ELIZABETH:
"Wednesday's child is full of woe,
Thursday's child has far to go . . . "
That's my brother John! . . . *(Teasing him.)* Because he's born on Thursday!
"Friday's child is loving and giving . . . "
That's Moliseng! . . .

THE SYRINGA TREE ❦ 145

"Saturday's child works hard for a living . . .
But the child that is born on the Sabbath day . . .
(Beaming, referring to herself! Swinging higher.)
Is bonny, blithe, good, and . . . "

• • •

Pasadena. Pouring rain now. Drenched, Elizabeth swings higher and higher.

ELIZABETH: Oh God I miss it . . . I *miss* it . . . I miss the smell of it . . . those sudden thunderstorms that make the whole world grow dark at four in the afternoon, the lightning and thunder that sounds like *four million drums* . . . the pouring sheets of water, every drop so precious to us . . . Africa has no fucking water! *(Slowing down as the swing comes to rest.)* And the sweet, sweet, soft smell of the steaming mud afterwards. You felt like you were part of the earth there, and like everyone was part of *you. (An old train whistle in the distance.)* I remember the sound of the train at Clover always made me feel like I lived nowhere, but I was really some-where then . . . I was really somewhere . . . And you write to me . . . my old dad . . .

DR. GRACE: *Every* place is part of you, my Lizzy, and you're part of *every place* . . . We're all just part of the earth, and we carry one another with us . . . wherever we go . . . for all time . . .

ELIZABETH: *(Stands.)* And I'm carrying my very own little George . . . stand-ing under *(Lightly.)* my berry tree in Pasadena . . . I fell in love with the tree not caring what the house was like . . . Andrew! It has a tree! . . . with berries! . . . It has a tree with berries! We could put a swing! *(To baby George.)* Daddy could put a swing for you! *(Calling into the house to Andrew.)* Coming! *(To baby George.)* Your Grandpa Isaac's on the phone! Your Grandpa Isaac's on the phone! Here, *(Hands baby George to Andrew.)* go to Daddy . . . *(Takes the phone.)* Hi Dad!

• • •

The old porch, Knysna, South Africa. Dr. Grace, his tea on an old table. This is an extraordinarily beautiful place, enormous old oak trees, vineyards for miles, the smell of lavender in the air.

DR. GRACE: Elizabeth, Lizzy . . . your old dad knows. John has come. John has told me about Moliseng . . . gone forever . . . your old dad knows. And I'm thankful he told me . . . and I'm thankful he waited until Eugenie could no longer hear it . . . Oh! You mustn't be angry with him, Elizabeth! Lizzy! Listen to me . . . I have news for you . . . It was extraordinary, Elizabeth, extraordinary! I'm sitting here with Mabalel, my old skeleton . . . I thought Salamina had fallen off the face of the earth, blown away in the wind . . . I had all my old patients combing Johannesburg for her . . . black, white, and in-between! They all came up with the same answer. And then I went down to have scones and tea at that little place under the oak trees . . . yes, we actually have a tearoom down here . . . and my ears almost fell off my head! Karel asked that woman if her maid was better, and she said, "Yes, thank you very much, we didn't have to take her to the doctor after all, Salamina's fine now" . . . Salamina! I thought I must be dreaming . . . you know, wishful thinking . . . But no! There I was searching the length and breadth of Johannesburg up north and there's a Salamina up the road! Of course I all but attacked the poor woman for information! Mr. and Mrs. Biggs . . . Turns out when they retired they asked Salamina to come down to Knysna with them, she's been with them in Parkmore since she left us, and she works for them to this day. *(Getting up from the table, looking out through the oak trees to the vineyards.)* I want you to go and see her, Elizabeth. Go and see her.

•   •   •

Pasadena. Elizabeth and Andrew.

ELIZABETH: *(Slowly.)* He wants me to come home, Andrew. God . . . I've tried to picture him, a million times, my old dad . . . in a farmhouse I've never seen. I'm sure it's unspeakably beautiful . . . enormous hundred-year-old oak trees, and the vineyards of course . . . It's funny . . . I can't seem to picture him without my mum, his beloved Eugenie. She wanders into every room I place him in, *(Graceful.)* bold as brass, *(Smiling.)* "making herself useful" . . . She always used to say that . . . my mum . . . He said the farmhouse will be surrounded by lavender, and the oak trees . . . I can't even picture the oak trees anymore, it's so faded to me now. I've never told you this, Andrew. Sometimes I dream I'm there . . . I dream I'm climbing in the mimosa trees, and the thorn trees, and the syringa trees, looking for somebody . . . always looking for somebody . . . I'll go there in my dream, Andrew. *(Shutting it out.)* I don't think I can go there. *(Suddenly*

flooded with her dream, searching through the leaves of a hundred trees.)
Salamina . . . *(Realizing who she looks for as she extends her arms like a child to be picked up.)* Salamina . . . ?

• • •

Jet engines soaring. Elizabeth, Andrew, and George depart on the journey home.

• • •

The airport runway, Johannesburg. Up on the balcony of the airport terminal, the new flag flying, John and Dr. Grace wait. Elizabeth and Andrew holding baby George, walk across the tarmac. Elizabeth breathes in deeply, smelling the air as if trying to inhale the place.

• • •

The terminal. Their greeting tearful, joyful, a celebration as George is held aloft for all to see.

ELIZABETH: I wish you'd have waited in Knysna for us . . . you shouldn't have come all this way!

DR. GRACE: Oh it's a short hop, Elizabeth. Thought I'd brave the madness of Johannesburg . . . see for myself . . . all the changes . . . *(Suddenly tears, embraces her.)* Oh my Lizzy, my busy Lizzy.

ELIZABETH: How is Mum . . . ?

DR. GRACE: She's doing fine, Elizabeth. I kissed her for you when I saw her on Sunday . . . whispered in her ears that you were coming *home! (Pause.)* She won't know you, Elizabeth. She doesn't know anyone anymore. But she's in a marvelous place, Lizzy, and they take very, very good care of her there, and I mean . . . you'll just see . . . it's for the best.

ELIZABETH . . . .Yes, I know that . . . I know. And look at your little American . . . Georgie! *(John hands him to the old man.)*

DR. GRACE: Oh Elizabeth! Oh! Hello, George! Well he . . . he has Eugenie's eyes Elizabeth . . . as blue as English violets . . . *(Walking away to contain his emotion.)* Hello, George! Well! Well, you have your Great-grandfather's name George . . . welcome my boy, welcome to these shores! Welcome to *you!*

• • •

V.O. of young Elizabeth. From her swing.

ELIZABETH: When she didn't bring the tea in the morning, we thought she was sick! *(Racing off down the path.)* So we *ran* down to her room, and . . . *(Standing at the door.)* everything is gone . . . just the bed up on bricks . . .

•   •   •

An old Cape Dutch farmhouse, Knysna. Mrs. Biggs, in her early seventies, wearing a soft blue cashmere twin set and pearls, steps out onto the veran-dah into the full bloom of wisteria. She hurriedly and excitedly calls to some-one in the house.

MRS. BIGGS: Salamina? Salamina! I think they're here. *(Running down the drive a bit.)* I *think* I see dust at the end of the . . . yes . . . yes! . . . They're driving up the driveway . . . *(Running back up onto the porch.)* Come on, come out! . . . They're here! Oh, you look fine! Come on, come out, they're here!

ELIZABETH: *(The car pulls up, bringing John, holding baby George, and Eliza-beth, all warmly welcomed by Mrs. Biggs.)* Hello, Mrs. Biggs? I'm Eliza-beth . . . This is my little brother John, and my baby, George! Thank you so much for having us here, today, to your home. *(Looking back to the gate.)* It's such a beautiful farm . . . I'm sorry, I'm so nervous! Is she here? *(Salamina, now in her sixties, appears quietly at the front door little by lit-tle out onto the porch.)*

SALAMINA: *(Tentative, a whisper.)* Miss Lizzy? . . . Miss Lizzy! *(Slowly, staring at Elizabeth through the settling dust, she extends her hand.)* Monkey? Mon-key . . . ?

ELIZABETH: *(Suddenly in her arms, laughter and tears.)* Sal? Sal . . . You're just the same. Sal . . . *(They are gathered into one another's embrace.)*

SALAMINA: No Miss Lizzy . . . I am old jhe? . . . I am too old! Yjo . . . *(Catch-ing sight of John and the baby, covering her mouth with her hand.)* You are *married* Miss Lizzy!

ELIZABETH: Yes . . . I'm married, Sal . . . almost ten years now! *(Realizing.)* Oh . . . oh, my husband is . . . *Andrew* . . . this is . . . you don't recog-nize John?

SALAMINA: *(Still holding her hand over her mouth.)* Master John . . . houw! . . . is it . . . *(Indicating a small baby with her palm up, close to the ground.)* Master John!? . . . Jyo . . . you are too tall! . . .

JOHN: How are you, Sal? . . . *(Takes her hands.)* What's this uniform!? I thought I'd find you running the country!

SALAMINA: *(Dignified, quiet.)* No, Master John . . . this one it's *my* work.

MRS. BIGGS: Salamina's absolutely marvelous! We are so grateful to have her, but of course, you all know that!

SALAMINA: *(Still staring up at John and holding his hand between hers.)* Jo, jojo . . . Master John! *(She stoops down in a remembered game with him, long ago joy. Pause.)* And this one, it's your picaninni?

JOHN: Well, I wish he was my picaninni . . . this fat boy! He's Elizabeth's . . . aren't you? Yes! *(To George.)* You're Elizabeth's! Here, go to Salamina . . . *(He hands George to Salamina, who starts to take him, and then cannot. She turns away.)*

SALAMINA: *(Gently.)* No, Master John. *(Silence.)*

MRS. BIGGS: Salamina and I spent the whole morning making *wonderful* scones for you, high jinx in the kitchen! . . . I'm sure you'd all love a nice cup of tea! Come along! Why don't we all go inside . . . I think . . . *(Salamina has walked away.)* I think let's go on in. Come along, come on . . . *(John with George in his arms follows Mrs. Biggs up the steps of the farmhouse.)*

JOHN: What a beautiful farmhouse, Mrs. Biggs . . . Georgie seems to love it here, Elizabeth . . . ! Elizabeth? *(He turns to Elizabeth. She is not there.)*

• • •

Under the hundred-year-old oak trees. Elizabeth finds Salamina, standing alone, her hands over her mouth. Salamina lifts her eyes to look at Elizabeth. They stand in silence together.

ELIZABETH: I brought you some things from America . . . they're in the car . . . And I brought you this . . . *(In her hands, a small gift.)* It's from my house . . . in America, from the tree at my house . . . berries from the tree . . . *(Extends her hands to Salamina.)* Sal . . . Salamina? . . . Moliseng . . . *(In the soft wrapping placed in Salamina's hands, a handful of berries on a little stem . . . Salamina is silent, slowly touching each berry in her hand, then smelling them, she sinks to her knees, burying her eyes in them. She rocks back and forth in a slow, gentle motion, the way she always rocked Moliseng to sleep. Elizabeth kneels down beside her, streaming in a well of grief. Salamina cradles Elizabeth in her arms.)*

SALAMINA: Oh jho, Elesebett, hje . . . ?

You must *not* cry for Moliseng, Elesebett jhe . . . ?

Moliseng . . . she is *with* us . . .

When the wind it blows, when the leaves grow and fall,

When we walk under the trees,

Moliseng . . . she is *with* us.

Calling to us . . . in the wind, Elesebett,

To be proud, to open our heart with joy . . . *(Quietly.)* We are free . . .
   We are free!

Moliseng she is with us forever, and ever, Miss Lizzy,

Forever and ever.

Eh, Monkey? . . . *(Elizabeth is inconsolable.)* Oh jyo . . . oh jho
yje? . . . *(She rocks Elizabeth in her arms, and then gently, laughing in remembrance.)* Oh Monkey Monkey ch! *(Salamina holds the berries to her
heart. Slowly she gets up, and extends her arms to Elizabeth.)* Come . . . Uppy,
Monkey . . . Uppy jhe? *lye* . . . Uppy Monkey . . . Yje . . . ! *(She quietly
helps Elizabeth up, till they are both standing, looking beyond the edge of the
trees, out into the wind . . .)* For ever and ever jhe . . . ? Moliseng . . .
(Quiet, to Moliseng, in the wind.) yhe . . . ! yhe . . . !

END OF PLAY

SOUND EFFECTS
Crickets
Beethoven's *Fifth Piano Concerto, Adagio*
Policemen shouting, dogs barking
Tinkling sound
African drums
Beethoven's *Kyrie Eleison* and splashing water
Knocking
Car engine
Screeching tires
Frogs and crickets
Tires crunching on gravel
Phone ring
Wind
Student protest march
Singing
Gunshot
Thunder, lightning, rain
Old train whistle
Jet engines
Soft wind

NOTE ON THE SONGS
In the tradition of folk music, some songs are passed aurally from one gener-
ation to another and are not notated. Hence, spellings and translations may
vary. Exceptions to this are "Ballad of the Southern Suburbs," a.k.a. "Ag Please
Deddy," by Jeremy Taylor and "Die Stem," the official national anthem of
South Africa until the end of the Nationalist Government.

"Ag Please Deddy" by Jeremy Taylor.
"The Click Song," a traditional song made famous by Miriam Makeba. Sung
    to young maidens on their wedding day, it is a song praising the dung
    beetle (Qonqotwane) — king of the road — placed on the path by lost
    herd boys tending cattle. The way home is whichever way it chooses to
    go. It is a play on rhythm and click sounds:
    "Iquira lendlela kutwa nguqonqothwane (twice)
    Sele qabel'eqith'apha haya nguqongqothwane."
"Thula Thula Baba," widely known South African lullaby.
    "Thula tu thula thula thula baba, Thula baba thula.

Samthatha sambeka

Samathata sambeka, samthatha ekhaya."

Loosely translated:

"Shush baby, don't cry, We took him/her home and said,

Hush baby don't cry, Your mother will be here in the morning."

"Shoshaloza." Originally sung by the migrant workers from Rhodesia, it has become associated with the gold mines. It is a song about a train that brings the workers through the mountains and wishes them well for their journey back home. However, the real meaning/agenda of the song is very political, a coded message about carrying on the struggle. "Shoshaloza" means "push the train," meaning the freedom train. It is a work song, sung in exquisite harmonies to accompany physical labor, usually by road workers and miners.

"Shoshaloza, Shoshaloza, kule zontaba,

Stimela siphum' eZimbabwe/Rhodesia . . .

(replaced with "South Africa" in newer versions)

"By the mountains, push the train from Zimbabwe

Do your work, get on with your life,

Good luck with your train journey out . . . "

"Die Stem." ("The Voice" or "The Call.") The official National Anthem of South Africa until 1994 when the Nationalist government ended. It was written by the Afrikaans poet C.J. Langenhoven in 1918. It is now, along with the English version, included in "Nkosi Sikeleli," the present national Anthem.

"Uit die blou van onse hemel, uit die diepte van ons see . . .

Ons sal lewe, ons sal sterwe, Ons vir jou,

Suid Africa."

The official English version is as follows:

"Ringing out from our blue heavens, from our deep seas breaking round . . .

At thy will to live or perish, O South Africa, dear land."

"Nkosi sikelel' iAfrika." The "prayer" song, adopted as the national anthem since the first free election in April 1994. First composed in Zulu in 1897 by Enoch Sontonga and completed by a Xhosa poet Samuel E. Mqhyai. Meant originally for schools and church choirs, it was used as the closing song for meetings of the banned African National Congress.

"Nkosi sikelel' iAfrica

Maluphakamis'u phondo lwayo

Yizwa imithandazo yethu
Nkosi sikelela
Thina lusapho lwayo."

"God bless Africa,
Let her fame resound/ let the horn of her people rise high up,
In your love hear our prayers,
God bless our people, help us
Your children."
Moliseng's song, traditional children's coming-home song, Zulu.
"Imithi goba kahle, ithi . . . ithi . . .
Kanje, kanjo . . . "

"Everything will be all right . . . say . . . say . . . This way, this way . . ."

GLOSSARY AND HISTORICAL NOTES

Jo, Yjo, Jheh — Exclamation like Hey or Oh!

Batho ba Modimo — Oh my God / People of God.

Pas de chat — French ballet term meaning "step of the cat."

Dumela . . . Aghe . . . Dumela — Greetings . . . yes . . . greetings/Hello.

Picannini — Never used pejoratively but as a term of endearment for children, like "kids."

Pass — Identity document required to be carried by blacks at all times but most especially in designated white areas. It was instituted in 1950 by the Population Registration Act. The Urban Areas Act had already located blacks to controlled areas, the then-called "homelands," to ensure separate development for black and white people. Townships like Soweto sprang up when people in the desolate homelands moved to the cities seeking work. They were not allowed to stay in white areas and organized themselves into townships that sprang up around the cities. Most townships had no electricity, no telephones, shanty housing, and poor transport in and out. In 1950, the government also passed the Group Areas Act, which implemented strict residential segregation, whites only in white areas, "coloureds" (government term for mixed race) only in "coloured" areas, blacks and Indian people in their respective areas. Anyone working in an area other than that designated to them had to register and carry a "pass" for such employment, for access and permission to remain there overnight. Children would not be issued a pass to remain overnight with a black parent in a white area, and for the most part black children remained in the townships and homelands, separated from their parents and cared for by aging grandparents. The policy became known as "White by Night" as it had the effect of clearing the black population, except those employed in these areas, out of the white suburbs at night. Blacks found in white areas at night without a "pass" would be arrested.

Tokolosh — A feared devil in African mythology, capable of stealing the spirit or harming one, usually at night. He is believed to be very old and extremely short, perhaps only two feet in height, hence the custom of placing beds up on bricks to escape his reach.

"Don't belong to the Queen anymore" — South Africa withdrew from the Commonwealth in 1961.

Francesco — A beloved South African circus clown who wore blue glitter ears.

Suurpap — Sour milk porridge, often made in a cast-iron pot on the fire outside.

Bignonia Cherere — Mexican blood vine with deep red, finger-length trumpet shaped flowers.

Blerrie — Curse word, Afrikaans pronunciation of English "bloody."

Dominee — Afrikaans word for minister, usually in the Dutch Reformed Church, which was originally brought to South Africa by Dutch settlers, and eventually branched into two groups, the Nederduitsch Gereformeerde Church and the Nederduitsch Hervormde Church. Both, but more especially the former, were involved with the National Party, with some Ministers belonging to the Broederbond, a "secret" group of influential politicians and members of the community affiliated with the policies of apartheid as originated by the National Party. This said, it is important to note that some Dominees of the Afrikaans church, were against these policies.

Kielie kielie kielie — Afrikaans for "tickle tickle tickle" and pronounced *killy.*

Nee — Afrikaans for "No."

Ja, O ja — Afrikaans for "Yes, oh yes . . . "

Ag shame man — Expression of sympathy or empathy.

Fokken jood — Afrikaans meaning "Fucking Jew."

Jou fokken kaffir — Afrikaans for "you fucking kaffir." *Kaffir* is an ugly, extremely derogatory word for a black person.

Mabalel — A famous Afrikaans poem written by Eugene Marais.

Baragwanath — Africa's largest teaching hospital. It is situated near Diepkloof, Johannesburg, and primarily serves the black population from the townships. The standard of medicine here is extremely high despite the crowded and impoverished conditions and surroundings.

"Special paper" — Elizabeth often refers to this, meaning the *pass* required for blacks, but also meaning special permission from the police for whites to enter the township areas.

Clover — From Clova, a farm in the Northern Transvaal originally known as Mahila's Hoek, after Mahila the Witchdoctor who first owned the land.

Rhodesia — Former name of Zimbabwe.

"War medals" — Awarded for service in the North African engagement of the Allies against Hitler.

"Gifts, friends, foes, lovers to come, journeys to go" — Unknown origin, probably English lore, taught to the author as a child.

"News that will not appear . . . " — Heavy media censorship was in place during the National Party's rule. A state of emergency was called as a way of controlling the media. Reports of unrest or violence were heavily censored if reported at all.

"Vote the Beloved Country" — Inspired by Alan Paton's novel, the actual headline on one of the major daily newspapers on the historic day of the first free election in South Africa in which blacks voted for the first time. The date was April 27, 1994, after which Nelson Mandela was elected President.

"Wednesday's child . . . " — Nursery Rhyme, unknown origin.

Knysna — Small town in Cape Province in the south of the country, pronounced "Nize/nuh," with a silent *K*.

Note: Best efforts have been made to ensure the accuracy of these facts, spellings, and translations, and they are offered with the understanding that some of the information is, by nature, subjective and might be subject to change. Sources include Jonathon Paton's *The Land and People of South Africa*. Spellings and translations by Tsidii Le Loka and Tsepo Mokone. Thanks to Alan Ralphs and JET, Tish Goldberg Hill, Paul Potgieter, and my father, Dr. Isaac Gien, for their kind assistance in gathering information.

SOUND CUES

Master Sound Cues from the New York Playhouse 91 production, Frederic Orner and Bill Dolive, stage managers. Sound design by Tony Suraci. They are included merely as a guide.

CUE	EFFECT	PLACEMENT
Q1	Birds	at rise
Q2	Dogs barking and police van sounds	"Moliseng, Moliseng, Moliseng, *Yhe*"
Q3	Fairy dust tinkling	"put on their fairy *dust* powder"
Q3 *out*	Chimes	"thought she could see *some*"
Q4	Drums	"bed after *dark*"
Q5	Drums	foot *touches* ground ("Fi fie")
Q5A	Beethoven Piano	"left*over* from my supper"
Q5A *out*	Concerto 5 adagio	"Good night. Good *night*"
Q6	Beethoven same	pat fires
Q7	Beethoven Kyrie (Baptism)	"nice and *warm*"
Q8	Knocking at door	"clean and white *again*"
Q9	Organ chord	"Let us bow our *heads*" crescendo (prayer) 2nd
Q10	Police Van (driving, door slams, dogs, drives off)	"stoke the fires in *hell*"
Q10 *out*		as Lizzie reaches for fairy dust
Q11	Birds, outdoors	"flour and brown *sugar*"
Q12	Crickets, night	"go with my *mom* to the drive-in"
Q12 *out*		"*boom* boom. boom boom"
Q13	Car trip	"not allowed to go in there"
Q14	Brakes!	"matter be, oh *dear*"
Q15	Wind	"God only knows"
Q16	Beethoven *Piano Concerto No.5 Adagio un poco mosso*	"You mustn't tell Salami*na*"
Q17	Car leaving	"my sweets for *Moliseng*"
Q17 *out*		"gate *closed*"

Q18	Night sounds	"sleeping outside *on* the"
	Return of black car	
	Footsteps	
Q19	Ominous wind	"no sour *milk*"
Q20	Phone rings	"pieces *and* quiet"
Q21	Farm sounds (cows)	"big wire *gate*"
Q21 *out*		"wrap your whole *face* up"
Q22	Phone party lines	"Luckily with the *party* lines we have"
Q23	Wind	"river of *blood.*"
Q24	Riot sounds	"nguqongqothwane"
Q25	Moliseng: "Kanje e"	"don't want you in *there*"
Q26	One gunshot	"Amand*la*"
Q27	Voice-over/	"I miss you both, *Dad.*"
	Thunderstorm,	
	Rain subsides,	
	Train whistle	
Q27 *out*		on train *whistle*
Q28	Airport runway	"Salamina . . . Sala*mi*na?"
Q29	Voice-over	"Welcome to *you.*"
		("When she didn't")
Q29A	Wind	"uppy, monkey" as she starts to *rise*
Q30	"Click Song"	curtain call

The Visible Horse

By Mary Lathrop

To Michael and To Daniel

THE AUTHOR

Mary Lathrop's plays include *Hell on Wheels,* which was commissioned by the Philadelphia Festival Theatre for New Plays, *The Six Basic Rules, Table Stakes — No Limit* and *A Bris Is Still a Bris. The Urn of Drew* was a finalist for the 1991–92 Susan Smith Blackburn Prize and was work shopped at the Seven Devils Playwrights Conference in McCall, Idaho. *Dreams of Baby* was selected as Best New Play of 1993 by the *Seattle Times* Footlight Awards. *The Eighteenth Mitzvah* received the 1999 Richard Hugo House New Play Prize. *Tales from the Salt Mines* was commissioned by A Contemporary Theatre in Seattle and work shopped at the Ojai (California) Playwrights Conference. Her plays have been produced by theaters in New York, Chicago, St. Louis, Milwaukee, Denver, and elsewhere. Her one-act play, *The Chicken Fight,* was translated into Thai and produced as a comedy special for Thai Television (ITV Network). Her short screenplay *Chocolate* was produced by No Cents Films in Los Angeles. She has received Playwriting Fellowships from the Washington State and Seattle Arts Commissions and Artist Trust. *The Visible Horse* was work shopped at the National Playwrights Conference under its earlier title *Undead* in 1996.

ORIGINAL PRODUCTION

The Visible Horse was first produced at Whidbey Island Center for the Arts, in Langley, Washington, January 2001. It was directed by Rachel Katz Carey with the following cast:

Scott . . . . Zach LeClair
Meg. . . . . Johanna Melamed

CHARACTERS

SCOTT: a twelve-year-old boy
MEG: his mother

SCENES

Thursday afternoon, outside the condo
Thursday night, Scott's room
Friday afternoon, outside the condo
Sunday afternoon, willow Lake
Monday afternoon, outside the condo

TIME

The Present

NOTES

In Scott's first monologue, he has a razor scooter; in the second, he's on roller blades; and in the third, he has a skateboard. It's very important that he use these things throughout so that the audience can always see him working to maintain his balance. Running time is approximately 95 minutes. There is no intermission.

THE VISIBLE HORSE

Thursday afternoon Scott enters on a razor scooter. He does some tricks, i.e., wheelies, balancing with no hands, etc.

SCOTT: Watch this . . . See? . . . No, wait, watch this . . . See, cool, huh? This is cool . . . Anyways, I figured out what being cool is. It's 10 percent popularity, 10 percent fashion — and that includes hygiene. Right? Also your hair, how you smell, and bad breath. Hey! no! nobody wants to talk to somebody with green teeth. See? White, right? And you should do three baths a week, only I'm on swim team, and chlorine kills underarm germs, so I don't take baths, cuz of the chlorine — hoo, I'm really glad of that. But I wash my hair in the shower after practice, right?

  (He takes a small sample-size bottle of mouthwash out of his pocket.) This is my mouthwash — Scope. *(He swills some in his mouth and spits it back into the bottle.)* Did you know you can use it more than once? Just swoosh and spit it back — a course, you gotta spit thin or you'll spill. Anyways, I've had this Scope since school started. It showed up in the mailbox, and my mom, she goes, "Hey, go ahead and have it." And it's still minty fresh. Still! Want to smell? *(He puts the bottle back in his pocket.)*

  So, 10 percent popularity, 10 percent fashion, and that includes what your wear, your shoes, oh!, and underwear. My mom, she bought me boxers; Jason, this cool kid on swim team, he wears boxers. *(He pulls his underwear band up out of his pants to show them off.)* His have blue stripes. Oh! And, know what? These are a lot more comfortable. I'm not shitting. Heck, how are you gonna be popular if your underwear's squeezing your balls off? Nobody's going to talk to you if you're grumpy all the time. I got four pairs: red stripes, green stripes, black lines, and socks. They're really hilarious, they look like all the socks in the dryer stuck to them. But I won't wear them on swim days. Hey, I used to think it was cool to wear GI-Joe jockey shorts, can you believe it? Only they squeezed my balls off, squeezed them flat! Man, I'm not kidding! *(He demonstrates his roomy boxers.)* See? Real roomy, right? All the cool guys wear boxers. And heck, my balls feel great!

  (He squats down and ties his shoelaces.) High-tops are cool, but don't lace them all the way: uncool.

  Anyways, the laces, you know, the laces are too short to tie that way. I think if the tongue's all messed up? That's pretty cool.

(He takes a comb out of his pocket and combs his hair.) I got a haircut. This is pretty cool. Only, see, I was gonna let my hair grow. I seen this picture of my dad when he was little, our age, and his hair waaaay long — man, it was awesome. I think he was a hippie or something. So I go, "Yo, Mom, I'm gonna grow my hair long, like that." And she goes, "Forget it. Nobody wears long hair anymore." Only when she takes me, we walk in, and the barber, right?, he has this hella long ponytail half ways down his back. For real! And I go, "So, Mom! Nobody's got long hair!" She was psyched out! And this hippie barber, he goes, "All the cool guys have short hair." So I go, "Yeah? Guess you're not cool" Right? And my mom, I thought she'd shit. I'm not kidding. And this barber goes, "I may not be cool, but I know what is cool. And short hair is cool." No, he was way cool; he wouldn't take shit. So I go, "Okay." Right? Only when he cut it, this hippie barber, he cut my sideburns, which I did not want. Anyways, I comb it back with gel, which smells good, and that's hygiene. Gel's way cool. Do you want to smell my hair? *(He puts his comb back in his pocket.)*

So, 10 percent popularity, 10 percent fashion, and 80 percent attitude. My mom goes, like, "Yo, be friendly." Puhhh! You got to know who to take shit from, and who you can waste right back on. You gotta know. With most kids do this: neutral, see? Or you can smile just a little, see? Most kids like if you look neutral or friendly. But with some kids, do this. Heck, you gotta! If you do this on one side, it's snarling, and that impresses them. A course, you do it on both sides, you could start a fight, right? Also, if there's some guy gives you shit, but he's part of a group, Christ! chill. If you waste back, they could all dump on you. And that's not popular.

Anthony, this mean kid, every time, well not in front of teachers, in front of teachers he's sooo polite — I hate this guy. I was taking a pee in the boys' bathroom, and he was taking a pee beside me, and he goes, "Ooooo, now that Jason taught you karate, why don't you beat me up?" But all those boys in Mrs. Winslow's homeroom . . . there's Josh and Chris, who everybody thinks is great, and Anthony's maybe tight with them. I don't know, but they're a tight-knit class and they don't take shit. They're all really tight, and if I wasted Anthony, they'd all waste me. I could waste him. He's a pussy. I could. If my dad was here, I know how he'd go. Like he'd go "Yo, Anthony, you pick the time, you pick the place, I'm gonna beat the crap out of you, you little shit." My dad, he'd, he'd go like that.

(He takes a smashed half of a sandwich out of his pocket.) I didn't eat

this at lunch. You want some? What you eat for lunch is cool . . . or maybe fashion, I'm not sure. Don't let your mom pack you cold stew and shit like that. Sandwich, chips, cut up fruit, cookies — plain shit, which you can trade. Know what's really awesome? Fruit roll-ups! Everybody trades for fruit roll-ups. I wouldn't shit you.

Oh! And, like, if your friend is the smallest kid, and someone's wasting him, and you're big, right? You gotta stomp on that bully, cuz it's your friend. People see you stick up for some guy and that's popular. Also, sometimes they'd waste on you so you have to waste back. They do that to prove you, and then they'll let you in. That can happen. It can.

(He adjusts his boxer shorts.) These boxers are great on my balls — it's good fashion and hygiene, both. That's it: 10 percent popularity, 10 percent fashion, 80 percent knowing who you can waste.

The best kids to waste are new kids, cuz they don't have any friends, but I think that's mean. Heck, I wouldn't waste some guy just for being new. His mom probably made him move, and he didn't want to, right? Like, he really wanted to stay at his old house, with his old friends and his old school, but his dad got killed, and his mom wanted a fresh start. Naw, you shouldn't waste some new kid, cuz you might find out that his dad got wasted and his mom made him come here even though he didn't want. And now he has to live in a condo, and they gave away his dog. I would probably be nice to a new kid — except if he dumped shit on me, I'd punch his guts just once so's he'd know I'm tough. Then we could be friends. And, maybe, he still has his bike, and we could ride bikes, do hobbies. That would be cool.

Know what? At my old school, building models was a hobby. A lot of guys built models, and me and some of my friends, sometimes we'd build together, even. Like this one time, me and my dad invited over my model friends and we built the visible horse. It was awesome. He looked just like a horse, only his skin was clear plastic and you could see all his plastic guts. And my dad, he goes, "Let's eat horsemeat burgers for lunch," which grossed us way out. And after, we brought it in and showed and telled. See, model building was known. I don't think anybody builds models at this school, so shhhhh. Right?

So, 10 percent popularity, 10 percent fashion and hygiene, right? And 80 percent attitude. Like if somebody stomps on you, you gotta stomp back or you're a wuss and that's not popular. Oh! And staring. Staring's the worst. If someone stares you, don't look away. If you look away, hoo, you're in for shit forever. I do staring in the mirror, to practice, right? You gotta practice, cuz you gotta look evil. They get way psyched if you look evil.

Man, I hate staring — it's really hard. Oh! and, check this: even girls do staring . . . but I don't know why. They stare weird, right? And you can't waste girls or you'll get shit forever, right? Anyways, I don't think you should ever waste a girl. I mean, I don't like them, right? But I probably will next year.

They had this dance in the gym, right? No parents allowed — it was awesome! You had to pay three bucks to get in, but then you could eat all the chips and crap you wanted. I only danced once, by myself. When they dance fast, everybody just dances, and that's pretty cool. Hey, I wouldn't dance slow for a million bucks!

Oh! And this girl stared me. I'm not shitting! I stared her back way evil, but she stared me for a half an hour. Every time I looked, she stared me. I was psyched.

My mom, she took me, right? But I wouldn't let her walk me in, cuz no parents allowed. Anyways, she made me wear this black shirt; she said it was cool. She shouldn't say that, right? When she says "cool," it's lame. But I wore my Simpsons shirt underneath, so I took it off. Simpsons shirts are fashion, but you gotta wear a clean one every two days — that's hygiene.

They had the lights turned way down at the dance and a strobe, but it was waaaay noisy. That mean kid, Anthony, he wasn't there — see, he really is a wuss.

(He nods his head, as if in time to music.) Head banging: I did this for the whole dance. That was being cool. Every time that girl stared me, I did this. *(He demonstrates a "staring" face.)*

They only played two slow dances, right at the end, cuz they couldn't find the slow dance music. Mr. Edwards, he was in charge of the music. Mr. Edwards, he's okay. If we get him for science next year, that would be really cool. You know what he does? Dissects cow eyes. Gross! That would be awesome.

I could of slow danced that staring girl, but they only played two, right at the end. What if my mom seen? See what I mean, right? If my dad was here, I would have danced her. My dad was cool. My mom! My mom would be, like, "Who's that little girl you danced?" But like, "Yo, Mom, stay in the car."

So, 10 percent fashion and hygiene, 10 percent popularity, 80 percent attitude. But, hey! With girls, I think it's 10 percent popularity, 10 percent fashion, and 10 percent hygiene. See what I mean, right? With girls you get an extra 10 percent for hygiene. And you can't be gross to a girl, cuz they get really grossed. Like you can't talk about cow eyeballs and such — they don't think it's cool. Girls don't like being grossed, right?

If I slow danced that staring girl, I'd go like, "Do you like my Simpsons shirt? It's clean." Right? Girls like stuff like that. And if her breath was bad, I'd let her use my Scope. That's friendly, and that's popular.

Oh! You want to see something? *(He takes a rock out of his pocket.)* It's got gold in it. See? Little tiny flecks of gold, for real! Hey, I found it at my old house. Me and my dad, we were digging this hole, and I just found it, right? See? And my dad, he goes, "Awesome! Maybe it's a magic rock. If you make one special wish, it might come true." I go, "Dad, chill — I'm not a baby. Magic rock? It's gold, and that's good enough for me." Right? I'm gonna keep it til I'm twenty-five, then I'm gonna sell it. Make fifty thousand bucks from one rock. I'm gonna give it to my mom. Like, "Yo, Mom, here's fifty thousand bucks. Buy a mink coat." Right? *(He puts the rock back in his pocket.)*

I found that with my dad; it could be magic. You ever had magic? Not that wussy, fakey stuff, like cutting a lady in half. My dad said that was fakey. I mean real magic, like some things in nature have power, right? I was wishing on this star at my old house, stars have power — until I found out it was a streetlight. Duhhh. You can't wish on streetlights. Well, you can, but you don't get nothing back — I found that out. I could wish on this rock, right?, like, if it really did have power.

You know werethings? Like werewolves and werebears and vampires? They're way cool. The undead: creatures that are living and dead at the same time, I believe in that. I do. You can be living and dead. You could be both at the same time, right? And if you could wish a guy back from beyond, that would be awesome, right? So's, I'd wish for my dad.

My mom, she goes, like, "Always remember your dad." "Yo, I'm not stupid, Mom." She goes, "You're gonna be all right. You're gonna grow up and be a fine man like your dad. That's what he'd want." Hey, my dad didn't care if you were fine or nothing. He liked you anyways. He'd go, "Yo, nobody's perfect. Give me five." He'd go like that. Unless you messed with his stuff, then he'd go, "Hey, man, that's my stuff: put it back."

He'd go, "Anthony's an asshole." He'd go, "You're my best pal." He'd go, "It's okay if you dance that staring girl. You can dance her if you want."

So, you want to chill? Wanna see my condo?

(Scott exits.)

Thursday Night

Scott's bedroom. It's a mess, the bed unmade, his stuff all over the floor. On a shelf or in some other place of honor is Scott's model of the visible horse. Scott is lying on his stomach on the floor of his room, holding some action figures. He's speaking for the action figures as he manipulates them.

SCOTT: . . . I'm gettin outta here . . . Anthony, you're dead, you buttwad . . . Kerpow . . . Ahhhhh . . . Kerpow . . .

(Meg enters and hands Scott a pair of pajamas. Scott pointedly ignores her as he plays with his figures.)

MEG: Scott, here, put these on. Scott. I really mean it tonight — you're not sleeping in your clothes again.

SCOTT: You'll never take me alive . . .

MEG: And just so you know: I know that you haven't changed your underwear for a minimum . . .

SCOTT: Surrender, you asshole . . .

MEG: . . . Of two days, so in the morning, you're starting from the skin out. You got it?

SCOTT: Captain, the escaping prisoner has been captured . . .

MEG: Scott?

SCOTT: . . . Good work, men . . .

MEG: Please?

SCOTT: Sergeant, I'm ordering extra rations for your men.

MEG: Or, if you really must sleep in underwear again, you can, but you have to put on clean ones. Okay?

SCOTT: I don't have any clean underwear. Captain, we're ready in interrogation . . .

MEG: Scott, you have a drawer . . .

SCOTT: . . . Prepare the prisoner . . .

MEG: . . . Full of clean underwear.

SCOTT: No Mom, what I got is a drawer full of jockey shorts with GI-Joe on them.

MEG: What if we buy you more boxers this weekend? I bet you'd like that.

SCOTT: It's not going to be easy to break him, Captain . . .

(Meg has run out of patience, and she grabs the action figures away from Scott.)

SCOTT: Don't!

MEG: That's enough, Scott. Get in bed.

SCOTT: I'm doing something.

MEG: Scott, I've had it — it's late; I'm tired. *(Meg herds Scott into bed.)*

SCOTT: Can I stay home tomorrow?

MEG: Bedtime's always such a pleasure, isn't it?

SCOTT: Is my throat red?

MEG: No.

SCOTT: You didn't look. *(Scott gets in bed, clothes and all. Meg tucks him in.)*

MEG: Your throat isn't red, and you're going to school.

SCOTT: I don't feel good, Mom. For real.

(Meg kisses Scott's forehead checking for a fever.)

MEG: You're fine. You've got to go — school's your job.

SCOTT: Then I quit!

MEG: You don't get to quit.

SCOTT: Right, like you didn't quit your old job?

MEG: I quit so we could move to this happy place. We're done with this argument, Scott. Go to sleep. *(Meg gives Scott a quick good night kiss.)* Oh. I was talking to Walter in the parking lot, and he wants to know if you'll help him move some furniture to his storage unit this weekend.

SCOTT: I guess.

MEG: And Scott, this time when he offers you money, say no, okay?

SCOTT: Oh, so if some guy wants me to do work . . .

MEG: He's our neighbor, and he's been very nice to us.

SCOTT: Uh huh. So, Mom, do you like Walter?

MEG: He's very pleasant. Go to sleep.

SCOTT: Okay then, I'm just blurting this out, right?

MEG: Good night, Scott.

SCOTT: Mom!

MEG: Will you stop?

SCOTT: This is important . . . It's really important.

(Meg gives Scott the floor.)

SCOTT: Okay, it's only fair if you're prepared, right?

MEG: Can we wrap this up?

SCOTT: You want me to go to school? I'll go to school, hey, I'll even go early, but the office is gonna call you tomorrow, because sometime, before school, morning break, sometime, I have to beat the crap out of Anthony.

MEG: Really?

SCOTT: Yeah.

MEG: Why?

SCOTT: Because he's a jerk.

MEG: Great reason.

SCOTT: He's a butt wipe.

MEG: Oh, well, a butt wipe. Of course! A butt wipe!

SCOTT: What are you mad at me for?

MEG: What am I supposed to say? Goodie gumdrops — crap beating! That all-American after-school activity!

SCOTT: Not after school. After school I come home. *(Scott puts his head under the pillow and snores loudly.)*

MEG: Scott!

SCOTT: I'm trying to sleep.

> *(Meg pulls the pillow off Scott's head. She sits him up and looks him straight in the eye. She isn't going to let him off the hook.)*

MEG: Do I even want to know what happened to you today?

SCOTT: Nothing. Forget it. *(Pause)* He said something he shouldn't.

MEG: What in the world did he say that made you want to hit him?

SCOTT: I don't want to; I have to. Didn't you hear me? I have to, which is not "I want to," which is what you said. I. Have. To.

MEG: You have to?

SCOTT: Yes. And I would of beat him up right then, but it was after school and he ran onto his bus, which he was standing beside, and which he knew I couldn't get on because you need a bus pass and I ride my bike.

MEG: Would you like to talk to Grandpa about it? Do you want to call Grandpa Ray?

SCOTT: Leave me alone.

MEG: Scott, what did he say?

SCOTT: Something bad.

MEG: Something bad.

SCOTT: Trust me, okay?

MEG: Trust you?

SCOTT: Oh, Jeez . . . Mom, he said something bad about . . . you.

MEG: About me?

SCOTT: Do you get it now?

MEG: People say all kinds of things.

SCOTT: People shouldn't say bad stuff about other people's mothers and if they do, then people have to stick up. Kids were laughing.

MEG: They were laughing at him.

SCOTT: No, Mom, they weren't laughing at him. So if I don't stick up, everybody calls me a wuss for the rest of my life.

MEG: Come on, Scott, I don't really care if some boy in your class insulted me.

SCOTT: He didn't insult you, Mom.

MEG: Hey, I don't care if he said I was a green witch with snot for brains and bad breath.

SCOTT: Yo, Mom, he said you had sex.

MEG: With him?

SCOTT: Duhhhh.

MEG: He actually said that?

SCOTT: Don't smile.

MEG: Just so you know: He was lying.

SCOTT: This isn't funny.

MEG: What kind of jerk is this kid?

SCOTT: Anthony — he's a massive jerk, and a wuss. And he has to take it back.

MEG: Scotty, my reputation was completely ruined long before you were ever born, so nothing that Anthony says can make it any worse . . . That's a joke.

SCOTT: Am I laughing?

MEG: No, you're not laughing.

SCOTT: I'm sorry if you don't like it, Mom, but I gotta stick up. I gotta.

MEG: Jumping some kid a day later in the playground isn't sticking up.

SCOTT: Mom, look, it's like a rule.

MEG: A rule? There's a rule at your school that if someone says they "had" your mother . . .

SCOTT: . . . Mom! . . .

MEG: . . . You are required by this school rule to beat them up?

SCOTT: You gotta be tough.

MEG: Another school rule?

SCOTT: It's a man rule.

MEG: Oh, listen to you: a man rule.

SCOTT: You gonna tell me there aren't any of those?

MEG: Oh, no, there are definitely man rules.

SCOTT: I didn't start this!

MEG: Always lower yourself to the other person's level.

SCOTT: I'm defending you.

MEG: Whenever someone picks a fight, jump at the chance.

SCOTT: He called you a whore!

MEG: Always take the dare, pretend you know everything . . .

SCOTT: He said he fucked you!

MEG: My God! Isn't it bad enough that some twelve-year-old creep is talking dirty about me? . . . I couldn't stand it if you got hurt.

SCOTT: Hey, a really, really famous man rule is don't fight guys if they're way bigger than you are, and Anthony's little.

MEG: Well, then, great; no sweat!

SCOTT: Okay!

MEG: No sweat.

SCOTT: Okay, I won't fight him.

MEG: Look me in the eye, and you promise me, Scott.

SCOTT: My dad would tell me to fight him.

MEG: No, he wouldn't.

SCOTT: No, he would. He would say, "You better get ready, Scott, cuz you're gonna take that guy down."

MEG: Some thug would maybe say that.

SCOTT: He would say to fight, but he would say to not tell you, also.

MEG: Oh?

SCOTT: He would say, "I humor her."

MEG: He would not.

SCOTT: He would, too. He would say that people have to draw a line and stand on it.

MEG: Yes, he probably would.

SCOTT: I said I wouldn't fight him

MEG: It's really late, Scott.

SCOTT: Mom?

MEG: Close your eyes.

SCOTT: Oh jeez, here we go — you're gonna cry.

MEG: I'm not sad.

SCOTT: Don't treat me like I'm a baby.

MEG: I know you're not a baby.

SCOTT: Because I understand a lot of things. Like, for example: in two more days, well, it's late, in one day and a half, will be exactly one year.

MEG: Oh?

SCOTT: I hate when you do that, Mom.

MEG: Yes, Scott, I know what day it is.

SCOTT: And surprise!, that one year after your husband got killed you would cry . . .

MEG: Well, I'm not crying, and you're going to sleep. Good night. *(Meg exits.)*

SCOTT: Mom? . . . Mom? . . . Hey! Mom!? . . . MOM!!!! . . .

(Meg comes storming back into Scott's room.)

MEG: You have to stop this, you have to stop. I can't do this every night, I can't, I can't.

SCOTT: But, Mom . . .

MEG: No!

SCOTT: But . . .

MEG: Stop!

SCOTT: . . . Mom!

MEG: No!!

SCOTT: But, Mom . . .

MEG: This is torture.

SCOTT: But all I want is . . .

MEG: No! I said no.

SCOTT: But I want to ask you if . . .

MEG: Are you deaf?

SCOTT: Mom, PLEASE . . .

MEG: Are you stupid?

SCOTT: I have to ask you, I need to ask you . . .

MEG: NO! THE ANSWER IS NO! *(Long beat.)* Oh, Scott, Scotty . . . I'm
    sorry, so sorry. I didn't mean . . . Scott? Scott, honey, can I put my arm
    around you, okay? Please?
    *(Scott turns to Meg. She takes him in her arms and they hold onto each other
    for dear life.)*

SCOTT: Mom?

MEG: Yes. What do you want to ask me, sweetheart? You can ask me anything
    you want.

SCOTT: What would of happened if my dad had got in the car later?

MEG: I don't . . . Hmmm . . .

SCOTT: Even one blink later?

MEG: I don't know, Scotty.

SCOTT: Or that drunk guy who hit him — what if he was early? Or if he passed
    out and couldn't drive?

MEG: You can make yourself go crazy, love.

SCOTT: Mom? When it's really late at night, and you're in bed, and you can't
    sleep, right?, and you're just lying here, I mean lying here . . .

MEG: Yes?

SCOTT: Do you worry?

MEG: Absolutely.

SCOTT: What about?

MEG: All kinds of things.

SCOTT: Yo, Mom!

MEG: Yo, Scott, I worry about bills. I worry about getting fat . . .

SCOTT: You're not fat.

MEG: I worry about work, worry about that funny squeak that the car makes in the morning. I worry about you . . .

SCOTT: Hey, I'm tough.

MEG: I worry that I'm not being much of a mother.

SCOTT: Really? Can I have more allowance?

MEG: I don't worry that much. Good night.

SCOTT: But this is creepy, isn't it? It's late and quiet, and your body's tired, but your brain thinks like it's now or never, right? I call this worry time.

MEG: What's your worry, Scotty?

SCOTT: What if I got kidnapped into a parallel dimension, where everybody looked the same, only they had evil souls, right?, and I'll never find my way back to my own world where people love me?

MEG: That sounds terrible.

SCOTT: It could happen.

MEG: No, Scott.

SCOTT: It could.

MEG: If you go into a parallel universe, I'll come get you — I promise.

SCOTT: But see, there'd already be an evil mother in that parallel universe ahead of you.

MEG: We'll make a password — so you can be sure it's me.

SCOTT: No. Because anything you know here, she knows there. Like, if I'm in this parallel universe right now, the evil you is tricking me into a password. See what I mean?

MEG: How can I prove that I'm me, instead of someone who looks like me?

SCOTT: And acts like you, and sounds like you, and is you except on the inside.

MEG: Heh, heh, heh . . .

SCOTT: Don't.

MEG: My little pretty.

SCOTT: Mom, don't!

MEG: Scott, I'll do whatever you want to prove to you that I'm your real mother. Just tell me what to do.

SCOTT: No, that's good; that could be it. See, an evil, parallel mother, you know how she'd go?

MEG: No. How would she go?

SCOTT: Well, she wouldn't go, "How can I prove?" like you just went. No! She would go "Yo, Scott, relax, you're perfect, you're perfect," deep inside my ear until I fell into a trance and then she'd pull my soul out of my mouth.

MEG: Oh, Scotty. You had a nightmare.

SCOTT: Do you ever have a dream when you think you wake up and everything seems normal and then you go, "Oh no, I'm still asleep," and then you dream that you wake up again, until you scream and scream without any sound, and finally you wake up for real and you're all twisted in the covers?

MEG: Yes, actually.

SCOTT: Mom, I feel like I dreamed my dad was killed in a car crash, and I wake up every morning, knowing he's in the kitchen, standing by the sink eating cornflakes and bananas, only he's never in the kitchen, he's always dead.

MEG: Sweetheart, it wasn't a dream.

SCOTT: If you could have Dad back for one day, what would you do? And you can say sex if you want to, I don't mind.

MEG: Would this be a day that I would spend alone with him, or would this be a day with all of us together?

SCOTT: I would want a day alone, no offense, but you can ask for a family day if you want.

MEG: Oh, I would. I would definitely ask for a family day. I would ask to wake up freezing, because, remember what a cover hog your dad was? I would wake up and I would yank the covers, and just then, you would run in and jump on the bed. And your dad would sit up and he would say, "Good morning, everybody."

SCOTT: No, he wouldn't. He'd go, "Where's my coffee?"

MEG: Right! So you and I make coffee, and it's a sunny morning so we sit on the deck, and Dad comes, just cleaned up, with wet hair, and smelling like shampoo and aftershave and toothpaste. And his skin would be cool, and the sun would be warm on our heads and the coffee mugs in our hands, hot.

SCOTT: And I would go, "Yo, parents, let's go for a picnic."

MEG: Oh, yes, a picnic!

SCOTT: And Dad would make tuna fish. You use too much mayonnaise.

MEG: My tuna fish is great.

SCOTT: I'm just being honest.

MEG: Okay, Dad's horrible, dry tuna fish sandwiches.

SCOTT: And potato chips, pickles, cookies, apples, juice boxes.

MEG: And a good bottle of red wine for your father and me.

SCOTT: I wouldn't really wish for a picnic day.

MEG: What would you really wish for?

SCOTT: I would wish for a regular day.

MEG: Oh?

SCOTT: I would wish for a day that started with my dad going, "Get up, it's time for school." A day when I couldn't find clean socks, a day when I missed the bus, and my dad takes me, so I get the big lecture about dawdling. I would wish for a day with nothing special after school and nothing great for dinner. I would wish for a day that, in the evening, you have a meeting, and Dad's too busy to help with homework, although I would wish we watch TV together and stay up late. No, I take it back, I wouldn't wish for that at all. I would wish that he makes me go to bed right on time, maybe even forgets to tuck me in.

MEG: Sounds dismal.

SCOTT: I would wish for a day so plain that I could forget myself right into it.

MEG: Scott, a whole year's gone by — what do you think your dad would want for you? . . . Do you think he wants you to pretend that your life isn't real because he isn't here? He wants you to have fun, to make friends, to grow up happy into a wonderful future . . .

SCOTT: What do you call a guy when his dad is dead?

MEG: When both parents are dead, you call that being orphaned.

SCOTT: Right. An orphan.

MEG: You're not an orphan.

SCOTT: Sure, no sweat.

MEG: You have me, both the grandmas, your Grandpa Ray. You're not an orphan.

SCOTT: Right.

MEG: Scott, you are not an orphan; you are not in a parallel universe; you are not in a bad dream.

SCOTT: Yeah? Maybe someday, someday, I'll wake up for real real, and my dad, he'll be sitting on my bed, going "Shhhhhh, everything's fine, and I'm right here."

MEG: Sweetheart, I'm sorry, but that's not ever going to happen. A car ran a red light and hit your dad's car from the side. It was a horrible accident, he never saw it coming, and he died right away. We didn't want him to leave us, but it really happened.

SCOTT: I want to go home, Mom.

MEG: Scott.

SCOTT: Come on — can't we go home?

MEG: Scott, we are home. Now, this is home. We moved here because maybe it wasn't going to hurt so much someplace else.

SCOTT: You mean we ran away.

MEG: I can't change it now. I'm sorry. I can't change anything . . .

SCOTT: . . . We ran away from my dad.

MEG: My God! You are so mad at me!

SCOTT: I have to look at his picture to make sure it's his true face inside my brain.

(Meg puts her hand on Scott's heart.)

MEG: No Scott, your dad is right here, inside.

(Scott knocks her hand away. He is infuriated.)

SCOTT: That's a lie!

MEG: As long as you remember him . . .

SCOTT: I wanted to say one more thing to him! Only you wouldn't let me. So answer me this, this one easy thing. Answer me why you didn't let me say good-bye to my dad.

MEG: Of course you said good-bye. We said good-bye to him together.

SCOTT: I wanted to go to the funeral.

MEG: You were at the funeral.

SCOTT: No, I wasn't! You wouldn't let me go! You wouldn't let me go! . . .

MEG: Scott, listen to me! I promise you, from the bottom of my heart, you were at the funeral. We were all at the funeral. Joe Gresham and Uncle Al both spoke about Dad. I really want you to remember this, Scotty. Uncle Al told the bike race story from when they were little boys, and even though we were crying, we were laughing, too. And remember riding in the limousine?

SCOTT: No.

MEG: You really liked that part. You sat backwards all the way from the funeral home to the cemetery. And remember the motorcycle cops? You had a big conversation with one of the motorcycle cops when we got to the cemetery.

SCOTT: It all sounds like fun and such, but it's some dream of yours, because I don't remember, because I wasn't there.

MEG: Why would I make this up?

SCOTT: How should I know?

MEG: Scott, don't you remember anything?

SCOTT: I remember when you came to school . . .

MEG: I told you first . . .

SCOTT: . . . Hoo, I remember that.

MEG: I told you before I told anybody else. And then we called the grandmas and Grandpa Ray. And remember how everybody came to our house?
And Grandpa Ray wouldn't go home — remember? And he wouldn't even
stay in the spare room; he slept in the living room. And remember all
the food that people gave us? Things we'd never eat . . .

SCOTT: Potato salad?

MEG: Yes! Several bowls full. And we picked out Dad's blue blazer and his red
Donald Duck tie and took them to the funeral home. We did that together. And then we went to the Disney store at the mall and we found
a matching one in yellow for you. That's your Donald Duck tie, Scott.
It's right in your closet, right now. And at the funeral home, at the funeral, remember how we sat in that little side room with the curtain, and
you said you liked being able to spy on everybody?

SCOTT: No.

MEG: Yes. And when we got to the cemetery, we all stood under a big tent
because it was raining. And about ten old aunties all came over and said
that heaven was crying, until we rolled our eyes at each other. And I had
a red rose and you had a white rose, and we laid them on the casket. And
then later, when we got back home, I told you how brave you were, how
much you had helped me, and I told you that Dad would live in your
heart and we would never leave you.

SCOTT: The biggest lie of all!

MEG: It's how parents feel, Scott.

SCOTT: Why did you promise that? You shouldn't have promised that.

MEG: You're right. I shouldn't have promised that. But I really am telling you
the truth. You were there, Scott.

SCOTT: Well, there's one thing.

MEG: What's that?

SCOTT: It explains the lame Disney tie in my closet.

MEG: Of course, your father was famous for his ugly ties . . . Don't you remember anything?

(Scott shrugs but won't answer Meg or look at her.)

MEG: You know, whatever that last thing you didn't get to say to him, you
ought to just say it. I'm pretty sure he'll hear you.

SCOTT: I don't know.

MEG: I love you.

SCOTT: Can I be by myself?

MEG: Yo Scott, sweet dreams, right?

(Meg exits. Scott takes the visible horse from it's shelf and looks at it for a

long moment. Making a decision, he crosses to the foot of the bed and puts the visible horse on the floor. He reaches under the bed and pulls out a box. He takes out an old T-shirt, hugs it to him, smells it, then lays it carefully and gently out on the floor. He gets a framed photo out of the box and puts it beside the horse. He gets up and gathers a star-shaped candle and a book of matches off his desk and lays them on the T-shirt. He takes his "magic" rock out of his pocket, holds it up and makes a silent wish, then puts it on the T-shirt. He listens to make sure Meg isn't coming back. He strikes a match. As he lowers the flame to light the candle, the lamp in his room blinks, then blackout.)

Friday Afternoon
Scott enters. He's carrying a pair of roller blades. As he talks, he takes off his shoes and puts on the roller blades. As the scene unfolds, he skates around the stage.

SCOTT: Hey! 'Member that magic rock I showed you? Right? I mean, magic, hoo, they don't even do magic on TV — it's too fakey. Like McGuyver. McGuyver wouldn't ever do magic, right? McGuyver's way cool — scientific. Like each time he gets shit, which is every time — he has to or it wouldn't be interesting, right? — he doesn't wuss out, cuz he knows chemistry and how to build bombs and that's science.

 This one time, McGuyver, he was locked up by these evil guys and he escaped by starting a fire with only a pocket mirror. Yeah!

 You really gotta know this stuff. And, heck, even little kids know you can start fires with mirrors. My dad, he showed me about a century ago. A course, most guys don't carry mirrors, but now I do, because of *McGuyver. (He takes a mirror out of his pocket.)*

 Hey, I lucked out. I got it out of a gumball machine for twenty-five cents. You can't see yourself good, but it reflects fantastic. And you can start fires, and do signals, and such. *(He puts the mirror back in his pocket.)*

 Everything McGuyver does is real, he explains it and that's educational. Heck, I can watch *McGuyver* whenever I want, cuz I told my mom it's science and she agreed. Only I liked it better before Peter Thornton was blind. See, that's fakey: McGuyver's not gonna have a blind sidekick. I mean, if my sidekick went blind, he'd still be my friend, but like, "Yo, Peter, don't drive the car."

I like *Quantum Leap* better, right? Sam Beckett, he's in deep shit. Every show he lands in a different body in a different time, but he can't ever go, like, "Help me! I'm a time traveler," which makes him have to do stuff he doesn't know how, and that's funny. Like, one time, he landed in this lady, and he had to have a baby! Gross! He had to, cuz it's his only chance to get out and get home. *Quantum Leap* is future, which is science, future science, but it makes sense.

Oh! And my mom made me watch this show about computers. She goes, like, "There's this cool show about computers." I go, "That sounds like school." But we watched it, and, anyways, they showed V.R., virtual reality, this new kind, like, you put on earphones and you put on goggles, and you go right into the computer, right? And you can play games, build houses, fly . . . it's awesome! And my mom's all, "Ooooo, that's magic," right? But I'm, "Mom, get a grip, it's science."

Like, I could go into a computer, and, there would be software and cables and such, and that's real. See, science is reasons, but magic is oooooooooo, which is creepy, and that's cool, but like, hey, I'm a reasonable guy.

Can I tell you something? It's kinda scary. 'Member I told you I'd wish my dad back, right? Anyways, last night I snuck a star candle, shaped like a star and matches and such. This was way late, okay? I got out my rock I showed you, this picture of me and my dad camping, and my dad's T-shirt I stole from the dirty clothes a long time ago. See, sometimes I miss my dad at night, is all. Only when I lit it, the match goes pooshhh, man, this hella huge flame from this little, tiny match, right? And my lamp goes out. I go, "Shit!" The candle, it goes pooshhh. It was waaay bright. And check this: I didn't light it with the match, and it wouldn't blow out.

So heck, if magic comes, you're stuck with magic, right? I go, "Yo, spirits, I want my dad back." Right? I go, "Yo, spirits" three times. Three's magic. Nothing. So I go, "Yo, Jesus, I want my dad back." I go, "Yo, Jesus" three times. Then I go, "Magic rock, full of gold, make my dad appear." See, my dad, my dad he knew, he knew it was magic, right? And the candle, right? The candle goes out. It was dark, heck, not even my night light — I don't even know what happened, but it was waaaay dark and scary. And then I hear something, whoa, it was bad. "Cchhhh . . . Cchhhh . . . Cchhhh . . . " I was freaked! "Cchhhh . . . Cchhhh . . . " I mean, what is that? "Cchhhh . . . " Right? And I go, "Who's calling, please?" I go, "Oh shit". "Cchhhh . . . "

Anyways, I keep a flashlight under my bed. Only when I stick my hand under, I feel hair. I'm not shitting. Thwonk! There's green glowing from under my bed, and it's my dad, yes! Holding my flashlight. So anyways, I go, "Dad! What are you doing here?" And my dad, he goes, "Cchhhh." And he spits out this hella hair ball. It was, like, this big. And he goes, "Help me out." Only when I pull, his hand comes off, and it was pasty and it smelled way gross.

Heck, I just wanted my mom, right? So I go, "Yo, I'm calling, Mom." And my dad, he goes, "What do you want?" Right? And I go, "I want Mom." And he goes, "What did you call me for?" So I go, "Duhhh, cuz you were dead."

Anyways, he climbs out from under and turns on my light. Right? And he's waaay ugly now, with skin all falling off and all red eyeballs. So I go, "How do I know you're Dad, man? Look at you; maybe you're some ghoul or ogyrn." See, my dad, he had good skin and blue eyes, and this guy from under wasn't anything like my dad.

Only, check this, he sits on my bed, right?, and starts singing *Sweet Baby James*, way creepy like, but that's what he sung me when I was little. Like when I was little and I had bad dreams, my dad, he sung me that, which is, a course, a baby song, but it was, like, a sign, right? Like in the CIA they have passwords and such.

So I go, "Dad?" And he goes, "Yeah." And I go, "For real?" And he goes, "Yeah." He goes, "Good to see you, man."

So I go, "Are you undead, now?" And he goes he guesses. I go, "Can I get Mom?" And he goes, "Naw, I smell gross." Cuz girls, 'member, they've got 10 percent just for hygiene, right? Moms have got waaaaay more, like I bet 90 percent, and my dad, he knows this. So I go, "You wanna use my Scope?" But he goes that liquid makes his skin fall off. Right?

And I didn't tell him, my dad, right?, but there's this guy in Building B named Walter. He's okay — not my dad, duhh — but pretty nice. And my mom, she smiles sometimes and they talk in the parking lot. And Walter, his skin and eyes are normal. Heck, my mom, she gets grossed by moldy bread. I can't go, "Yo, Mom, here's Dad. He's undead now, give him a big kiss." What if his lips fell off?

My mom she went, "Do you like Walter?" And I was like, "He's okay. Do you like Walter?" And she's all, "He's very pleasant." I'm not gonna tell her about my dad.

Oh! Like if Walter wanted us to help move stuff to his storage unit, I could go, "Walter, you want a hand moving stuff?" And then I give him my dad's hand that fell off. That would be great! "Yo, Dad, let's give Walter a hand."

When my dad got killed, my mom, she came and got me at school, right? She goes, "I got to tell you something sad. Your dad was in an accident." So I go, "Quick! We gotta go to the hospital." Only, she goes, "He's not at the hospital. Your dad is dead." Man, I went totally off. I go, "Shut your shit; you're lying." And I never say shit to my mom, so that's how freaked out I was. Then later I felt way bad, cuz I made her cry, and it was her husband, right?

If I tell her about my dad's undead, what if she don't want? Heck, she hardly ever talks about him — and like my dad always went that it was too hard to figure out what she was thinking. Anyways, my dad goes, "One thing — you can't ever tell your mom I'm undead. I'm only here for you." Right? I go, "Are you taking me away?" And he goes, "I'm staying as long as you want." All right!

Then he goes, "What month is it?" And I go, "November." Then he goes, "What day is it?" And I go, "Thursday." And he goes, check this: "Hey, you get in bed; you got school tomorrow." So I know it really is my dad, cuz creatures don't care if you're tired in the morning, but parents do.

Then my dad, he crawls back under and turns off the flashlight, and goes "Cchhhh . . . . Cchhhh . . . " again, and this time I kind of liked it, only I couldn't sleep all night, cuz, heck, he smells rotten.

Anyways, he's still under my bed, and he stinks! I mean, I'm glad to have my dad and such, but eewwyyee. See, I don't think this is science. Or maybe it is — see, if this is science, I can cure the smell, and that's what I'm hoping. Heck, I could be famous, and that would be awesome. I don't think anybody's ever really brought back a guy from the dead before for real — I could be wrong.

See, what I'm wondering: What would McGuyver do? McGuyver knows chemistry and such, and you know that experiment? You mix two things that don't smell together and they smell like rotten eggs? McGuyver knows this — I saw him do it on TV. He was taken prisoner by some way evil dudes, and they locked him in a kitchen, and he made stink bombs so's Peter Thornton and the police could find him and save him. I bet he also knows how to mix two stinky things together and have them smell good, right? I wish I could just talk to McGuyver, just for a minute, or, heck, even Peter Thornton. He may be blind, but he's way smart, also.

Oh! And this morning, right? My mom knocks my door to wake

me up, and she goes, "What is that smell?" And I go, "Nothing." And she goes, "Have you been eating in your room again? If you don't have it clean when I get home, I'm bringing in the bulldozer." Know what? She means it. One time at my old house, she threw out my pet snake. A course, he was in a shoebox under my bed and he was dead, but I didn't know — I just thought he smelled bad.

See? She hates smells. And tonight, she's coming in to check my room, and she always looks under my bed. I was thinking I could hide him in the dumpster, they got waaay big dumpsters at the condo and they stink plenty — my dad, he'd fit easy, but how'm I gonna get him? Like, we just take the elevator down — doe de doe de doe . . . Man, they didn't even want to let us in, cuz they hate kids. Anyways, I can't put my dad in the garbage, right? See, I can hide him in my closet, she won't look there, but, Christ! How're you gonna hide a smell? Like, "Yo, Mom, come check my room, but wear nose plugs."

Anyways, I skipped school today. Heck, I had to. My dad, he wouldn't let me use soap and water, cuz liquid makes his skin fall off, so I don't blame him. Oh! And I went to the store and got Tidy Kat. Hey! You ought to know: Tidy Kat? — They're lying. Tidy Kat does not absorb odor, trust me. And my dad, now he's got kitty litter stuck on all the moldy spots, so he's looking way, waaaaay bad. And every time he moves, he dribbles Tidy Kat on the carpet, and I can't find the vacuum.

My dad, today, he goes, "Maybe I should go away." No way! He has to stay as long as I want. He promised! See, I'm glad I got my dad back and such, and I'll get used to how gross he looks and stinks, I will. Only, I can't let my mom find out, right? I'm going to Al's Auto Supply. You know those car air fresheners that look like trees — they're green? You know how many I can buy with five bucks? After the Tidy Kat, that's all I got left. You wanna come?

Sunday Afternoon
Meg is in the rowboat at the dock. She's wearing a life jacket. There is a picnic basket in the boat.

MEG: Scott . . . Scott! . . . Will you just put it on and get in the boat?
    (Scott enters. He's holding a life jacket.)
SCOTT: I don't see why I have to wear it.

MEG: It's the rule.

SCOTT: I got my swim club card in my wallet — I'm gonna show him. *(Scott turns to leave.)*

MEG: He doesn't want to see your swim club card, Scott. He doesn't care how well you swim.

SCOTT: But life jackets are for babies.

MEG: Am I a baby?

SCOTT: Hey, I swim way better than you do.

MEG: You heard him: If we want to rent a rowboat, we wear life jackets. No exceptions. It's probably not even him; it's probably his insurance company.

SCOTT: *(Mimicking.)* It's probably his insurance.

MEG: What is with you? You've been grousing about everything.

SCOTT: Hey, I wanted to stay home, and you wouldn't even tell me where we were going. And we drive forever and then some lake?

MEG: I get it, Scott. You've made your point — several times. Oh, come on, please? For me?

(Scott puts on the life jacket and gets in the rowboat.)

SCOTT: I'm not zipping it up.

MEG: Scott, get out of the boat.

SCOTT: Okay, okay, I'm zipping. Jeez, don't go nuts or anything. *(Scott zips up the life jacket.)*

MEG: Shove off, matey.

(Scott shoves the boat off from the dock. Meg rows.)

SCOTT: Well?

MEG: Let's just get out onto the lake.

SCOTT: Can't I, at least, row?

MEG: You can row later.

SCOTT: This is so much fun . . . Yo, Mom, you're gripping the oars wrong. You're gripping 'em wrong. Look, you're supposed to grip them with your thumbs over the ends.

MEG: Don't . . .

SCOTT: Here, move, let me row . . .

MEG: Look out!

SCOTT: Mom, I really know this from my old scout troop . . . Mom! You're rowing lame; you're supposed to rotate your wrists.

MEG: Will you stop?

(Scott backs off.)

MEG: It's just that I want to row.

SCOTT: Row.

MEG: No, I'm sorry. You row.

SCOTT: Forget it.

MEG: No, really, row.

SCOTT: What's the best thing to do here? Row or not row?

MEG: Row. I want you to.

SCOTT: I could get blasted either way.

MEG: I'm not going to blast you.

SCOTT: Promise?

MEG: I won't if you won't.

SCOTT: Ah . . . I guess we're gonna have to drift.

MEG: Please. Row.

(Scott and Meg switch places in the rowboat. Scott rows.)

MEG: Back before you were born, your father and I used to be very young.

SCOTT: Ah, jeez . . .

MEG: I, of course, was quite beautiful, and your father, he was fairly hand-some, except that he had a goatee, a little beard on his chin.

SCOTT: I seen pictures, Mom.

MEG: And nobody could call him Bill or Billy, either. He was William.

SCOTT: No!

MEG: Yes.

SCOTT: Shocking!

MEG: And his hair was dark, dark brown, no grey, and there was lots of it. Anyway, we were taking a trip one time. This was a long, long time ago, back before we got married, back before you. And we camped for a whole week at a little lake right here in Oregon. The water was warm, the bottom sandy, not muddy. It was a wonderful spot, with a big flat rock for sunbathing, with woods all around, and nobody else in sight. And up by the road, there was a store that sold soda pop and giant pretzels and rented rowboats. And the last day, we bought a picnic there — crackers and cheese and wine — and we rented a boat, and out there rowing around, Bill said, your dad said to me, "If I died now, I'd die happy. Just pour me in with the best bottle of red wine you can find." Anyway, this is that very lake. Welcome to Willow Lake.

SCOTT: Why did we come here? That's a horrible story.

MEG: Horrible?

SCOTT: *(Mocking.)* If I died now I'd be happy. I'm sick of it. I don't want to hear about dying.

MEG: No, love, it's a story about a time when we thought we'd live forever.

SCOTT: Yeah, sure. Nobody lives forever.

MEG: You're right: Nobody lives forever. *(Pause.)* All this year, I couldn't think about Bill, I couldn't think about your dad, but I couldn't not think about him, either. You did me a great favor. Remember the other night when you asked me what I'd do if I could have one more chance, one more day?

SCOTT: So?

MEG: Yesterday, God, I bet I cried as much as every tear I've cried all year, and then this morning I woke up knowing — I can have one more day, I can have one more chance. I can pack up my kid and all the feelings in the world, and bring them to Willow Lake. *(Meg opens up the picnic basket and takes out a bottle of wine and a corkscrew.)* Remember that your father told me to pick the best wine I could find, the best red wine?

SCOTT: I don't want to hear this!

MEG: Scotty, please! . . .

SCOTT: No!

MEG: Please — just a little drum roll, please? Sweetheart, this is DRC — Domaine de la Romani Conti. And not only is it DRC, but it's a prized vintage. This is the single most sought-after burgundy on the face of the planet. Finding this was my errand this morning.

SCOTT: Yeah?

MEG: Yes. To a very exclusive wine store, which opened just for me on a Sunday morning, so I could give them a sinful pile of money, after which they went and got this very bottle from a temperature-controlled, locked vault at a secret location somewhere in the bowels of the city.

SCOTT: So how much did it cost?

MEG: A lot.

SCOTT: Tell me.

MEG: I don't think your father would have said what he said if he'd known it was possible to spend this much money on one bottle of wine.

SCOTT: How much?

MEG: Well . . . Not as much as his funeral.

SCOTT: Whoa!

MEG: But more than his casket.

SCOTT: A thousand bucks? . . . More?

MEG: Way more.

SCOTT: Yo, Mom, are you sure you want to do this?

MEG: I have this picture in my head. It's so clear. "If I died now, I'd die happy. Just pour me in with the best bottle of red wine you can find."

SCOTT: Like you're keeping a promise.

MEG: Like I'm keeping a promise.

SCOTT: No, that's good; I can see it. It's, like . . . holy to make things right. Like in the video of *Star Trek Four, The Voyage Home,* they bring whales into the future.

MEG: Whales?

SCOTT: Well, a course, the original reason is because they need a whale to talk to the alien probe and save Earth, right? But at the very end, the whales are jumping around in the future San Francisco Bay, right? And everybody is on top of the Klingon ship and they're way wet, but laughing, also. Whales and oceans belong together, and Captain Kirk and the crew of the Starship Enterprise, they learn this.

MEG: Do they?

SCOTT: Yes. Just like you want Dad's spirit in this place where he was happy with you. Heck, I'd sure rather Dad is here at Willow Lake than in some cemetery.

MEG: It's pretty here, isn't it? See that big outcrop of rock right by the shore? Remember I told you that Dad and I camped here a long time ago? I think that's the spot where we camped.

SCOTT: I wish we brung the tent and stuff.

MEG: To go camping in November?

SCOTT: We're tough.

MEG: No, thanks. Besides we have to turn around and drive right back. You've got school tomorrow and I've got work.

SCOTT: I'd be okay to miss a few days — no, for real, I wouldn't mind, if it would help you, Mom.

MEG: What a nice boy.

(Scott rows. Meg opens the wine bottle. She smells the wine.)

MEG: Mmmmm. Scott, this smells like heaven. *(Meg holds the bottle out to Scott.)*

SCOTT: Whew! It's kind of strong.

MEG: I think it smells pretty good. I think it smells very good. *(Meg speaks to the wine bottle.)* Well, Billy, here we are sitting in a rowboat, getting ready to pour your wine into Willow Lake, just like you wanted.

SCOTT: You should drink some first.

(Meg takes a drink.)

SCOTT: Well?

MEG: Tasty.

SCOTT: Make a toast.

MEG: Okay . . . Here's to you and here's to me and may we never disagree, but if we do — to hell with you and here's to me! *(Meg laughs at her own joke.)* Dad taught me that about a century ago. *(She takes another drink and holds the bottle out to Scott.)* Your turn.

SCOTT: You're kidding.

MEG: No.

SCOTT: You're saying, "Sure, Scott, go ahead, you can drink"? You're saying that?

MEG: Sure, Scott, go ahead, you can drink.

SCOTT: Mom!

MEG: Down the hatch — go ahead.

(Scott takes a drink. He doesn't like it.)

MEG: Oh, in about twenty years, yes, shortly after you turn thirty, you'll be telling someone how once upon a time you tasted one of the great French burgundies. And you are going to lie and say how wonderful it was, how memorable, how you loved it, big shot.

SCOTT: And you like this stuff? I don't get the deal.

MEG: Help me do this, Scotty.

(Scott and Meg pour the wine into the lake.)

MEG: See . . . *(Pause.)*

SCOTT: It looks like blood. *(Pause.)*

MEG: Yes, it does.

(Scott takes his hand away. Meg finishes pouring the wine into the lake alone. After a moment.)

MEG: You all right?

SCOTT: Sure.

MEG: Thank you, Scott.

SCOTT: For what?

MEG: For coming here with me. Now I'll always remember being here with you, too.

(Scott turns away from her.)

MEG: Talk to me, Scotty. We just did this ceremony in honor of your dad . . .

SCOTT: And, oh right, magic, suddenly everything's great, perfect.

MEG: Come on, don't. You have to tell me how you feel.

SCOTT: Yeah? Tell me how you feel.

MEG: How I feel? Sweetheart, maybe it doesn't have a name.

SCOTT: Lucky you.

MEG: Scotty, please don't be sad.

SCOTT: This is your rowboat, Mom, your bottle of wine.

MEG: Your dad and I, we never dreamed it would be like this. You believe me, don't you? We never wanted it to be like this. *(Pause.)*

SCOTT: Mom, what if my Dad was undead and hiding under my bed and I could talk to him?

MEG: And could he talk back?

SCOTT: Yes.

MEG: I would say, "Tell your Dad something for me."

SCOTT: I did something bad, Mom.

MEG: Sweetheart . . .

SCOTT: That morning, he yelled at me all the way to school about missing the bus, and when he dropped me off, I slammed the car door and I never even looked at him.

MEG: Oh, I see . . . So, you're still, what? Still mad he yelled at you?

SCOTT: No, not me. It's just that he, he . . .

MEG: Scotty, if you're not still mad at him, why would he still be mad at you? Scott, your father loved you. He knew you loved him back. It's everything; it's all that matters. If he was here right now, he would tell you that.

(Scott shrugs.)

MEG: Scott . . .

SCOTT: It's good we didn't bring the tent. November's too cold for camping.

MEG: We'll go camping next summer. *(After a moment, Meg picks up the wine bottle. She starts to throw it into the lake.)*

SCOTT: Wait! Can I have it?

MEG: I thought I'd . . . Yes, sure. Of course you can. *(Meg hands the bottle to Scott. Scott leans over the side of the boat, fills the bottle with water, then puts the cork back in the bottle.)*

MEG: What are you going to do with it?

SCOTT: Nothing. Probably, maybe, I don't know, keep it under my bed.

MEG: Row us to shore.

(Scott hands the bottle to Meg and rows.)

Monday Afternoon
Scott enters on a skateboard. He's pissed off.

SCOTT: My teacher, I hate her. I "beeswaxed" her, okay? "Beeswax," right? See, at my old school, if you wanted somebody to leave you waaaay alone, you'd go, "None of your beeswax." And nobody'd freak, like, if you said "fuck off," which, a course, is what you meant. "Beeswax" was polite and that was popular. Heck, you could even say "beeswax" to a teacher. But not here. If you say "beeswax" here, she sends you to the office, and they send you home, and you can't come back unless you bring your mom, and have a conference, right? And you got to apologize, which I don't mind, but you got to tell them what the "beeswax" was, which I do mind. If I didn't mind, it wouldn't of been a "beeswax!"

So my teacher, right? She goes, "You're in a fine mood today," right? And I go, "Yo, chill." Then she goes, "You can talk like that on the playground, but not in my classroom." So I'm all, "I'm just in a weird mood," right? Which should of been enough. Only she goes, "What's the matter?" Like I'd tell her, Christ! She's only been my teacher for two months. So I growled, grrrrr!, and, man, she freaked! She goes, "You tell me what's with you right now." Heck, I had to go, "None of your beeswax." I had too.

Sometimes I think, like, I'm the visible horse, like my guts are showing through my skin and they might read my mind, which I DO NOT WANT!

Anyways, my teacher goes, "I've had about enough of you." You know the worst? I don't mind the office, I'm tough, but I had to sit there for the rest of the day, cuz my mom couldn't come and get me.

When she gets home, it's, like, all over. Because my mom, right? My mom's already had enough grief for one lifetime. So like, "Yo, why'd you beeswax your teacher, Scott?" "Yo, Mom, because I was up all night with my Dad, saying good-bye."

You ever been sad and angry both at the same time? They both fit inside together, right? Like this one time, my mom and dad were having an awesome fight, and I go, "Shut up," to them and they made me go to my room, which wasn't fair, cuz THEY were fighting, and I was sad and angry, both. Well, mostly angry. When my dad got wasted, I felt sad and angry. That makes sense. It does.

But my mom — I don't get it, I don't get it . . . Man, it's so weird. She's sad, right? But kind of, like, happy, both. What is that? Sad, but smiling, crying, but laughing?

Oh! And I got to tell you this one other thing. And, believe me, I am not shitting you on this at all. Okay, we're in the middle of this lake in a rowboat, right? And my Mom opens up some wine, in honor of, like, my dad, right? And she hands the bottle to me! She goes, "Make a toast."

I go, "Mother! You're breaking the law!" She goes, check this, she goes, "Go ahead, you can drink!" No, really. It was awesome.

It was tasty.

Anyways . . . So last night, way late, when I got home, my dad, he looks me right in my eye. And he doesn't even go, "Welcome back" or "I missed you." No. He's just, "How come you never cried when I got wasted?" And I'm, like, "whoa," cuz the undead, the undead are different, I guess, and they can know all kinds of things. I go, "You know that?"

But my dad, man, he's just on me, right? Like his red eyeballs start glowing, and he's all growing large, like his head can touch the ceiling of my room, and his smell — eweeyeeww — times, like, a thousand . . .

So I go, "Stop it, man, this is too scary."

And he's all, "Answer me why you didn't cry."

But I'm, "Christ! How should I know?"

And this ghoul father is going, "Chhhhhh, chhhhhhh, chhhhhhhh . . ."

"Okay!" I go. "Okay."

See, at the time my dad got wasted I almost cried, but 'member I told you that after his car wreck I felt sad and angry, right? It's not like, duhhh, I didn't notice he got killed. Only, this part here, oh! and here, too, here, no, mostly my entire guts felt burny. And at that time, sometimes I almost cried, I did, but if I had then that burny would have burned me away, and I'd have died, also. So I just held my breath. Be, because of my mom, right? Because she was crying all the time and she needed me. That was all — not like it was some big insult, like I didn't love my dad.

Then he goes, "Hold on, kid, I gotta get really gross for a minute." And I'm, "You already are — you're disgusting."

And check this: My undead dad, he sticks his hand into his stomach, kind of skkllerrrrsh, and he brings out this rock, right? And he goes, "This is my heart. Only now I'm undead and such, it's a stone." And he goes that all of his guts — heart, lungs, stomach, everything — they're petrified. Like this one time, my dad, he took me to the petrified forest, where we saw trees that are minerals, not wood. And he goes, "They don't work, but hey!, I'm undead, who cares."

And I'm getting this awesome, creepy feeling, like my hairs on my neck stiffen, right? And I'm all, "Stop! You're freaking me out!" And my dad, my dad's all, "Come on, kid, hold out your hand. Gimme your hand."

But I'm, "Oh? And why would you want my hand, Father, dear?" Only he's just, "Chhhhhhhh, chhhhhhh . . . " And I'm thinking if I touch this thing, right?, this rock heart, what if my guts become stone, too, like, cold, gone? He just keeps going, "Touch it, kid, just touch it. Touch it."

Anyways, this was not like talking stuff and goofing around on Saturday. I go, "Hey, man, it's, it's, it's cool with me if you're undead."

And my undead dad, he's all, "But if you touch it, we can be together. Together, kid, forever."

So I tried to touch it. I almost touched it. I wanted to . . . But NO! I go, "I need to be alive. Please, I have to be alive." And figure, cuz he's just been trying to get me to come be dead with him, my dad's all, "Good. Alive is good."

And he yawns, only cuz he's undead and such, it comes out like moaning. He was so creepy. I go, "Can't you just be a pleasant monster, like yesterday?" Only he's all, "I'm sorry, kid, I gotta go be dead again."

But I'm, "If you go be dead again, I'm all alone." And he's all, "No, you're not." But I'm, "I am, too." And he's, "Am not." "AM TOO!" Only he goes, "Say you're at a swim meet, right? And the starter gun goes off." Right? I'm all, "What are you talking about?" And he goes, "You dive in and you're racing — what do you see?"

Whatever. I go, "Backstroke or freestyle?" He goes, "Freestyle." So I go, "The bottom of the pool, duhhhh." And he goes, "What do you hear?" And I go, "My breathing. And my heart pounds . . . I don't know. Man, racing's hard; you gotta pay attention."

Then he goes, "So when you're racing, is your mom jumping up and down and cheering?" "Well, yo, Dad, a course she is." My mom, she's at all my meets. She always goes that she's my very best fan. But my dad, he's all, "Are you sure? Cuz you're busy swimming, right? She could be picking her nose. You positive she cheers you?"

Heck, I know she cheers me. I go, "Shut your shit! She just does, okay? I don't have to prove."

And my guts, right? They were getting waaay burny — heck, right then, they were on fire — so I started holding my breath. Only there I am, looking right into my dad's awful, red eyeballs, and they were soooo ugly, but they were so kind, so sorry.

And he says, "Between a dead dad and a live kid, it's like at swim meets. I'm your dad, I'm there, you don't ever have to wonder. But you gotta pay attention, Scott, swim your event, race like anything. Afterwards, you'll see me again. Hey, you couldn't miss me. I'm waiting right at the finish, son, and I'm cheering you the whole way."

And saying it, it wasn't my undead dad with the peely skin and guts all showing, though. No. It was my real father, right there, right in front of me. I saw my dad.

Anyways, I cried a way long time, hoo, maybe I shouldn't say so, but anyways . . .

And my dad, he goes, "Shhhh, shhh," like when I was little and I had bad dreams. And then he sung me *Sweet Baby James*, til I go, "Yo, Dad, you're way out of tune."

I go, "Anyways, I can't keep on hiding you in my room." Right? And my dad, he goes, "This is best." He goes, "Bedtime."

And 'member how my guts were burny? Anyways, now they were warm, like sometimes my mom, she makes me hot noodles with butter and cheese. And in my heart I felt like . . . Like late at night, when my parents would talk soft in the front seat and I'd be in the back seat, and we'd be driving home from the cousins, right? I felt like, like when I was walking through my old house after all the furniture was in the moving van. Felt like having to stay inside cuz it's raining outside, right? But also like, like falling asleep on my best pillow. Yeah. And I feel all of these things together. All of them at the same time. All of these feelings, they are all one feeling. One real feeling which is inside of me. There may be a name for this, but, heck, I don't know what it is.

Dad. The Dad feeling. Yeah.

So I get in and he climbs under and he's all, "When you wake up, you won't see me any more." And I'm all, "Night, Dad." And my dad, he says so soft, so only I can hear, "I love you."

(Meg enters. She's just gotten home from work.)

MEG: That must have been quite some time you had at school today.

SCOTT: Oh, man, here we go — I'm busted.

MEG: Well?

SCOTT: I had to sit in the office 'til the final bell.

MEG: I was in meetings all day today, Scott. So, excuse me if you were inconvenienced.

SCOTT: No, that's cool.

MEG: We have an appointment at 7:30 tomorrow morning in Mrs. Golden's office. What are you planning to say for yourself?

SCOTT: I guess I'll just say . . . I'm sorry. Hey, Mom, watch this.

(Scott does a trick on his skateboard. Meg is unmoved.)

MEG: Scott, you need to come inside, go to your room, and stay there 'til dinner's ready. You got that?

(Meg turns to leave.)

SCOTT: Yo, Mom? *(Scott skateboards past Meg, giving her a kiss on the cheek.)*

MEG: Yo, Scott. *(Meg exits. Scott takes a beat, then turns back to the audience.)*

SCOTT: I, uh, I gotta go in. My mom — you know . . . *(Scott turns to leave, comes back to say one more thing.)* Wait! See, tomorrow at school, when we go in about the "beeswax," I know exactly how I'm gonna go. Like I'll be all, "I'm sorry and I had a headache and I love school so much that I didn't want to go to the nurse's office." And then I'm gonna do this — see? Little tiny smile. And my teacher, man, she'll be, "What a nice boy." And the principal, right? She'll go, "And just think, poor little boy, his dad's dead." And my dad, right? My dad — he's laughing. *(Scott exits.)*

END OF PLAY

Strangers and
Romance

Two plays by Barbara Lhota

For my parents, Jim and Marilyn Lhota,
and for Janet Milstein, a generous, talented artist,
and a damn fine manager!

THE AUTHOR

Barbara Lhota is an award-winning playwright as well as a screenwriter. The Studio's production of her play, *Third Person,* was selected by the *Boston Herald* as one of the top ten plays for the 1993–94 season. She received the Harold and Mimi Steinberg award for *Hanging by a Thread* at the Crawford Theater at Brandeis University. *Green Skin,* her most recent collaboration, was staged at the Producers Club with Theatre Asylum in New York. Her plays have been seen at various theaters across the country including the Ritz Theater in New Jersey, the American Stage Festival in New Hampshire, the New England Theater Conference, and the Wang Center in Boston. In addition, her shows have been performed at several off-off-Broadway Theaters, including Tribeca Lab, Madison Avenue Theater, Phil Bosakowski Theater, and Love Creek Productions at the Nat Horne Theatre. She received her MFA in dramatic writing from Brandeis University, where she was an artist-in-residence and taught playwriting. Barbara now lives in Chicago, where she has had the opportunity to see *Family Portrait* performed at the Bailiwick's Directors Festival, *Third Person* with Symposium at National Pastime, *Morbid Curiosity* with Women's Theater Alliance at Chicago Dramatists and with Writer's Block at The Theater Building. Barbara is currently collaborating with Ira Brodsky on a screenplay called *The Long Shot* and co-writing with Janet Milstein a *Forensics Duo Series for Young Actors* for Smith and Kraus Publishing, Inc.

ORIGINAL PRODUCTION

Strangers was originally developed at Brandeis University under the direction of Susan Dibble. The Chicago premier was produced with Jupiter Theatre under the direction of Kristy Kambanis. The casts for the original productions were as follows:

Brandeis University

MADDIE . . . . Robin Weigert
MADISON . . . . Jay Scully

Jupiter Theatre

MADDIE. . . . . Nicole Soltis
MADISON. . . . . Matthew Hahn

INTRODUCTORY STATEMENT

Strangers began as a brief assignment to myself. I was to write a short play with two actors and a bench. I wanted it to be easy-to-produce, actor-focused, and in real time. I had no idea that the characters were not strangers when I embarked on this adventure or that they were entrenched in a game that allowed them to escape their shared tragedy. I admit it was a bit disconcerting, at first, to realize that the characters seemed to know where this was going when I did not. My brief assignment, many years later, was not quite so brief, but it does fulfill all original requirements. When all things go well once, it's good to try them again. *Romance* was written with the same stipulations. Both *Strangers* and *Romance* were written with the help and support of many actors, writers, and directors along the way. A big thanks to the Brandeis workshop and Martin Halpern.

CHARACTERS

    MADDIE: 30, a copy editor
    MADISON: 32, a security guard

SETTING

    The commuter train station in Boston. North Station.

TIME

    The present.

STRANGERS

SCENE: A commuter train station in Boston. A bench is center stage. On the wall behind the bench a map shows various color-coded train routes. Below the map is a wooden stand full of schedules. Upstage right, a garbage can overflows with coffee cups. There is a small chalkboard with a Christmas tree drawn on it and the words "Have A Happy Holiday from Mass Transit!" Before the lights come up, a garbled voice over the speaker announces "Last train to Fitchburg on track six!" There are voices, footsteps, and doors slamming shut.

AT RISE: The stage is dimly lit. Maddie, in a tight red dress, takes a long drawn out puff on a cigarette. She notices the handsome Security Guard who quietly whistles, "Jingle Bells" as he paces behind her. They exchange eye contact for a moment. Uncomfortable, the Security Guard returns to his pacing. Maddie takes another long sexy drag off her cigarette. He can't help but turn to her several times. Finally he goes over to her.

MADISON: You got a light?

MADDIE: Me? Yes. *(Maddie starts to rummage through her two shopping bags.)*

MADISON: You do know that's the last of 'em? Trains. I thought maybe you were deaf or handicapped and didn't hear them announce the last boarding call for the last train out of here. Very last. That's it. That's all. No more.

MADDIE: *(Still searching through her bag for a lighter.)* Oh well. I don't mind staying here for the night. There's something sexy about train stations. The vibrations from the rumble of the train. All that steam.

MADISON: We're talkin' Christmas Eve, lady. Nothin's goin' out this late on a night like this. You'll be stuck. I could call you a cab.

MADDIE: I'd rather you call me Scarlett. That's my name. *(Pulls out a four-inch lighter with a ship's steering wheel on it. You turn the wheel and it lights.)* Found it!

MADISON: What's that?

MADDIE: It's an antique. Picked it up today. I love anything that has to do with transportation. I find it romantic. See? It's a miniature ship's steering wheel and it lights cigarettes. *(She demonstrates it.)* Take it.
(Madison looks at it strangely.)

MADISON: You don't happen to have a cigarette too, do ya?

MADDIE: You're unique. Most people ask for the cigarette first. You did it the smart way. Asking for a cigarette is much more costly than asking for a light. But once you have people involved in getting you the light, they've admitted they're smokers. Nonsmokers rarely carry lights, unless they're romantic. And once they've admitted they're smokers, it would be too cheap to say they don't have a cigarette. It's easy to lie and say you don't have a cigarette when a lighter isn't involved yet. And this lie would spill out of your mouth with no remorse but soon, you'd begin to feel hot and turn red in the face. The lie would linger much longer than you expect in the back of your head pounding. BOOM. BOOM. BOOM! And then you'd explode in a hysterical fit of tears or laughter! I'm glad you didn't put me through that. Thanks. *(Maddie pulls out a cigarette.)*

MADISON: Welcome.

MADDIE: I only smoke on occasion, in places where it seems appropriate.

MADISON: Nowhere legal lately. *(Lights up.)*

MADDIE: Like in this place. It's old and romantic. It's a place for hats, blues, sex, and cigarettes. Important things seem to happen in places of travel. Train stations are the oldest and the most romantic. Don't you think?

MADISON: Yeah, I think, quite a bit. It's not a brainless job.

MADDIE: What are you talking about?

MADISON: Oh, I know your attitude. Security guards are not dumb. You have to be a quick thinker. Good reflexes. Got a lot of keys to keep track of. I've read Nietzsche. I've listened to Mozart. And I've seen several Woody Allen movies. I'm not dumb.

MADDIE: I didn't say you were.

MADISON: Oh. *(Madison smokes his cigarette and begins to whistle "Jingle Bells." He moves away from her.)*

MADDIE: What's that tune you're whistling? It's so familiar.

MADISON: This? *(Whistles it.)* "Jingle Bells."

MADDIE: Must have blocked it out. Used to be one of my favorites. Now I'd just like to forget it.

MADISON: You know, lady, this place is gonna be, uh, closed in about thirty minutes. I lock the doors after maintenance cleans the bathrooms.

MADDIE: I realize this is odd

MADISON: Are you feelin' okay?

MADDIE: Christmas has been hard for me ever since . . .

MADISON: Let me call you a cab.

MADDIE: Let me call you one. CAB! I'm sorry. And here you are being so concerned.

MADISON: It's not concern. I have to wait until everyone leaves. I have the responsibility of locking up. I hold the keys. See?

MADDIE: I understand. You want to get home to your wife.

MADISON: Uh, no. I'm not married.

MADDIE: Oh, really?

MADISON: You?

MADDIE: Not at all!

MADISON: Why are we talkin' about all this?

MADDIE: Conversations sometimes take the oddest turns. Isn't that funny? Mr. Uh?

MADISON: Rhett.

MADDIE: *(Thinking he's very clever.)* Rhett. I like that. I like the unique.

MADISON: Do you think I can just chat away while I'm on duty? I have a tense job. It's not easy.

MADDIE: Liking the unique is the reason I'm in trouble.

MADISON: What trouble? I've got a gun. I know how to use it.

MADDIE: Don't pretend you don't recognize me.

MADISON: No need to pretend.

MADDIE: Oh, Rhett, you can do better than that. Certainly you saw my face splattered across every newspaper five years ago?

MADISON: *(Straining for an answer.)* Oh yeah, yeah, I read the papers. I'm informed. Now, that I look at ya, I think I did. Five years ago? Sure.

MADDIE: *(Surprised.)* You did?!

MADISON: I admit it's a little vague in my memory.

MADDIE: It's crystal clear in mine. It was on Christmas Eve. In Turkey. I used to be much taller. The plastic surgery did wonders. Thank God my face remains intact.

MADISON: Yeah. I remember the color photos of you in uh, uh . . .

MADDIE: *Time.* The explosion wasn't the worst of it.

MADISON: No, I read about it, it was the uh, uh . . .

MADDIE: Burning of the paintings and the manuscripts that they made me read over and over. But especially the crazy rituals. They had me going mad!

(Madison raises his hands above his head and snaps his fingers.)

MADISON: *(Blandly.)* Elvis is alive.

MADDIE: Why'd you stop?! It was going so well, Madison!

MADISON: Follow the rules. Give me the signal. *(Madison raises his hands above his head and snaps his fingers.)* Elvis is alive.

MADDIE: *(Puts her hands above her head and snaps her fingers.)* And living in Canton, Ohio.

(They both put their hands down.)

MADDIE: Now, why'd you stop? It was going so well!

MADISON: No, it wasn't. How were you going to put together that pitiful story?

MADDIE: I was improvising. That's how you do it.

MADISON: I wasn't turned on, Maddie.

MADDIE: Not even by the red dress?

MADISON: And mentioning sex repeatedly just adds pressure.

MADDIE: I didn't know that.

MADISON: You were trying to make me look stupid. Why would I believe such a stupid story?

MADDIE: You weren't supposed to. I was going to be a pathological liar. I thought it was sexy. I thought you'd like it.

MADISON: I didn't. Besides you weren't following the rules.

MADDIE: Which rule? There's so many I get confused.

MADISON: Rule number one. You broke it three times. You're not supposed to bring up things that remind us of reality, Maddie.

MADDIE: Name one thing that was from our life together.

MADISON: The paintings for one. You know how bad I feel about burning your painting with the candle. It wasn't on purpose!

MADDIE: Oh, wasn't it? It took you long enough to notice. Flames were shooting up toward the refrigerator.

MADISON: You should have brought that up earlier then. You're not supposed to bring up anything real during our meetings.

MADDIE: You didn't even say you were sorry about burning it.

MADISON: It wasn't intentional. I'm sorry.

MADDIE: Fine.

MADISON: Secondly, you brought up reading manuscripts and that makes me think of proofreading. Then all I think of is you and your job.

MADDIE: You get to use your real job. Every time we do it, you're a security guard.

MADISON: That's cause I'm working. And not every time! Sometimes I'm something else in disguise.

MADDIE: You should have to come up with as many new professions as I have for this.

MADISON: Thirdly, the crack about the crazy rituals. I know you were talking about this. That's a rule in itself. Never bring up the game during the game.

MADDIE: I didn't break that rule. A ritual is a set form. It's supposed to be always the same. Our meetings are totally different. They're supposed to be always new and exciting.

MADISON: But it's always the same really. We're supposed to meet each other as strangers.

MADDIE: I'm so sick of this. I'm trying my best to please you and all you can do is pick on me. I think you burnt that painting to get back at me.

MADISON: That's ridiculous!

MADDIE: Well, maybe I'm just going crazy then. Here it is Christmas Eve and we're doing this again. It's crazy. Almost everyday now.

MADISON: Holidays are romantic.

MADDIE: Romantic? I'm not sure this is romantic anymore. It was kinda fun every once in awhile, but I'm not sure it's fun anymore. It's certainly not romantic or spontaneous.

MADISON: Would you rather give up on us completely?

MADDIE: *(Beat.)* Maybe we should try a new place. I feel stale here.

MADISON: Stale? We love train stations. Things begin and end in places of travel. Like when we moved to Boston together.

MADDIE: Yeah. *(Thinking.)* But then it was just for a laugh.

MADISON: You were so creative and so beautiful.

MADDIE: How about meeting at the airport? Playing it there.

MADISON: Too many people will distract us.

MADDIE: What about the bus station?

MADISON: We'll probably get killed.

MADDIE: That would be a dramatic way for strangers to meet. Those that die together, lie together.

MADISON: I don't like that.

MADDIE: Why?

MADISON: Let's just try it again. I know we can make it work perfectly again!

MADDIE: We have so many real connections between us now that it's hard to come up with something in the game that doesn't remind us of our life. It's hard to be strangers when you know how someone looks every morning.

MADISON: *(Looks through the bags.)* Maybe you should wear your hair up? How 'bout a different prop? *(Madison hands her an antique book.)* A book is perfect. You approach me this time. *(Maddie pulls some glasses out from her bag as Madison prepares himself. They look at each other for a moment and clap their hands. Suddenly, they break eye contact. Maddie begins reading her book. Madison starts whistling "Jingle Bells" while he paces.)*

MADDIE: Excuse me, sir, do you have a light?

(Madison turns to looks at her.)

MADISON: No!

MADDIE: Look who's not following the rules?

MADISON: *(Lifts up his hands and snaps his fingers.)* Elvis is alive.

MADDIE: *(Lifts up her hands above her head and snaps her fingers.)* And living in Canton, Ohio.

MADISON: Beginning with a light reminds me of the last one. And the last one was a failure. Try again.

(They look at each for a moment and clap their hands. They each go back to their position before. Madison reads and Madison whistles "Jingle Bells.")

MADDIE: Wait a minute.

MADISON: Rules, rules.

MADDIE: *(Snaps her fingers over her head.)* Elvis is alive.

MADISON: *(He does the same.)* And living in Canton, Ohio.

MADDIE: How come you get to whistle "Jingle Bells?" You did that in the last one too.

MADISON: Does it distract you?

MADDIE: Yes!

MADISON: Fine. I'll whistle something else.

(They look at each for a moment and clap their hands. They each go back to their positions from before. Maddie reads and Madison whistles "White Christmas." It's a very hard song for him to whistle, and he doesn't do it very well.)

MADDIE: Excuse me, sir, but could you stop whistling.

MADISON: That's rude.

MADDIE: I'm glad you said that. I think it's refreshing when people say what's on their mind. Sometimes I wish my old lover could say what was on his mind, so I'd knew what bothered him.

MADISON: I don't like to talk about old lovers.

MADDIE: Good honesty. Allow me to introduce myself. *(Offering her hand.)* Dr. Hall.

MADISON: A doctor? Why would a doctor wait for a train? You people rake in the bucks.

MADDIE: Humm. You sound bitter.

MADISON: That's cause I used to be a doctor too. I know how you lie to people. And act superior. You remind us of our mortality.

MADDIE: You were a doctor? Where?

MADISON: I don't have to answer your questions. In a hospital.

MADDIE: Oh, well you misunderstand me.

MADISON: I understand perfectly. You women doctors are really uppity.

MADDIE: I'm a psychologist.

MADISON: Oooh. A looney then.

MADDIE: You say whatever's on your mind, don't you? Seems you carry some animosity about women in authority.

MADISON: I don't have any problems. You women just like to create problems by quoting men your salary.

MADDIE: Hummm. You say "you women" like we all get together and have little clubhouse meetings on men. Don't flatter yourself. I know what you're referring to and I don't like it.

MADISON: You couldn't know what I was referring to because you don't know me, Dr. Hall. Or at least you're not supposed to!

(Maddie puts her hands over her head and snaps her fingers.)

MADDIE: Elvis is alive.

MADISON: *(Puts his hands over his head and snaps his fingers.)* And living in Canton, Ohio.

MADDIE: So what if I got a little promotion at the publishing company, and I'm making a little more money than you. That should make you happy.

MADISON: I am happy! I'm so happy! But do you have to push it in my face?

MADDIE: You were breaking the rules. You were bringing in our real life. You don't like the fact that I got a raise and you didn't.

MADISON: It's been hard for me. I don't think you had to make such a deal of it.

MADDIE: What was I supposed to do with the extra money? Hide it? I wasn't trying to threaten your masculinity.

MADISON: Oh, weren't you? Then why did you choose to be a doctor in this one? Why do you always remind me that all I am is a security guard?!

MADDIE: I don't do that. It's you who always makes that such an issue. I don't care what you do.

MADISON: You know I bring in less money than you. You know your little paintings have taken off while I can't convince anyone that I have good business ideas. So why don't you make me look strong in one of the games? Do I have to be the weak and stupid one when we play too?!

MADDIE: Stop being so defensive about your intelligence. If I thought you were stupid, do you think I'd marry you?

MADISON: You didn't know what a loser I was then. I can't get through half the business courses.

MADDIE: You've got to face it, Madison; it's hard to be in school while working sixty hours a week.

MADISON: But if I'm ever going to own a theater, I have to get through these classes.

MADDIE: No one person owns their own movie theater anymore. They're owned by huge companies.

MADISON: Yeah, but I'll give them something the new companies won't. We'll only show old classic movies, Laurel and Hardy, Abbott and Costello, Burton and Taylor.

MADDIE: Classic movies aren't in demand.

MADISON: Well, who would've thought your stupid little cat paintings would take off? Why would they be in demand? But they are. Ever since that woman from that cat specialty store bought them.

MADDIE: It was a fluke. You know it had nothing to do with money. I needed a release because of our loss. It was just good luck that I sold them.

MADISON: Why couldn't I have some luck? Why can't I now?

MADDIE: Maybe you will. I just don't want you to get your hopes up.

MADISON: But you should be getting my hopes up. My movie theater is all I have since . . .

MADDIE: Say it, Madison. You've got to accept what happened.

MADISON: I don't accept it. I can't accept it. I won't. *(Picks up the book and puts it in her hands.)* I think we should use the prop more. I think that's the problem.

(Maddie gets up to go.)

MADDIE: I have to get home and wrap Alfred Hitchcock's presents.

MADISON: I'm sure Alfred's doggy bones can wait.

MADDIE: You wouldn't want our baby's present to go unwrapped on Christmas, would you?

MADISON: Don't talk like our animals are our children again. I hate that.

MADDIE: Why? Why do you hate that?

MADISON: Let's do it right just once tonight, Maddie.

MADDIE: Why don't we just talk?

MADISON: Not now. Later. After we get it right.

MADDIE: Okay, I'll try to get it right then.

(She pulls a handkerchief from the bag. Madison strikes a manly pose. They look at each other for a moment and clap their hands. Maddie hides behind her book and sniffles.)

MADISON: What are you reading?

MADDIE: *Camille. (She coughs, and then cries into her handkerchief.)*

MADISON: Why are you crying?

MADDIE: I cry very often. Every night when I'm alone. It's because I'm lost and weak and looking for a man who will be strong for me. I'm also dying of an incurable disease.

MADISON: I've sent letters that have been unanswered. I've come for you.

MADDIE: Could it be you? *(Feels his face as if blinded by her sickness.)* You're the only one who could cure my sick heart. I've been waiting so long.

MADISON: You remember me then?

MADDIE: Somehow I knew you'd always come back. I knew. I'm so frightened really. I feel safe in your arms.

(Madison notices his arms aren't around her, so he puts them around her.)

MADISON: My real name's Madison but most people call me Robin.

MADDIE: Robin? Batman's Robin?

MADISON: NO! NO! After Robin Hood! *(Madison puts his hands over his head and snaps his fingers.)*

MADISON: Elvis is alive!

MADDIE: *(Does the signal back.)* And living in Canton, Ohio. Why'd you stop that one?

MADISON: It had no honesty.

MADDIE: And you think real life does? *(Pause.)* You stopped it because he loved Batman and Robin.

MADISON: We need a script. Something tried and true.

MADDIE: Let's face it, Madison. We can't get through it for a reason. Can't we try it without the game?

MADISON: *(He looks at the book.)* Romeo and Juliet! They were just strangers when they met.

MADDIE: Aren't we all?

(They look at each other briefly and clap. They stare with each other intensely. She takes his hands.)

MADDIE: Dance with me? *(She takes him up to dance.)* Could I give you an angelic kiss?

MADISON: If there was anything angelic about you, you'd settle for my hand.

MADDIE: Don't angels have lips?

MADISON: They also have hands, which they place together to pray with.

MADDIE: So why don't we put our lips together like their hands and have praying lips and then we could do the same with our bodies.

MADISON: Listen, you move too fast. Where do you come from?

MADDIE: Verona. It's near Detroit.

MADISON: Figures.

MADDIE: My father owns General Motors. I could buy you whatever you want.

MADISON: What?! I don't want your filthy money. My father works for the union. You laid off half my family. They'd like to kill you.

MADDIE: Frankly, my family would like to kill yours also, with all those salary and benefit increases.

MADISON: Why don't we skip the family problems and run off together?

MADDIE: Yeah, you wouldn't mind that, would you? You never had a good relationship with your family like I did.

MADISON: I gave up as much as you. I was young too.

MADDIE: Next thing I know, we'll be faking suicides.

MADISON: Hadn't thought of it, but now that you mention it.

MADDIE: I'm attracted to you physically, but it doesn't seem mutual. I don't think I could make a commitment.

MADISON: Don't you think we can outlive our fate?

MADDIE: No. Things happen that we have no control over!

MADISON: *(Madison snaps his fingers above his head.)* Elvis is alive! This isn't working either.

MADDIE: *(Snaps her fingers over her head.)* And living in Canton, Ohio. The whole thing is a farce.

MADISON: It would've helped if you would have allowed me to be Romeo instead of Juliet.
(Maddie laughs.)

MADISON: You need to be serious. You're not serious enough. That's our problem.

MADDIE: I think it's a sign of our sanity. Let's quit.

MADISON: Forget the props. Let's not talk about it. We'll just go.
(They clap their hands. Maddie goes back to the bench and pulls a hanky out of the bag. Madison stands at a distance.)

MADDIE: Mister, I'm not a nut case but a tornado blew our house apart and my husband's body was never found. I think he's left me. He used it to leave me. He's been missing for the last four months. I think he's gone forever, and I feel so alone.

MADISON: Where'd you come from?

MADDIE: Kansas.

MADISON: Long way. How'd you expect to get around?

MADDIE: Click my heels. No, but seriously. I had faith. Crazy, I guess.

MADISON: I wouldn't say that. Why do you think your husband left?

MADDIE: He started to get distant a few months ago.

MADISON: Did you ask him about it?

MADDIE: Yes. All the time. He didn't want to talk about it.

MADISON: Maybe it was too hard.

MADDIE: It was hard for me too.

MADISON: So tell me about Kansas.

MADDIE: I think he still blames me.

MADISON: I saw a great rainbow there once.

MADDIE: For the death of our child.

MADISON: *(Hands over head, fingers snapping.)* Elvis is alive!

MADDIE: Don't stop! We never talk about it. You pick at things that have nothing to do with the real problem between us.

MADISON: Say it. Say it! "And living in Canton, Ohio!"
(She shakes her head "no.")

MADISON: Then start a new one. *(He claps his hands together.)*

MADDIE: Could you tell me when the first train leaves tomorrow?

MADISON: Won't be one. It's Christmas.

MADDIE: The next one then?

MADISON: I'm not a security guard really.

MADDIE: What are you then? Look, I'm desperate. I have reason to believe my husband hates me!

MADISON: *(Madison lifts his hands above his head and snaps his fingers.)* Elvis is alive!

MADDIE: *(Maddie lifts her hands above her head and snaps her fingers.)* Please, Madison!

MADISON: Go again!
(They clap their hands. Madison stands by the bench. Maddie reads over a brochure.)

MADDIE: I've seen you before, I think.

MADISON: Nice line. You ever even been here before?

MADDIE: Yes. I even remember the date, August twenty-first, my son's birth

MADISON: *(Madison lifts his hands above his head and snaps his fingers.)* No real life!

MADDIE: We've grieved enough. I've said I was sorry 'til I was blue in the face.

MADISON: Go again! No reality!
(They clap their hands.)

MADDIE: Sir, I'm color-blind and that's why I've been missing all these trains. The map is color-coded. Can you tell me if that's as blue as my son's eyes?
(Madison lifts his hands and snaps his fingers.)

MADISON: No! Go again!
(He claps his hands several times.)

MADDIE: Sir, my son, Michael began choking on food —

(Madison snaps his fingers over his head.)

MADISON: Go again! *(Madison claps.)*

MADDIE: I tried to help him —

(Madison snaps his fingers over his head.)

MADISON: Go again! *(Madison claps.)*

MADDIE: I was asleep —

(Madison snaps his fingers over his head. He then claps his hands again.)

MADISON: *(Claps.)* Go again!

MADDIE: He died.

(Madison snaps his fingers over his head. Maddie snaps her finger over her head repeatedly. Madison claps his hands over and over.)

MADDIE: *(Screams.)* It wasn't my fault, Madison!

MADISON: *(Puts his hands up in the air and snaps them.)* Elvis is alive!

(Madison claps his hands. Beat. He claps again. Beat. Claps again and again.)

MADDIE: I won't do it again.

MADISON: You have to.

MADDIE: I don't have to do anything. I've stopped playing. I can't please you. You're trying to punish me for something I couldn't stop.

MADISON: I don't know what you're talking about.

MADDIE: That's the problem. You won't admit it. You can't stand to be with me unless I'm some stranger somehow. And that's sheer torture for me because I love you. You.

MADISON: I loved him, Maddie!

MADDIE: I know. I did too.

MADISON: He was my buddy. I miss carrying him to bed at night. We played so hard.

MADDIE: I know.

MADISON: I don't want to blame you.

MADDIE: Then don't! *(Beat.)* Why don't we try again? We could try to have another child.

MADISON: *(Angered.)* We can't replace him!

MADDIE: I know that!

MADISON: I don't want to have another one. He made my life special.

MADDIE: Mine too. I'm sorry. *(Maddie begins to walk out without the bags.)*

MADISON: Where are you going? Hey, I got ten minutes still. We can get it right. *(Madison claps his hands. He runs toward her.)* Stop, lady! This is the police. Put your hands up! *(Madison grabs Maddie and pushes her down to the ground. He claps his hands louder and harder. He's on the edge, even a bit dangerous.)* Okay, lady, a little kid died four months ago and I want to know what you saw! And what you did! *(Beat.)* Come on, lady! I want to know who's to blame! *(Claps his hands more.)* C'mon talk! It's either talk now or go to hell! Did you hear? Say anything! Come on now, talk! TALK, TALK, TALK!

MADDIE: *(Quietly.)* I woke up to Michael choking. I ran into his room, but he wasn't there. I started screaming when I saw my baby in the kitchen on the floor. His face was all blue. I did all the things you're supposed to. I squeezed under his ribs so I could get whatever it was out of his throat. But he'd stopped breathing. I pumped his stomach over and over, calling his name. I cried for help. I couldn't leave his side to call anyone cause I knew he was already dead. And my heart was beating in my head so loud. Maybe I did it all wrong but I tried. I tried. I tried. God, I tried. *(Madison moves away.)*

MADISON: If I was there, I could have saved him.

MADDIE: And I wish with all my heart that you'd been there with me.

MADISON: Where you going, Maddie? It's Christmas Eve.

MADDIE: I can't live being always guilty. Things always begin and end here, right? Good-bye, Madison.

MADISON: If I had more money, maybe you wouldn't have had to work so much. Maybe you wouldn't have been so tired, and you would have heard him.

MADDIE: Maybe.

MADISON: If I were smarter, I would've had my own business and we'd live in a house where he couldn't wander into the kitchen so easily.

MADDIE: Maybe.

MADISON: He was all I had to be proud of, and I should have been home! I should have been with you!

MADDIE: No.

MADISON: *(Madison reaches for her.)* I know that Michael's death wasn't your fault. I've always known that, Maddie. But it wasn't my fault either. Was it?

MADDIE: No, it wasn't. Definitely not. No. *(She hugs him close.)*

MADISON: I'm sorry it took me so long to say it. *(He pulls her tight to him.)* I love you. I love you so much!
(They cling to each other tightly.)

MADDIE: Umm. Remember the first time we ever met?

MADISON: *(Smirks.)* Blind date.

MADDIE: *(Lifts her head from the hug.)* Ohio.

MADISON: *(Cringes.)* I was sooo boring.

MADDIE: Yes, but I couldn't forget a word you said. You were sincere.

MADISON: *(Starting to release her.)* You too.

(They look at each other in silent communication for a moment and then they both clap their hands.)

MADISON: Hi.

MADDIE: Hi.

MADISON: Hi.

MADDIE: I'm fine.

MADISON: Me, too. Are you?

MADDIE: Yes! I mean, I don't know? Who?

MADISON: Maddie?

MADDIE: Yes. That's me. So . . .

MADISON: So. *(Madison takes out a cigarette.)* You want a light? I mean, a cigarette. Forget it. I don't want to smoke.

MADDIE: I don't smoke either. Much. This is nice here.

MADISON: This is where I work. Just got off. Won't work here for long though. I'm gonna own a movie theater someday.

MADDIE: That's nice.

MADISON: Yeah. So, you want to go some place?

MADDIE: Sure. Where?

MADISON: I don't know. To dinner?

MADDIE: Yeah.

MADISON: Good.

MADDIE: Great.

MADISON: So, uh . . . did you hear Elvis is alive?

MADDIE: Right. And he's living right here in Canton, Ohio. You don't believe that shit? . . . I mean, stuff.

MADISON: No. I just didn't have anything else to say.

MADDIE: Oh. I like nervous tension in a man.

MADISON: You do?

MADDIE: I mean, it's honest.

MADISON: I'm full of it. Nervous tension, I mean.

MADDIE: I bet you are.

MADISON: So there's a diner around the corner. You want to eat?

MADDIE: Sounds perfect. *(She puts her hands over her head and snaps her fingers. He snaps back.)* I love you, Madison. *(She kisses him passionately.)*

MADISON: *(Beat.)* You want to go home and try?

MADDIE: This isn't part of the game?

MADISON: No, maybe we could have another one.

(She hugs him.)
MADDIE: Now that would be a Christmas present.
(They leave together. Madison tosses the book back into the shopping bags.)
MADISON: I guess Elvis is dead.
(She looks to him. He takes her hand as the lights fade out and the music fades up.)

END OF PLAY

ORIGINAL PRODUCTION

Romance was originally produced with the Jupiter Theatre under the direction of Mathew Hahn. The cast for the original production was as follows:

MIRIAM .... Kristy Kambanis

MICK .... Steve Ratcliff

CHARACTERS

MIRIAM: 34, a college professor

MICK: 36, a mail carrier

SETTING

A small chapel in Boston.

TIME

The present.

ROMANCE

SCENE: The stage is dimly lit, and there is a large wooden pew center. An antique kneeler with a portion of a decorative black metal altar rail stands in the down stage right area. In front of the kneeler are rows of candles for lighting. A sign by the candles asks for a donation of ten cents for each candle. In the down stage left area, parallel to the candles, there is a small statue of the Virgin Mary on a wooden pedestal. The lighting is filled with warm colors, dim and reddish, like the innermost part of a small side chapel, in a much larger church. A small Christmas wreath is hung on the kneeler and two poinsettia plants frame the altar.

AT RISE: An attractive woman, dressed in a wool skirt with matching jacket, sits smack in the middle of the pew. Her winter coat, hat, and gloves are draped over the armrest. Beside her is a classic black suitcase with wheels. She nervously clutches the bottom of her seat beneath her knees. She sits silently for a moment and then begins to hum "Jingle Bells" slowly and quietly at first and then louder and more franticly. Suddenly, she stops humming and gets up and goes to the kneeler to light a candle. She strikes a match to light the candle and then notices the sign for a donation. She immediately blows out the match and in doing so, several other candles.

MIRIAM: Shoot!

> *(There's a loud thud offstage.)*

MICK: Shit! *(Pause.)* Sorry.

> *(Miriam quickly moves over to the bench. She crouches down, so that no one can see her. As Mick enters she slips to the side of the pew so he can't see her. Mick enters in his wrinkled tux covered by a winter parka. He speaks as if he's talking to a good friend, occasionally gesturing with his bottle of beer.)*

MICK: You know what I've been thinkin', God. The reason our whole world has gone to crap and the idiot politicians keep gettin' re-elected and the ozone layer turned into a greenhouse thing, and the Red Sox keep losin' is that there are a lot of words with no meanin' out there. You follow? Words people use to create misunderstandings, to confuse instead of to *(Several arm gestures.)* uh, uh, uh, communicate. *(Pause.)* You want examples? That's fair. But remember this is uh, uh, an embriotic idea. Naaaah, it's new idea. Forget the embryo, it has too much to do with women. And that's a whole other mess. Okay, so examples. There's plenty.

I just have to think. *(He leans against the pew and pounds his head with his fist.)* Pre-boarding. A perfect example. What does it mean? Flight attendants call passengers on planes to pre-board. Logic says, there is only boarding and not boarding. But they use the prefix "pre" meaning before. So pre-boarding would be before boarding. Only that's not what it means because the pre-boarders actually board the plane during pre-boarding. Now, these pre-boarders are really special people. They're people with first class seats. Rich people. Somehow people with first-class seats don't have to truly board. They magically float onto the plane during PRE-BOARDING! Get it?! But the word doesn't mean what you'd think it would. Does it?! It confuses! It should be called early-boarding or first-class boarding, or take-up-all-the-storage-space boarding! *(Pause. He looks down at the bottle.)* I was gonna be pre-boarding tomorrow for the first time. For the first time, I was gonna be a special person, a first-class passenger who could pre-board. I could still do it, but it wouldn't have the same meaning. Would it? *(He sits, puts hands in head.)* Shit! *(Mick suddenly becomes aware of a presence looking at him. He lifts up his head to see Miriam. He jumps up.)* Jesus Christ, what the fuck are ya doin?! *(Putting his hand out.)* Uh, sorry. Sorry, bad mouth. *(Hits his mouth.)* Are you a nun? Forget that. Doesn't matter. One shouldn't be shootin' off their mouth in a chapel. But what the hell are you doin' down there? Ya scared me.

(Miriam looks out. Pause.)

MICK: What are you moot, or somethin'? *(Pause.)* Great. If there's one thing I need tonight, it's a listener. Course an occasional "uh-huh" for reassurance wouldn't be so damn awful. *(He laughs. Pause.)* How'd you get in here? It was locked. *(Pause.)* Oh, right. Moot, thing. *(Notices her suitcase.)* Goin' some place? Lucky you. I'm not. I almost . . . aw nothin'. *(Pause.)* It must be awful hard to be moot. All those thoughts and comments and jokes that have to stay unsaid. You could write 'em but they wouldn't have your voice inflections like on 'em. Yep . . . so much left inside. *(Pause.)* Maybe I know what it's like to be moot. *(Pause.)* I kept completely moot today when . . .

MIRIAM: Mute!

MICK: What?

MIRIAM: Mute. The word is mute. Not moot. Mute, meaning not speaking. While moot, the word you keep using over and over, means a discussion, an argument, debate, or proposal. You complain about the lack of distinction in the use of words and their then abstracted meaning, and you have the nerve to use *moot* when you mean *mute!*

MICK: You are a nun, aren't ya?

MIRIAM: *(She begins picking up her bag.)* No. I'm a teacher.

MICK: Same thing.

MIRIAM: I think you should go home. You smell like alcohol.

MICK: I knew I was in for more than an "uh-huh" if you weren't truly a moot person, pardon me, mute.

MIRIAM: *(Worried.)* I don't look like a nun, do I?!

MICK: I don't know. They don't wear those habit hats anymore. So you might look like one.

MIRIAM: Yes, but they do have a look.

MICK: They do?

MIRIAM: Yes!

MICK: Well, what would that be?

MIRIAM: They wear a lot of navy and powder blue suits. Usually polyester suits. Polyester because it's cheap and it shows that they are frugal. They wear white blouses, also made of polyester, to go with the blue suits. They wear their hair short with no curls, and they always wear stickpins on their slightly large collars.

MICK: Haven't thought about this much, have ya? *(Pause. Looks at her.)* Well, I figure the points mute anyway.

MIRIAM: I don't find that funny, frankly.

MICK: Why are you so defensive about this? It would be so bad for me to think that you were a nun?

MIRIAM: No, no, it's just that I think that I . . .

MICK: What?

MIRIAM: *(Gestures to her body.)* Well, that I have a certain . . . at least, I hope I'm . . . I am . . .

MICK: Lots of fill in the blanks for a woman with dictionary definitions.

MIRIAM: I'm not stuffy like you presume. *(She picks up her bag from the floor.)*

MICK: Where're ya goin'?

MIRIAM: I don't know you. I don't have to answer that. It's almost rude that you ask.

MICK: Hummm? Almost rude? I wonder if it's almost rude to eavesdrop on somebody spilling their guts to God?

MIRIAM: *(Clears her throat.)* I had no idea who you were. I thought you might be dangerous. Of course, you still could be. This chapel is closed and . . .

MICK: That's right. The chapel is closed. So how did you get in here?

MIRIAM: I came in much earlier.

MICK: You mean you sat here and let the janitor lock up around you?

MIRIAM: I didn't hear them lock up. How'd you get in, buddy?

MICK: I was so blind that I didn't see the door. Came crashing right through it. Wouldn't ya know?

MIRIAM: I find that hard to believe.

MICK: Me, too. But then, a lie for a lie is fair. *(Pause.)* Quite honestly, I picked the lock. You?

MIRIAM: *(Sounding worried.)* Why? What do you want here?

MICK: You act as if I'm gonna to rob the place. What would I steal? Holy water? *(Points to the statue.)* Yeah, I've heard the Mary stiff is a hot item on the street. Right up there next to Barry Manilow eight-track tapes.

MIRIAM: Okay, I lied!

MICK: Come again?

MIRIAM: I heard them lock up. I did. Okay? Every echo, every clamor! Happy? *(Starts rustling through her bag.)*

MICK: You're a little nervous, aren't ya?

MIRIAM: And you know what the sad part is?

MICK: No clue.

MIRIAM: I felt so relieved. Alone, but so relieved.

MICK: Jesus, I wish I could feel that way.

MIRIAM: *(Takes out a piece of chewing gum and chews. Tearing the gum paper nervously.)* But one cannot hide. One cannot hide from the things they must confront. And if one finds it impossible to confront, if one finds an unwilling ear, one must, no alternative, leave. *(Pause. She blows a bubble.)*

MICK: What is that? Bazooka?
   (She nods. Pause.)

MICK: Can I have a piece of that?

MIRIAM: *(Taking out piece for him.)* Sure.
   (He puts in the chewing gum.)

MIRIAM: I feel sad. So sad.

MICK: Me, too.
   (They both chew.)

MIRIAM: Somehow you forget what you had and you try desperately to return to it . . .

MICK: *(Reading comic.)* I want a job workin' at Bazooka doin' their comics. You don't have to draw well and you don't have to be funny.

MIRIAM: It's impossible, though.

MICK: Maybe they'd put me in their fortune division. I'd be good at that. I'd get specific. None of this, "Today you will have a startling discovery." So the hell what? Too general.

MIRIAM: I had to leave. It was a lie—all of it.

MICK: *(Pretends to read off comic.)* Mine would read . . . today you have a startling realization that carrying mail is a pitiful job with lousy benefits, and the one part of your life that seemed set, wasn't, so you go out and buy a case of Mic and you drink. While watching *Gilligan's Island* reruns, it occurs to you. Why is life so random? Like why did they name it *Gilligan's Island* instead of *Professor's Island*? He's the smart one. He deserves to have the island named after him. Why do some people find love while other people remain completely alone? Then you think maybe it isn't so random. Maybe it's the choices, the decisions we make that cause our downfall. We can't feel hopeless. *(Standing.)* You rise up from the couch determined to go out and find love. Triumphant and happy, you are! Secure!! And then a bolt of lightening comes through your window and strikes you dead. *(Pause.)* At least that fortune's more specific. *(Pause. Sits.)* Come to think of it, being general never hurt anybody.

MIRIAM: Well . . . you can't mope forever. *(She spits out the gum.)*

MICK: Lose its flavor already?

MIRIAM: No, it's just that I can't taste anything. Do you know where a pay phone is?

MICK: I don't think churches have 'em? It's too immoral. Too many shady things happen on the phone.

MIRIAM: *(Looking about.)* It's been many years.

MICK: Like phone sex. That's done on the phone. Aw, you don't want to hear that.

MIRIAM: Years since I've been in a—*(Suddenly hearing what he said.)* I'm not a prude.

MICK: Pardon?

MIRIAM: I like sex. I like it very much. Just because an individual has a well-developed mind, is a professor, does not mean that they have a numb body. You think that my only stimulation is spreading my fingers over a European historical reference list while listening to *Carmen.* I'm aware of my erogenous zones. I giggle. I masturbate. Sometimes I spontaneously scream or rant. And I have even performed intense sex acts illegal in most states! I am incredibly sexy.

MICK: Oh, I believe the rantin' part.

MIRIAM: *(Gathering up her stuff.)* So have you seen a pay phone or not?

MICK: Who ya gonna call? I know, I know, it's none of my business. But it's not as if I'm nosy. This is an unusual situation. Us being in this chapel. The whole situation skips us over real formalities. It's like when you puke in front of someone. Suddenly that person cannot be an acquaintance anymore, because they've seen you through the very personal act of puking. It brings you closer to being intimate. Get it?

MIRIAM: I can't stay here.

MICK: There's a station on Tremont that might have a phone.

MIRIAM: Good.

MICK: Though it's closed.

MIRIAM: Already?

MICK: It's two in the morning, lady.

MIRIAM: It couldn't be. I came in here at four.

MICK: In the afternoon?!

MIRIAM: It's impossible. I need to do something.

MICK: If you were here at four. Then that means . . . *(Counts on hand.)* You were here for ten hours?

MIRIAM: The bus station. How far is it?

MICK: You can't walk. Not in this neighborhood.

MIRIAM: No choice. I'll find a phone. Then I'll call a cab.

MICK: But it's freezing cold out. Besides it's too dangerous.

MIRIAM: So, light a candle for me. *(Struggles to pick up her heavy suitcase.)*

MICK: I'd have to set the chapel ablaze to save ya. This is not the place to wander around.

MIRIAM: I'm aware of that. I'm from the city myself, sir. I know how to walk in a manner that looks threatening. And I can smoke a cigarette.

MICK: What does that do? Relax you as you get pulverized?

MIRIAM: It makes me look intimidating. *(She holds the suitcase with both hands.)*

MICK: *(He gets up.)* I'll get my car.

MIRIAM: No! Thank you, but no.

MICK: It's no trouble. It's not a big deal.

MIRIAM: I couldn't.

MICK: I told you, I don't mind.

MIRIAM: I can't. *(Pause.)*

MICK: Are you scared of me?

MIRIAM: I don't know anything about you. Except that you broke into a church, somewhat drunk.

MICK: But I keep the hatchet well hidden. Got to give me credit for that. *(Pause. She starts to exit.)* Do you believe in God?

MIRIAM: I really must . . .

MICK: *(He grabs her arm.)* Please! This won't take any time. Just answer. Please!

MIRIAM: God is exactly like Santa Claus.

MICK: Well, thank you for your time. I didn't expect that. I didn't expect that from someone who spent 10 hours in a chapel. But I've been caught off guard so many times today. It fits. Good-bye, lady.

MIRIAM: No, I don't think you . . . *(Pause.)* Good-bye. *(She exits.)*

MICK: Good-bye. Heard that before. *(Goes to the candles and strikes up a match. He begins to light all the candles.)* One candle for me. Two candles to forgetting her. Three and four candles for the crazy woman with the suitcase to look intimidating. *(Miriam re-enters quietly.)* Five candles for Mom, six candles for her. For her who leaves so easily and that I can't ever forget. Ever.

(Miriam clears throat.)

MICK: *(Doesn't turn.)* Eavesdrop much?

MIRIAM: I believe in Santa Claus.

MICK: *(Now he turns.)* What?!

MIRIAM: I couldn't leave here with you thinking the wrong thing. I believe in the spirit of good. *(She laughs.)* Call me crazy.

MICK: I already did.

MIRIAM: *(Pause.)* I wanted to tell you that. *(She turns to leave.)*

MICK: Wait! So do you believe in an afterlife?

MIRIAM: No. I believe we live on in the hearts of those that love us.

MICK: Oh, don't give me that crap! I guess, that means you figure when we croak, that's the end.

MIRIAM: I think it's pretty egotistical to assume we go on forever.

MICK: So what? Is it egotistical when we don't walk in front of a car or that we stop someone from stabbing us with a knife? We want to go on, live. We don't call that egotistical. It's called self-preservation. And all us healthy ones believe in it

MIRIAM: I really don't know the answer.

MICK: I do. I believe in anything that keeps us goin' on after this lousy life. Reincarnation, heaven, any of that stuff. Of course, I'd like to be reincarnated with the same name. Then you're used to answerin' to it. *(He holds out hand.)* The name's Mick. You got a cigarette before you go?

MIRIAM: *(She hands him the suitcase. Then goes through her purse.)* Miriam. Sure.

MICK: And you don't have a clue of how to get to the bus station, do you?

MIRIAM: *(She continues to look through purse.)* A little clue. See, I'm used to having no direction, literally and figuratively.

MICK: So stay, at least, until it quits snowin'. I couldn't hurt a flea. I light candles for my Mom. And she wouldn't think it was very nice if I killed somebody

MIRIAM: Yeah, and I'm sure that's what Norman Bates said to his mom too.

MICK: I like you. I trust you. That's rare.

MIRIAM: *(Pause.)* I'm sorry I've been abrupt. I know you mean to be nice. But talking isn't . . . well, it's not easy. *(She hands him the pack.)* Here.

MICK: Could have fooled me. *(Looks at pack.)* Lucky Strikes? Wow, very intimidating. *(He offers her one.)*

MIRIAM: I know. I hate smoking. I just bought them for the rough neighborhoods. And because I thought it would be dramatic to offer them on occasion. I guess I've been looking for drama in my life.

MICK: *(Sarcastic. Lighting cigarette off the candles.)* And look how cheaply you got off. Two bucks for "dramma." Some of us aren't even looking for it, and we end up payin' a lot more.

MIRIAM: I'm married.

MICK: And what does that have to do with the price of eggs in Iowa?

MIRIAM: I just thought you should know. I mean, I heard you before when you were talking . . . out loud to . . . I mean, accidentally, I heard you mention that you were sad because some her was leaving and that you'd never forget her.

MICK: Wait? You thought I was talking about you?

MIRIAM: *(Pause.)* No. No! Did I say that? Don't be ridiculous. We've only just met. I only meant that whoever the her is I might be able to offer some advice about her. Being a married woman and all. *(Pause.)* So what happened to her if you don't mind answering?

MICK: *(Takes a drag.)* Where's your ring? *(Coughs.)*

MIRIAM: Pardon?

MICK: If you're married, where's your ring?! *(Mick coughs.)*

MIRIAM: Well, I'm not sure I'm technically anything right now. I'm in the midst of a separation. I think. Though my husband doesn't know it. I imagine.

MICK: And I'm coming to you for advice? *(Touches his head.)* Oh, boy. *(He puts his cigarette out.)*

MIRIAM: What's the matter with you?

MICK: I think I'm gonna be sick.

MIRIAM: The drinking?

MICK: *(Lies across the pew.)* I didn't think it would still have this effect on me.

MIRIAM: Still? You mean this has happened before?

MICK: Only a few times. Maybe a dozen or so.

MIRIAM: *(She comes over to him.)* Oh my God, you really are sick. Here, take off this tie. *(She loosens his bow tie.)* Wow, you're all dressed up.

MICK: Yep, you can dress me up, but I still puke everywhere. *(Cough.)*

MIRIAM: Don't be contemptuous. Here put your head here. *(She pulls his head on her lap.)*

MICK: Ow. Not so rough.

MIRIAM: Breathe deep. *(Pause.)* So what was the occasion?

MICK: *(Adjusting on her lap.)* When were you gonna tell your husband you split?

MIRIAM: Why don't you just relax for awhile? Close your eyes.

MICK: When he started posting signs up for your whereabouts? After he poured millions into search helicopters? After he quit his job, worried sick, exhausted and half-dead? Were you gonna wait till the very last minute?! Till it caused him the most pain and embarrassment?

MIRIAM: You've got the wrong Morris. I don't even think it will disrupt his patient's appointments.

MICK: *(Sits up.)* How do you know? *(Touches his head.)* Ow.

MIRIAM: Maybe you ought to lay your head down again.

MICK: No, I'm fine. Answer. How do you know?

MIRIAM: I pick up his hair follicles in the shower. I know.

MICK: So what! What does that prove? You don't know his every thought. People are surprised every day to discover mysteries and secrets about their lovers. Nothing is set in concrete. Especially when the day comes that they are put on the spot. Wham! *(He slaps his hands. Touching his head.)* Ow. Anyway, that's when the truth comes out. That's when you really know.

MIRIAM: I didn't mean he wouldn't be concerned. He's not that cold. He'd probably assume that he'd forgotten that I had one of my literature conferences. After a day, he'd figure out that the lovely sweet smell in our room comes from my powder spray, and he'd discover that he has to put his own tea on in the morning. By the second evening, he'd begin to miss the sound of Beethoven's *Moonlight Sonata* playing over and over with the taps of my typewriter. He laughs at the primitiveness of me still using one. And then he'd get a case of heartburn, but he wouldn't know why. He'd feel as if he'd lost something, but wouldn't know what. And then he'd remember that he'd felt as if I should be home by now. After which, he might feel a slight pang. A pang of longing. Longing for only me. But he'd brush it off quickly. So quickly. Too quickly. Finally, he'd call my mother. *(Pause. Laughs sadly.)* And she'd get the helicopters out.

MICK: You can't think like that. You can't make all those assumptions. It's not fair not to give him a chance to respond.

MIRIAM: Oh, but I have!

MICK: No, you just think you have! You've never laid it on the line. You never came right out and said, "Do ya love me, or don't ya?! Cause if you don't, I'm leavin'!" Never since you've been married, right? *(Pause. She goes back to her suitcase.)*

MIRIAM: But why should I have to? If you love each other, you know.

MICK: Oh, it's just like a woman to think like that! You assume mental telepathy. You say, "I've been so upset. How could you not know?! My hand was on my hip like this all night." We're supposed to read hand gestures?

MIRIAM: You ought to. I read yours—I mean his.

MICK: No, you just think you do.

MIRIAM: When he's angry he puts his head back, his shoulders tense a bit, and he strokes his hair out of his eyes.

MICK: Maybe he had a crick in his neck, his shirtsleeve was wrinkled wrong and his hair was buggin' the hell out of him.

MIRIAM: He seems so angry with me. But it all remains polite. Civilized. Just like a doctor.

MICK: Maybe he thinks you don't want him anymore. Maybe that's what makes him angry. Makes him furious to think you don't love him anymore. *(She moves away from him.)*

MIRIAM: You don't know. You've never been married!

MICK: No. I haven't. *(Pause.)*

MIRIAM: I didn't mean that insultingly.

MICK: It must feel powerful to be so beautiful.

MIRIAM: *(Pause.)* Beautiful? Are you talking about me?

MICK: Yes, you and . . .

MIRIAM: It's been a long time.

MICK: So remind him. Be blunt.

MIRIAM: He used to say it all the time when we first got married.

MICK: When was that?

MIRIAM: Seven years, and about thirty-three hours ago. But who's counting?

MICK: Did he forget the anniversary?

MIRIAM: No, he bought me a new briefcase. One I had admired. It was lovely.

MICK: But . . . ?

MIRIAM: That was all.

MICK: All?

MIRIAM: Well we didn't . . . . I mean, I expected . . . . Where are those cigarettes? *(She begins rummaging through her purse.)*

MICK: *(Pause.)* Would you dance with me?

MIRIAM: *(Looking around.)* I don't think that would be appropriate.

MICK: And sitting in here smoking at three in the morning, is? *(He takes her
hand.)* Besides who would know? Other than Santa Claus. Come on.

MIRIAM: *(She stands.)* Why?

MICK: Because I want to. It was something I wanted to do. *(He takes her gently.)*

MIRIAM: Sorry that my hand's so cold.

MICK: Well, you know what they say about that.

MIRIAM: And it's true. *(He twirls her a bit.)* This seems really silly.

MICK: I don't feel silly.

MIRIAM: I don't keep rhythm so well. No music.

MICK: Here's one you might know. *(MICK hums "Jingle Bells.")*

MIRIAM: *(She laughs, humming along.)* When we went on our honeymoon,
my husband, Morris, told me he had a great Christmas present for me.
And I was guessing like a necklace or some real big thing . . . Oh, I can't
tell this. I'll be embarrassed. *(She stops dancing.)*

MICK: Don't be.

MIRIAM: Okay . . . Oh, I can't!

MICK: Don't worry. You'll probably never see me again.

MIRIAM: *(Pause.)* Why?

MICK: I don't know. Does it matter?

MIRIAM: Yes. *(Pause.)* Well, he wrapped himself up in Christmas paper, he was
nude, and he tied a jingle bell on his . . . well, you know. And it was great.
The best. I mean, not the jingle bell. We took it off for safety reasons.

MICK: And now . . .

MIRIAM: And now . . . what?

MICK: No more bells?

MIRIAM: You could say that. *(She stops dancing.)* You know I realize that I still
haven't finished my Christmas shopping yet. Isn't that weird?

MICK: Why'd you stop?

MIRIAM: *(Pause.)* The day I was supposed to get it done, I bought this red
dress instead. Perfect. Low-cut but sophisticated. The kind that shows my
legs off just perfectly. *(She pulls her skirt up a tiny bit to show him her calves.)*
I have nice molded calves; the thighs aren't so fine.

MICK: Um, it all looks pretty fine to me.

MIRIAM: Thanks. *(Beat.)* Anyway, I was so anxious. I waited for him. I felt
so, so red in it. So voluptuous. You know? I wanted him so bad. I didn't

mean to have him be uncomfortable. I never intended that. This red dress was supposed to cure his problem, OUR problem. So I tried to remain hopeful while he seemed both humiliated and terrified. I knew it was a problem, but we both figured it would go away. But it doesn't. And he blames me. Like I cause it. Like maybe, I don't want him bad enough. Isn't that crazy? And the months go by and it becomes harder to talk about. I thought the dress would . . . I gave it away to a friend. I couldn't look at it. It reminded me of our failure. My failure. I try, I try to get him to talk about it. To go get help. But he shuts down. And I can't take it anymore. I'm so lonely without him. I'm so so lonely. God, I'm lonely. *(Mick hugs her. He slowly begins dancing with her again.)* I can't, I can't do this with—

MICK: Shhhs. For a few seconds close your eyes and dance with me. You can be anywhere you want, with whoever you want. Just dance.

MIRIAM: You smell nice.

MICK: Thanks

MIRIAM: *(Touches his breast pocket.)* What's this in your pocket?

MICK: *(Stops.)* Nothing.

MIRIAM: What's the matter?

MICK: Nothing. Just tired.

MIRIAM: You never answered why you were all dressed up. Was it a wedding?

MICK: The weather must be clearin' up out there.

MIRIAM: Did you have to go to a wedding and just broke up or something?

MICK: The car's down the street.

MIRIAM: So where are your first-class tickets to?

MICK: Look, no one got God damn married today!

MIRIAM: Men don't often dress in tuxedos looking so handsome.

MICK: It was a funeral.

MIRIAM: *(Pause.)* Oh God. Why didn't you tell me?

MICK: I liked having my mind off of it. Where are you goin' on the bus?

MIRIAM: I don't know. Maybe, Detroit. Do you mind me asking . . .

MICK: Yes. Why Detroit?

MIRIAM: That's where the family is. Was this the . . .

MICK: So did you plan to call Morty from home?

MIRIAM: Morris. No, *(Pulls out letter.)* I've written him a letter.

MICK: A letter? A lousy letter? Letters are for love, Miriam, not for ends. Letters are to be read over and over.

MIRIAM: What makes you an expert on love?

MICK: I don't claim to be. Just on mail. Just correspondence. Just mail carrying.

MIRIAM: So who was that her?

MICK: I suppose you want me to deliver your nasty little note?

MIRIAM: I've poured out my whole heart to a complete stranger. And you don't even trust me enough to tell me.

MICK: She got dozens of letters. Mushy ones. And white roses. I even listened to this security guard who works down at the train station. He tells me that women love classic romances. Take her to a classic and she's your for forever! And I did. Took her to *Casablanca, It Happened One Night, Philadelphia Story, Rocky*, on and on. I did everything you're supposed to. Everything!

MIRIAM: And what happened? You were to be married?

MICK: *(Picks up the suitcase.)* What's in here?

MIRIAM: Did she die?

MICK: Feels like a God damn typewriter.

MIRIAM: Answer me, Mick!

MICK: *(Pause.)* No.

MIRIAM: Then who did?

MICK: Me.

MIRIAM: I thought you said there was a funeral?

MICK: There was. The family was spread over the pews. He isn't Catholic exactly, but close enough. The brothers and sisters, all married, sat right here. And there . . . *(He points.)* there sat Mom, hair done up high. So they do the whole walk down the isle, everything's smooth. Everybody's pretty. Until they get to the part where ya got to, where ya gotta . . . *(Slaps his hand.)* Wham! You know, tell it like it is. And he gets to askin' her if she wants to spend the rest of life with him and there's this pause. And he thinks, "Wow, she's makin' this dramatic!" But the pause goes on. He looks over at her and she doesn't move. She stands there. Still. Only he can hear her breathing. He tries to catch her eye to see if she's just nervous, but she ignores him. He looks over at Mom and her forehead's all wrinkled, tense, and her hair starts unraveling. And then, this knot forms in his throat like a lump, but kinda twisted, and it gets real dry. And he thinks, he can say something, do something, tell a joke, he can stop this. But the only thing that comes out of his mouth was a little moan. A little cry, a noise, so small. You can barely understand that he's sayin' "Marie, Marie." She turns to him with a face so full up of sorry. His sisters, his brother keep tellin' him that it was cold feet, cold feet. But in that instant, he knew she didn't love him. She wanted, wished, hoped to, but she just didn't. She wanted to, but she didn't. Didn't love him. And the whole thing turned into a God damn funeral. *(Pause.)* So don't tell me about lonely.

MIRIAM: *(Pause.)* Okay, so you win. But do you think that's your last chance?

MICK: Who's gonna want me? I mean, look at me. I'm not exactly what you call handsome. I don't make a lot of money.

MIRIAM: *(She looks at him.)* I'm looking at you now. And I think you're very attractive.

MICK: *(Embarrassed.)* You do not.

(She moves in closer.)

MIRIAM: Yes, I do. *(She touches his face and then suddenly stops.)* Wow, I better go. *(She picks up her suitcase.)*

MICK: Why are you picking that up?

MIRIAM: I have to.

MICK: *(He puts his hand on hers.)* Don't.

MIRIAM: Why?

MICK: Because, because the damn thing has wheels!

MIRIAM: Where were you going for your honeymoon?

MICK: *(Pulls envelope out of his breast pocket.)* We wanted Disney World, but we got a deal on tickets to Venice. We settled for that.

MIRIAM: Are you going?

MICK: No. I don't like to travel alone. But I can't even return the tickets at this point. *(Looking at the suitcase.)* That thing feels heavy as a typewriter.

MIRIAM: It is. It seemed like the most essential thing to bring.

MICK: I would've thought underwear, silly me.

MIRIAM: How long was the trip for?

MICK: I could only afford a week. Travel's hard on the savings.

MIRIAM: Take me.

MICK: I told you no problem. I'll give you a ride to the station.

MIRIAM: On the plane.

MICK: Funny.

MIRIAM: Take me to Venice.

MICK: You need some sleep.

MIRIAM: You won't go alone and I need some place to go. Why not?

MICK: You're not bull shitting, are you? You want to go to Venice?

MIRIAM: It beats Detroit.

MICK: Gee, let me think about this. *(He walks around a little. He pulls the ring out of his pocket, and puts it on stand with the candles.)* It might be nice. Yeah, yeah, I like it. You and me, and Venice and pre-boarding.

MIRIAM: When's the flight?

MICK: At ten this morning. I'd have to pack.

MIRIAM: So you throw your underwear drawer in the suitcase and we're off!

MICK: What about you?

MIRIAM: Well, I'm sure you have a few extra pairs.

MICK: That's not . . .

MIRIAM: Let's just say we could be there for each other. Good friends. *(Pause.)* Oh gosh.

MICK: What's the matter?

MIRIAM: Using a lavatory is imperative. Do you suppose this place has one?

MICK: Down the stairs and to the right. It's the men's. I picked the lock.
(Miriam exits. Mick hums a little "Jingle Bells" as he looks at her purse with the letter in it. He takes his envelope with the tickets out.)

MICK: It wouldn't be the same, would it? *(He goes over to Miriam's purse and takes out the letter to Morris.)* No stamp. Figures. *(He replaces the letter with the tickets to Venice. He closes up her purse and puts the letter to Morris in his breast pocket. He goes to the candles.)* That's me. Always sorting.

MIRIAM: Are you ready?

MICK: *(Pause.)* When we were dancing, who did you imagine you were with? *(Pause.)* You still love him. Give it one more chance.

MIRIAM: Why did you come back here tonight?

MICK: Cause I wanted to die. Not suicide. Nothing like that. I just wanted to die. I can't imagine going through my whole life alone. *(Sarcastically.)* What a loss that would be to the world, huh?

MIRIAM: Yes, it would be.

MICK: *(Pause. He looks at her.)* I'll take you home.

MIRIAM: Promise me you won't let those tickets go to waste.

MICK: I promise. *(He winks and then starts to pick up the typewriter.)* Now, let's get out of here.

MIRIAM: Wait! *(She grabs his ring.)* You don't want to forget this. It's worth too much.

MICK: Remember to show that Morty of yours that letter in your purse first thing. He should know how you feel.

MIRIAM: And what about . . .

MICK: Tonight? We had a romance, a little romance. I guess it's still possible for me. *(He kisses her hand.)* Thank you.

MIRIAM: No, thank you. *(She kisses him long and hard on the lips.)*

MICK: *(Blown away.)* Wow. Okay, lightening strikes again.
(She laughs, and they both start to exit.)

MICK: I wouldn't mention that to Morty. *(Offstage.)* But you're definitely no nun.

(Lights fade out and the music fades up.)

END OF PLAY

Notes

By Jennifer Laura Paige

For Heather Stone, who asked for it.

THE AUTHOR

Jennifer Laura Paige is an actress and writer who has lived in Minneapolis since 1995. Her Twin Cities acting credits include *Arcadia* and *Good Night Desdemona (Good Morning Juliet)* at Park Square Theatre, *The Adventures of Herculina* at Frank Theatre, and *The Adventures of Mottel* at the Children's Theatre Company. In addition, she has been featured on Minnesota Public Radio's *This Minnesota Century* and can be seen in the independent feature film, *Twin Cities*.

Jennifer holds a BA in English from the University of Minnesota, where she was the recipient of the DeWitt Jennings Payne Award for outstanding undergraduate literary study. She is also an active volunteer with the Women's Prison Book Project. Her essays *Red Light People* and *Moving Day* recently appeared in the anthology, *Minnesota Memories*. *Notes* is her first published play.

AUTHOR'S NOTE

A quick note on the "hand gestures/sound effect notation" — to me, the comedic timing of the piece works most effectively when the actress gives each "hand gesture" or "sound effect" the same rhythmic emphasis she would give to a one-syllable word, rather than gesturing while continuing to speak the rest of the line. Also, we *have* to hear "Herman Melville was her uncle," or else nothing that comes afterwards is going to make any *sense*, OK?

ORIGINAL PRODUCTION

Notes premiered on April 1, 2001, at the Center for Performing Arts in Minneapolis as a part of Theatre Unbound's Women's Work Series. It was directed by Heather A. Stone and performed by Kourtney Kaas.

CHARACTERS
A Drama Teacher

NOTES

A drama teacher sits on the stage in a metal folding chair, holding a yellow legal pad and a pen.

DRAMA TEACHER: Okay. Is everyone done changing? *(Scans auditorium.)* Good. Okay. First of all, I want to thank you all for being so *present* tonight and for sticking with it, and keeping one foot in front of the grindstone, and *yeah*, and . . . *especially* for just . . . completely . . . putting yourselves *up there*, through a really, really *(Hand gesture and/or sound effect in place of adjective. She does this often. These can sometimes be big and descriptive; they can also be as simple as an exhalation or the wave of a hand, a placeholder for the word that's being bypassed.)* dress rehearsal. *(Clap, clap, clap.)*

I know we went a bit over. *(Checks watch.)* And I know you all have school tomorrow morning, so thank you, thank you, *thank you* for that. Because getting through the whole show finally was, *I* think, very, very valuable. And the *good* news is . . . well, you may or may not *know* this, but among *theater* people, it's generally believed that a dress rehearsal like the one we had tonight is a *sign*, and what that sign *signifies* is, that your opening night tomorrow night is just going to . . . *(Sound effect or hand gesture.)* You know, so anyway. Congratulations. You should all be very proud.

I just have a few quick notes, but first off, let's have a round of applause for Jamie, our student playwright   there she is, round of applause, for challenging us with such an *ambitious (Hand gesture.)* that takes us back to a time in history that's never been seen before by anyone, so thank you, Jamie. *(Clap, clap.)*

Okay, our running time tonight was four hours and twenty-three minutes. Um, general note, if you can, *try to think about pacing.* I know that we had a lot of stops and starts tonight, that, hopefully, we won't experience again in the future and Randy? Where's Randy? How's your head? Good. And, I *know* that the show tomorrow night will . . . *(Hand gesture.)* you know, as certain things just fall into place. But I still want each and every one of you to think about what you can do as far as cues, that's the biggest one, cues, scene changes, *know* your lines, *jump* those cues, and just generally . . . *(Hand gesture.)* You know? That's what we need. More . . . *(Repeat hand gesture.)* OK?

Shelly, watch the mouth thing. Rachel, don't upstage yourself.

Caitlin, we HAVE to hear "Herman Melville was her uncle" or else nothing in Act II is going to make *any sense*, Okay?

Hanna, read Plug . . . Hanna, red Frog, Hanna . . . What *is* this? I can't read my writing. Well, *that's* really helpful. Does anyone know? Something like . . . Rent . . . Flag? *(Pause.)* This would be right after the mead hall . . . *(Hand gesture indicating natural or man-made disaster of actor's choosing.)* Hanna's line? Anyone? Anyway.

Everyone, good spider-dance. Everyone, watch for broken glass. Everyone, projection, volume, energy.

Rachel, how's your knee? Well, when you get home, put some ice on it.

"April foods"? *(Rechecks notepad.)* "April *fools! April fools!* The rats are running down the hill and a reign of holy terror is upon us!" It's a mouthful, Caitlin, but we've Got. To. Hear. It. Or else nothing in Act III is going to make any *sense*, Okay?

Shelly, mouth thing. You're also doing *this* a lot. *(Strange convulsive movement.)* It's another one of your *actor habits. (Repeats movement along with one of Shelly's lines.)* "My godfather once reaped the dark harvest." No, really, I'm exaggerating, but that's basically, *you* know, and sometimes, with the character, it works, but remember that if it's not a choice, then you want it to always *be* a choice. Understand?

Okay. End of the dream ballet. End of the dream ballet. Jared, how can we *get you off*, there? *(Pause.)* People, as we all witnessed, Jared could not get himself off tonight after the dream ballet. Is anyone *backstage* free to give him a hand with that? Molly?

What's funny? What's funny? Tell me.

Okay, kids. Kids. People. Settle down, people. I know I asked Molly to "Get Jared off" and yes, it has a double meaning, and it's *funny*. And that's okay, we all laugh, and that's . . . that's . . . perfectly normal. *(Pause.)* But we all know what I MEANT to say, and so if, if . . . *as* . . . mature people that I know we all *can* be, if we could just move on now, and just . . . just *(Hand gesture.)* Yeah. Guys. Guys. If we could settle down, now and—Madison, Courtney, eyes up here, everyone . . . Shelly, Carlos . . . one person talking—come on, now, everyone, everyone, everyone . . . focus . . . focus . . . focus . . . focus. *(Stands, and without warning throws metal folding chair against the floor or wall with a thunderous and dramatic crash. Silence. Beat.)*

Now, after the dream ballet, Jared—who has a big metal *bucket* on top of his head—is going to need some help getting offSTAGE during the partial blackout. Or *else*, he is going to knock over the Gondola again and BLEH! *(Hand gesture.)* Molly, can you help him? Good. Moving on.

Caitlin, volume. Molly, cheat out.

Shelly. Mouth thing. You're also doing *this* a lot . . . *(Different strange convulsive movement.)* If you're not playing the Elephant Man, you don't want to be doing it.

Carlos? How's your eye? Well, go flush it out with some cold water. Jesus.

(Reading.) Madison, don't laugh when burning at the stake. Courtney, don't laugh when burning at the stake.

General Note: When Madison and Courtney are burning at the stake, absolutely no one *on*stage, *off*stage, or *back*stage should be *laughing*. At all. Understand? Good. Because burning at the stake is very *(Hand gesture.)* you know? And I want you all to keep that in mind. Because there really was a real time in history when this sort of thing took place on a daily basis. And, back then, let me tell you, *nobody* was *laughing*. When my husband and I got *(Hand gesture.)* on our honeymoon — and this is kind of — anyway — but it's short, so, anyway, on our husband . . . on our *honeymoon*, my husband and I went to this little village in *Germany*, where many, many people, and women especially, were burned at the stake at one time in the past. And now, they've built this little museum, a memorial, you know, to commemorate those . . . events in history. And, like I said, my husband and I, *on our honeymoon—we were there.* And saw many, many vivid and graphic historical documents, and woodcuttings, and dioramas and . . . *woodcuttings*. All about people, and women especially, who burned at the stake at one time in the past in a very vivid and graphic way. And let me tell you something, *Courtney*. *Madison*. Nobody was laughing. *Nobody was laughing.* Not me, not my husband, not German *tourists*, not *Dutch* tourists, not *American* tourists, which *I was* at the time, not my *husband*, not *me*, not my husband, not *anybody*. And then later on comes part *two* of the story. And it's not really *you* know, but *sort of* it is. Because, part *two* of the story (and this happened very recently) is that I came home one day after six years of marriage, and found this *same* husband at home, in bed, in *our* bed, in MY Bed, doing some vivid and graphic things of his OWN, along with my *butt-naked stepbrother*. And you can *rest assured* no one was laughing then either. *(Silence.)*

(Snort.) Although, actually, I think *that is* kind of . . . *(Giggle, hand gesture.)* I mean, it's not really *funny*, but it's *(Hand gesture.)* you know. Because — *(Losing battle not to laugh.)* because, if you picture — no, scratch that — no *really*, if you picture — and this is *so* inap*pro*priate — but *(Laughing fit.)* — Sorry! It's just — can you *picture* the two of THEM doing the *(Hand gesture.)* with their? *(Hand gesture.)* And then, and then, and then, and then . . . here's a *thing*, you know: They've both always worn the *exact* kind of shoes, like *for-*

ever, you know, like those dorky brown *loafers* with the *tassels* and all of these, *(Hand gesture.)* you know, and the question *I* have is—the question I'm *left* with is, *aren't gay men supposed to have good fashion sense? (Suddenly very emotional.)*

(An awkward moment. Beat. Forced merriment.) April fools! April fools! Got you, Hanna, Caitlin, everyone. That *(Waves hand.)* just now, was just my attempt to be . . . Not really funny, I guess, but . . . moving on. Oh. Hey. Did you guys ever see . . . that one when Mary and Rhoda did that *(Hand gesture.)* back then? Are you all too young? Because, it's *just like that.* Just . . . punchiness. Punchiness. No excuse, really, but . . . punchiness. Because . . . we *actually* went to Niagara *Falls*, so clearly . . . I'm . . . Just making sure you're awake after all of these . . . *(Pause. Tone shift.)* Notes. *(Pause. Softly.)* That's a lie. Just now. It's a lie. Sorry. Not *exactly* a lie, just a really clumsy . . . attempt, on my part, to cover up my *(Hand gesture and sound effect.)* back there with a really . . . blatantly . . . not . . . true . . . thing, or in plain terms . . . a *joke.* Or . . . a really bad . . . joke. Not exactly a joke, but, you know, a . . . *(Hand gesture.)* A reference to the *play*, an *inside* joke, *that's* what it was . . . supposed to be. "April fools, April fools! The rats are running down the hill and something, something, something, something . . . "

(Beat. Reading verbatim from notepad.) Anyway, Caitlin, volume. Caitlin, volume. Caitlin, volume. Hanna, cues. Caitlin, volume, Shelly, mouth thing. Shelly, arm thing, hand thing, face thing.

Madison, don't laugh when dead. Courtney, don't laugh when dead. Molly, don't laugh when dead. If I see any laughing or smiling corpses tomorrow night, they're all going to be *(Hand gesture.)* . . . Anyway. Moving on . . .

END OF PLAY

Saint Lucy's Eyes

By Bridgette Wimberly

As a girl, the statue of Saint Lucy standing in the church connected to my elementary school frightened me until I stepped back and re-evaluated the pair of eyes lying on her plate. Eyes I once found judging, now looked forgiving. I was inspired to do a play exploring judgment: the law and judgment, forgiveness and judgment, sin and judgment, judgment by others and self-judgment. I wanted to explore the process of forgiveness, a woman who had to re-evaluate a pair of eyes watching her. This play is dedicated to my mother, Conchita Wimberly, for her watchful eyes.

THE AUTHOR

Bridgette Wimberly began writing *Saint Lucy's Eyes* in a workshop while a fellow in Lincoln Center Theater's Directors Lab. She became a 1999 Mentor Project Fellow at the Cherry Lane Alternative when Wendy Wasserstein chose this play to mentor culminating in a workshop production at the Kauffman Theater. *Saint Lucy's Eyes* went on to a sold-out production at the Women's Project and Productions starring Ruby Dee and moved to The Cherry Lane Theatre. Bridgette was also the 1998–99 Van Lier Playwriting Fellow at Manhattan Theater Club. She has commissions from Manhattan Theatre Club *(The Mark)*, The Cleveland Playhouse *(Forest City)*, and a Sloan Science Commission from the Ensemble Studio Theater *(The Separation of Blood)*. Bridgette recently won a 2001 fellowship in poetry from The New York Foundation for the Arts. She has written a book of poetry entitled *Ghetto Music*.

INTRODUCTION *By Ruby Dee*

My friend Billie Allen asked me to read *Saint Lucy's Eyes*, a play she had just agreed to direct, and to consider playing the lead role. The playwright reminded me strongly of Lorraine Hansberry, taking on the issues of a new generation. I'd never read a play dealing with abortion before — about more than abortion really. It was about temptation, sacrifice, ambition, redemption, regret; about love, callousness, forgiveness, and second chances. I was drawn to the young woman struggling to blossom beyond unwelcome circumstances. I understood, from my own experiences living in Harlem, the character of Grandma, caught up in personal moral and religious complexities. I had to play the part.

ORIGINAL PRODUCTION

Directed by Billie Allen with the following cast:

GRANDMA . . . . Ruby Dee
YOUNG WOMAN . . . . Toks Olagundoye
BAY . . . . Willis Burks II
WOMAN . . . . Sally A. Stewart

CHARACTERS

YOUNG WOMAN: A very fresh, naïve young woman of seventeen dressed in modest clothing in the play's beginning who progresses to a sophisticated well-dressed lawyer of about thirty.

OLD WOMAN GRANDMA: A middle-aged woman about fifty to sixty who will age to sixty to seventy at play's end.

BAY: A middle-aged man.

WOMAN: A young woman, somewhere in her twenties. She is more sophisticated than Young Woman, i.e., she may smoke, wear her hair dyed, dress flashy.

SETTING

ACT ONE

A small tenement apartment. We see a worn easy chair adjacent to an old black-and-white TV with a coat hanger as an antenna on top. There is a large table center stage with a couple of chairs at this table. We see a couple of doors. One leads to a rest room, the other to the hall outside, and there is another opening with a curtain covering it that leads to the kitchen, which is just visible through the split in the curtain. There is a sofa bed in the corner of the room. There is a wooden folding table, folded against the wall or the kitchen window that can be extended. We see a large window with a fire escape behind it. It is raining very hard. The room is dimly lit by a few lamps. Periodic thunder can be heard and lightning can be seen illuminating the window. There is music in this act. Popular rhythm and blues hits can be heard faintly.

ACT TWO, SCENE ONE

A room in the Lorraine Motel in 1980. The hotel has fallen into disrepair and is used as a transient's motel.

ACT TWO, SCENE TWO

A prison interview room. We see a large table with a couple of chairs. Windows with bars on them. Periodic thunder can be heard and lightning can be seen illuminating the window.

SAINT LUCY'S EYES

ACT I
Scene One

The time is April 3, 1968, in Memphis, Tennessee, in a small tenement apartment. As the curtain rises, we see two women. The younger woman is standing with her overcoat on. The much older woman is at the table stringing string beans.

YOUNG WOMAN: *(Clutching her coat.)* It's been raining all day.

OLD WOMAN: *(Stringing beans, she nods affirmatively.)* All day. Gonna rain all night.

YOUNG WOMAN: I hate it when it rains. It's dark and dreary. Sad and lonely.

OLD WOMAN: I've had some of my best times on a dark rainy night.

YOUNG WOMAN: Not me. There's something spooky about the night and I've always hated thunder and lightning.

OLD WOMAN: I'm not talking about sitting at home with a cat and a good book. Suppose you ain't been with somebody special? Somebody make all that thunder and big old lightning go away. The rain could be pouring down cats, dogs, rats, and roaches . . . you with the right somebody . . . like a sunny day on the beach, yes ma'am. All curled up cozy. I can remember some beautiful rainy nights. *(Stops stringing beans and walks toward kitchen.)* Had myself a ball. So did he.

YOUNG WOMAN: Who? Who are you talking about?

OLD WOMAN: I don't know who child. Can't remember who. Besides I never kiss and tell. I tell you this though, he was something fine. With a pocket full of dollar bills. That's the one thing that can turn a perfect rainy evening ugly . . . a broke man. *(Shaking her head.)* Ain't got two quarters to rub together. Can't spend nothing but the evening. Remember, you heard it here first. Show me the money or you won't see no honey. Speaking of money. Did you bring it?

YOUNG WOMAN: Yes.

OLD WOMAN: The whole fifty?

YOUNG WOMAN: *(Clutching her coat.)* Fifty dollars. That's what you asked for. Fifty dollars.

OLD WOMAN: Well, I have to ask, honey. Don't take it personal. Some of these girls come up in here think I take credit. Come in here all they got is twenty, twenty-five dollars. *(Stands and crosses around to Young Woman.)* This ain't Petries. I ain't got no lay-a-way plan. This a cash-and-carry operation here. You hear what I'm saying?

YOUNG WOMAN: *(Gives an envelope to Old Woman.)* Yes ma'am. I brought the fifty. The whole fifty. Just like you asked.

OLD WOMAN: *(Takes the envelope from the Young Woman, counts the money, and puts it in her bra.)* You sure have, child. The whole fifty. Well, take your coat off and hang it up over there. *(She motions to the coat hooks on UR wall. Young Woman hesitates.)* That is if you plan on staying. Can't nobody accuse me of kidnapping nobody. You free to go anytime you please. But it's still gonna cost you the fifty. My time. You gotta pay for my time. Somebody else could of used it. It's all about economy. That's what's wrong with colored folks today. Why we take two steps forward and fall half a mile backward. Don't know nothin' 'bout no business. *(Moves to the SL side of the table and picks up the bowl and pot of beans; then walks DL toward the kitchen.)* You have to excuse me. You came a little earlier than I planned and I gotta get my old man's supper on. I didn't think you were coming, way it's been raining. *(Exits into the kitchen. Young Woman looks about the room clutching her coat, then walks to the front door.)* Like in the bible, forty days and forty nights. *(Re-entering from the kitchen and crosses toward Young Woman.)* You ain't got your coat off yet? What you hidin' under there? *(Grabbing Young Woman.)* Let me see. Let me see. You ain't hiding no buffalo are you?

YOUNG WOMAN: *(Moving away from Old Woman, her coat comes off in Old Woman's hand.)* No! No! I ain't hiding nothing. I'm just cold that's all. I'm cold.

OLD WOMAN: Well, honey, I have to ask. Don't take it personal.
(Young Woman takes it and hangs it on the wall coat hook.)

OLD WOMAN: Some of these girls come up in here look like they trying to hide a whole herd of buffalo up under there. Think I'm suppose to do a roundup and perform rodeo tricks I guess.

YOUNG WOMAN: *(As she returns to her chair SR of table.)* I'm just cold that's all. And I hate it when it rains. I hate it when it rains. I just hate it.

OLD WOMAN: Well, don't have no tantrum up in here, gal. Won't do you no good. Life's a natural born bitch. Seems you get more things you hate than those you like. I know it's been that way for me anyway. *(Thunder rumbles in the distance. Young Woman jumps and crosses down to the SR chair. Old Woman crosses US of the table to Young Woman.)* Woo! We as jumpy as a kitten. Just some thunder. *(Walking over to comfort and to get her to sit down.)* Just some thunder, child.

YOUNG WOMAN: When I was younger, on rainy nights like this, I would curl up in mama and papa's bed. *(Wrapping her arms around herself.)* Right between them. I'd feel so safe. Like nothing could ever touch me. It wouldn't matter how loud the thunder got or how much lightning lit up the sky because I knew they wouldn't let anything harm me.

OLD WOMAN: *(Sitting in the chair SL of the table.)* Safe huh?

YOUNG WOMAN: Yes.

OLD WOMAN: I know what you mean. Everybody need to feel safe. That's how my old man makes me feel. He ain't much to look at. Broken down old thing. Hard working though. Give me his left eye if I couldn't see out my right one. *(Beat as she comforts Young Woman.)* Sounds like your mama and papa love you.

YOUNG WOMAN: Yes. I thought Tyrone loved me too.

OLD WOMAN: Tyrone? If that ain't a player's name, I pray for lying.

YOUNG WOMAN: Guess he didn't. Love me I mean. Told me I was going to hold him back. He had plans all of a sudden. Big plans. He didn't want to be married. Not to me, not to anybody. He wanted to go to college. So he went and joined the army for the GI bill.

OLD WOMAN: Vietnam!

YOUNG WOMAN: *(Nods.)* He sent me a letter with your address and phone number and fifty dollars in it.

OLD WOMAN: Sound like he sent somebody here before?

YOUNG WOMAN: I don't know. I don't think so.

OLD WOMAN: You still love him?

(Young Woman shrugs her shoulders. Then shakes her head negatively.)

OLD WOMAN: If you want, I can put some hoodoo on him for you. Cost you another twenty-five, but it will be worth it. I'll have him barking at the moon and chasing cars.

(Young Woman smiles and shakes her head negatively.)

OLD WOMAN: Well, at least I got a smile out of you. Hell, maybe he'll get his worthless butt blown up over there in Vietnam. That'll make him wish he stayed here and did right by you. Course don't listen to me. I ain't got no kinda heart for cowards. *(Exits into the kitchen for a stack of newspaper sections.)*

YOUNG WOMAN: This isn't going to hurt is it?

OLD WOMAN: *(Re-enters with several newspaper sections.)* Honey, everything hurts, eventually. Eat too much cake, you get a bellyache. *(Laying out the sections to cover the top of the table.)* Spend too much money, you go broke. Drink too much good whiskey, you get a hangover. Love a man when you shouldn't, well.

YOUNG WOMAN: I'm just scared.

OLD WOMAN: Every young gal and some not so young come up in here scared. Some been in here three, four times before. *(Finishes laying down the sections of paper over the tabletop.)* Course I can understand if it's an occupational thing. You can only be so careful 'fore the odds catch up with you. But some of these girls ain't working girls and I see them more times than I should. Stupid. And stupid scares me. I can go to jail for what I do. *(Crosses ULC to the front door, opens it, looks out and closes it and locks it; then crosses RC to the window to look out; and crosses to the DL corner of the bed.)* And when you so stupid that the first time don't learn you not to have a second time, I don't want to see you no more. Now I need the money, but stupid people do a lot of stupid things. Like open they big stupid mouth to the wrong stupid people. Get me thrown in jail 'cause of some stupid heffa couldn't keep her stupid legs or her stupid mouth shut. Now while you're here, you're welcome. I ain't gonna force you to do nothing you don't want to do. You can think of me as Grandma. Fact, that's what many call me. But I'm only your grandma while you're here. And when you walk out that door, you a orphan. I don't know you. You don't know me. I ain't never laid a eye on you before. Is that clear?

YOUNG WOMAN: Yes.

OLD WOMAN: Yes what?

YOUNG WOMAN: Yes, Grandma.

(A teakettle can be heard whistling in the distance.)

OLD WOMAN: Well, there goes the kettle. I guess we can get started. *(Old Woman stands and heads for the kitchen. Re-enters and crosses UR of the SL chair.)* Go and remove your underwear and stockings in the bathroom there, and cover yourself with that sheet.

YOUNG WOMAN: *(Standing.)* My underwear?

OLD WOMAN: Yes, child. How you expect me to get to it? Go head. This ain't gonna be no day at the beach. But I ain't the bogey man. This a teach you be scared of men bringing flowers and a whole lot of promises and baby I love yous, but no ring. Men want to go to college and got big plans and you ain't got nothin' but a hard way to go. Remember you heard it here first. Show me the ring, or you won't see no thing.

YOUNG WOMAN: *(Upset and confused.)* Go where? Go where?

OLD WOMAN: *(Pointing toward the bathroom.)* The bathroom, child. Over there. Over there. *(Young Woman exits DL behind screen.)* And don't take all day. I gotta get my old man's supper on. He's a hard-working man, don't ask for much. Love him some string beans and white potatoes. He got high blood, so I try not to use too much fatback. *(Continues talking, as she crosses to DR wall, shifts a picture in order to access a jar of money from a hole in the wall behind the picture; takes the jar DR and sits on the DL corner of the bed. She takes the money from her bra, looks back toward the bathroom, then stuffs the money in the jar, and puts the jar back into the hole in the wall.)* His favorite dish peach cobbler. Man love him some of my cobbler. I'm telling you. Right now he out playing poker. Gambling. That's his contribution to the war on poverty. Um. Least that's what he expect me to believe. He gambles hours. So he'll be late tonight. But I still gotta get you out of here, 'fore I have to listen to his mouth. Make tonight's storm sound like a pea drop in a bucket. Lord knows I got all the headache I need for a lifetime.

(The lights flicker and thunder is heard in the distance. Young Woman comes out from the bathroom behind the folding screen. She is wrapped in a sheet and tiptoes DR of the recliner.)

OLD WOMAN: Oh! You startled me. I thought you were still in the bathroom there. *(Crosses DL of the table.)* You like some little cat sneakin' around here. What you sneaking around for?

YOUNG WOMAN: I thought somebody was out here. I heard music.

OLD WOMAN: Oh Lord. That's that woman upstairs. She play her music loud enough for everybody and I can't stand a lot of noise. She get her electricity from off the lights in the hall. Always blowing the fuse, 'specially on nights like this when it's raining. *(Gets a knife from the drawer on the SR side of the table.)* She know this old raggedy building can't take this overload. Stupid. Stupid people scares me. *(Crosses UC to the water/steam pipes in the corner US of the front door.)* Seem to me if you gonna bootleg you some electricity, you do it on the Q-T and not play all that boogie-woogie loud ass music. *(Shouting toward the ceiling and banging on the pipe with the knife.)* Hey, hey! Some people ain't got the brains they was born with. I swear I got to move out of here. Tomorrow wouldn't be too soon. *(Walks back to kitchen table and puts the knife back into the table drawer. Young Woman watches her looking scared to death.)* Get me some place peaceful and nice. Somewhere that's mine. Somewhere I own. Paper got my name on it. That ain't too much to ask nobody for. Don't wanna be one of those people, whole life ain't owned neither pot to piss or window to throw. *(Points upward, then to Young Woman.)* You understand what

I'm sayin'? *(Crossing toward Young Woman.)* Well, let's hope we don't have no trouble tonight. You want a drink of whiskey 'fore we start?

YOUNG WOMAN: No. Thank you.

OLD WOMAN: It's covered in the fifty, honey. As bug-eyed as you are, I'll throw in an extra shot on the house. Like I said, this ain't gonna be no day at the beach. But it ain't gonna blow you mind neither. You ain't the first, you won't be the last. I ain't trying to scare you none. But I have to tell you. You gonna wish you found something better to do with your night then visit with old Grandma here. A drink or two always makes things a little easier.

YOUNG WOMAN: My papa always said whiskey was the way of the devil.

OLD WOMAN: Your papa said? Well listen to old Grandma here. *(Crossing LC to the shelves and picks up a bottle of whiskey and two shot glasses and crosses US of table and puts the whiskey bottle and shot glasses down on the table.)* Ain't nothing wrong with a little help when you need it. Besides, I know you don't always listen to dear papa or we wouldn't be making our acquaintance here tonight. Would we, Miss Do-Everything-Her-Papa-Say?

YOUNG WOMAN: *(Shyly.)* No.

OLD WOMAN: Say what?

YOUNG WOMAN: *(Louder.)* No.

OLD WOMAN: Um hummm. Whiskey is the way of the devil. Well, I ain't the only one with horns and a tail in here. Are you drinking or not?

YOUNG WOMAN: I'll have just a little whiskey. Thank you.

OLD WOMAN: That's better. I'll pour us both a drink. *(Pours two drinks.)* I work better after a taste or two. There we go. *(Puts a glass in front of Young Woman, who sits in the SL chair at the table.)* Now drink it . . . slow. *(Shifts the SR chair to the US side of the table and sits.)* You don't want to choke yourself. *(Pours and sips her drink.)*

YOUNG WOMAN: *(Takes glass and swallows all of the whiskey at once.)* Oh, this stuff's like fire! *(Coughs.)*

OLD WOMAN: Listen to yourself. I told you to sip it. You throwing it back like a pro. My mama always said a hard head make a sore ass. And I can amen that. *(There is a sudden burst of lightning seen in the window followed by a loud thunderbolt. Young Woman drops to the floor screaming and crawls under the table.)*

YOUNG WOMAN: Ahhhhh! It's the Lord. It's the Lord. It's the Lord.

OLD WOMAN: What's wrong with you? You gonna get me thrown out of here. Will you calm yourself down. *(Lightning is seen again in the window followed by another thunderbolt.)*

YOUNG WOMAN: It's the Lord. It's the Lord.

OLD WOMAN: What's the Lord?

YOUNG WOMAN: Ahhhh! The Lord. Oh Jesus. Oh Jesus.

OLD WOMAN: The lightning? Are you talking about the lightning?

YOUNG WOMAN: Yes. Yes. I hear his voice in the thunder. His power is in the lightning. Oh! Oh!

OLD WOMAN: Child, I told you to sip that whiskey. Now that whisky's done gone to your head. Now you acting stupid. Ain't the Lord, it's the storm. It's just the storm. Don't turn stupid on me. You know how stupid people scares me.

YOUNG WOMAN: I don't want to be stupid, Grandma. I don't. But how do you know it's not Him? How do you know? I can hear Him talking to me. I hear Him.

OLD WOMAN: Everybody drink more whiskey than they can handle hear the Lord. They think they hear somebody. How old are you?

YOUNG WOMAN: Seventeen.

OLD WOMAN: Um. Seventeen. That's younger than I can remember. What's the Lord saying?

YOUNG WOMAN: That I'm bad. That I'm going to hell and burn for all eternity.

OLD WOMAN: Why? Why would the Lord say that?

YOUNG WOMAN: Because, I didn't keep His Ten Commandments. I lied and I cheated and now I'm going to kill. I'm going to kill.

OLD WOMAN: Going to kill? Who you gonna kill? I'm the one going to kill. Me. *(Crossing DR of the table and turning to Young Woman who is still under the table.)* I'm going to do it for fifty dollars. Me. And I don't have no shame in it. I help people. People in trouble. People come to my house and pay me to help them. They come to Grandma's house for help. Yes, ma'am. *(Crosses UL of table and shifts SL chair at the table so she can look at Young Woman.)* I've done so many, what's one more. *(Helps Young Woman crawl out and sits her in chair.)* See, child, the Lord ain't gonna punish you. *(Crosses UL of table.)* If there's any punishing to be done, He gonna punish Grandma. Me. Grandma ain't worried. So don't you worry your little seventeen-year-old head off. Grandma do for people what the Lord won't do. I know the Lord gonna forgive me. He forgives everybody. *(Crosses around the the UL side of the table.)* He's gonna forgive you too. So wipe those tears from off your face. Ain't no point of it raining in here too.

YOUNG WOMAN: But how do you know? How do you know? I can't keep it. It will kill mama and papa if I had a baby without a husband. I'm suppose to graduate in June. They got such high hopes for me. I want to go to college. I don't want it. I don't want it. Okay now I said it. *(Beating her stomach.)* I don't want it. There I said it. I don't want it.

OLD WOMAN: *(Pours a drink.)* Okay. Okay. You got some fight in you after all. *(Hands her the glass; then sits at table.)* Sip it this time. This ain't Kool-Aid. You take your time and sip it. Ten years ago I would of told you what's the difference. Have the baby. All most colored women could do is have babies. But you can do something special now. Not that having babies ain't special. I had a couple myself. But be somebody else too besides somebody's mama. Graduate from high school and go to college. Matter of fact, I think it's a sin if you don't. A bigger sin than killin'. *(Finishes drink then shifts her chair around to the SR side of the table and sits.)* I learned how to set women straight working for this white woman. I helped her by keeping house most days. Every now and then though some women would come to her house, stay a while, and then leave. Sometimes they come by theyself. Sometimes they come with another woman. They never looked happy, coming or going. Always looked serious. But grateful. Serious, but grateful. I thought she was a voodoo white woman at first putting spells and roots on somebody for these women. 'Cause women were always coming in, paying her, and going home. Serious.

YOUNG WOMAN: But grateful. A voodoo white woman?

OLD WOMAN: Well turn out, she was helping these girls, like I'm going help you. She taught me how. I was scared first time I see what she was doing. But I didn't say nothing. I almost wet my pants standing right there. But I kept my eyes open. She gave me a drink of whiskey. I swore I heard the Lord talking. Just like you. Afterwards she would go to this Catholic Church around the corner and pray. I don't know who for, 'cause I was too scared to ask. But as much as she was in there, the preacher thought she was some kind of holy woman. *(Takes a sip of whiskey, encourages Young Woman to take a drink by nudging her glass.)* You ever been in a Catholic Church before?

YOUNG WOMAN: No.

OLD WOMAN: Well it's no day at the beach, let me tell you. It's real dark in there. Candles and the light from the stained glass windows are the only source of light. They had all these statues around in life-size marble painted to make them look real. There was this one statue named Lucy. Saint Lucy. She was a pleasant enough looking woman, but she had a plate in her hand with somebody's eyeballs on it. These eyeballs would follow you around the church if you looked at them. Worse then them pictures of

Jesus. I mean they would actually move. Roll real slow when you moved slow and real fast when you moved fast. One day, I dozed off and she left me in that church all by myself. I tried to find my way out, but got lost and found myself right in front of St. Lucy. Her with those eyes laying in that plate, staring at me. Judging me. Following me everywhere I went.

YOUNG WOMAN: What did you do?

OLD WOMAN: I closed my eyes and I started running like I had some sense. Up one row and down the other. I was too scared to turn around. I knew St. Lucy was behind me with those judging eyes. I tripped and fell between the benches. I felt a hand on my shoulder and I screamed. Loud. The door to the outside just opened and the sunlight came in. I walked out. When I got outside, I got enough courage to turn around and look to see if I saw St. Lucy with her plate of eyes, but there was nobody there. Just the benches. Just the benches.

YOUNG WOMAN: Who was it that touched your shoulder? Who opened the door?

OLD WOMAN: I don't know child. But I tell you this, ever since that day, I could see more clear. Now I'm going to help you see. I'm going to help you face this fear, walk out that door, and see a whole new life. Walk out that door and shine. You hear me, girl? Shine like a new silver dollar. Can you do that?

YOUNG WOMAN: Yes.

OLD WOMAN: Now finish your drink. We gotta get started 'fore my old man get home expecting his supper. OK? *(Extends her hand to Young Woman.)*

YOUNG WOMAN: *(Taking Old Woman's hand and shakes it.)* OK.

OLD WOMAN: It ain't gonna rain no more. You hear me, child. It ain't gonna rain no more.

(Fade to black.)

Scene Two

April 4, 1968. As the lights come up, Bay is seated in his recliner in front of an old black-and-white television set with a coat hanger for an antenna. The volume is on very low. Bay is attempting to get the television to work better. He is aggravated and begins hollering and beating on the TV.

BAY: Come on. Come on now. Oh man! Oh man! This piece of shit.

OLD WOMAN: *(Entering apartment carrying a shopping bag.)* Bay? Bay?

BAY: *(Does not look at her as he fidgets with coat hanger.)* Yeah, yeah, baby, in here.

OLD WOMAN: *(Walking into apartment closing door behind her.)* I know where you are. I could hear you clear downstairs. Who are you fussing at?

BAY: This damn old TV. Ain't worth the electricity it takes to turn it on.

OLD WOMAN: *(Walking toward table, putting her bags on it.)* Well, it'll have to do for now. Ain't like it's nothin' on there worth watching anyway.

BAY: *(Mumbling and beating on TV.)* Awwww! Come on. Damn it. Come on.

OLD WOMAN: *(Walking over to Bay.)* Move, Bay. Let me see if I can fix it.

BAY: Yeah, baby, work your magic. Thing's giving me a bad headache.

OLD WOMAN: Umm hmm. I got the magic fingers. *(Begins to fidget with TV.)*

BAY: *(Watching her.)* That may be true, but what we need is a new TV or at least a new used one. This one's had it.

OLD WOMAN: *(Fidgeting with coat hanger.)* Don't start, Bay, hear. This TV will have to do. We agreed.

BAY: You agreed. As usual, I got to go along with it.

OLD WOMAN: Ummm hmmm.

BAY: *(Mimicking her in a woman's voice.)* Ummm hmmm.

OLD WOMAN: Look! Look! Here we go. Here we go. There's the picture. We cookin' now, Bay. We cookin' with gas.

BAY: OK! OK! Magic fingers. Yes! Yes! My baby got magic fingers. *(Kisses her.)*

OLD WOMAN: *(Walking away.)* Now don't touch it. Hear, Bay? Don't touch it and it'll play.

BAY: *(Sitting in front of TV.)* Don't touch it. Don't talk loud around it. Don't even breathe hard on it. You hear me, Bay? You hear me, Bay? *(Old Woman unpacks bags, picks up some of her groceries, and walks through curtain into kitchen ignoring Bay.)*

BAY: We need a new TV. A new TV. *(Shouting toward kitchen.)* Nothing that ain't breathing and paying rent should be this ornery.

OLD WOMAN: *(Offstage Left, in kitchen.)* Oh, Bay! Please don't start with me, hear. I had a long day.

BAY: Well, am I right? *(Looks back at TV, raising his hands.)* Awwww man! Look at this worthless piece of shit.

OLD WOMAN: *(Re-enters from kitchen.)* What? Did you touch it?

BAY: Naw, I didn't touch it.

OLD WOMAN: *(Walking over to Bay.)* Well, what's wrong?

BAY: I can hardly hear the damn thing. And I sho' can't read no colored folks lips.

OLD WOMAN: *(Crosses US of his recliner.)* Colored folks? On television? What you watching? *(Leans over the back of the recliner, rubs his shoulders.)*

BAY: King. They talking about the march Monday. Young suppose to go to court and get that injunction removed so we can march and end this damn strike. How long it's been?

OLD WOMAN: *(Picks up paper bag and exits into kitchen.)* Eight weeks.

BAY: Eight weeks. No money. I know I'm tired of trying to convince white folks I'm just as much man, got just as much bills, babies, and want just as much life he do. I'm screaming, I am a man, eight weeks.

OLD WOMAN: *(Re-enters with cloth to wipe table and tablecloth.)* And four hundred years.

BAY: He don't want to hear it. And this lifting job I got part-time is harder and nastier then emptyin' garbage ever been. And don't pay squat. I'm too old for this, baby.

OLD WOMAN: *(Wiping off the top of the table.)* It's gonna be all right, Bay.

BAY: I'm beginning to wonder.

OLD WOMAN: King's gonna fix it. He's like a bulldog. Put his teeth in your tail, *(Spreading table cloth over top of table.)* won't turn loose 'til you cry justice.

BAY: You think so? He ain't got Johnson in his pocket no more. Johnson worried 'bout making that war look good. And now that King done spoke out against it, last thing he wanna hear about is King and a bunch of garbage-emptyin' Negroes in Memphis.

OLD WOMAN: *(Adjusting the tablecloth.)* We lucky he came here. You got to have some patience, Bay.

BAY: Need the patience of Job and then some to live through this shit.

OLD WOMAN: *(Exiting into kitchen to stir pot and get bowl of peaches.)* And praying don't hurt.

BAY: Ummm. *(He continues to adjust TV with a piece of tinfoil as Old Woman comes out of the kitchen carrying a bowl of peaches and a hand towel.)*

OLD WOMAN: Look at these peaches, Bay. Ain't they the prettiest peaches you ever see?

BAY: *(Continues fussing with the TV.)* Peaches. This time of year?

OLD WOMAN: I got them from Mr. Ralph's Market out there by Ms. Allen.

BAY: Way out there? Is that where you been all day?

OLD WOMAN: *(Sitting SR side of table, wiping peaches with a cloth.)* Mmmm hmmm. She needed me to do some washin'. I always stop at the market when I'm out there. Mr. Ralph thinks I'm buying stuff for Ms. Allen. Only reason he sell to me. I swear they sell white folks the prettiest fruit. And cheap. Peaches they sell in colored neighborhoods look like they gone fifteen rounds with Cassius Clay. And cost the price of the ticket take to see him do it.

BAY: Mohammed Ali. Man name Mohammed Ali.

OLD WOMAN: Well whatever. Should be against God's law to change the name your mama give you.

BAY: Man got a right to call himself whatever he want to.

OLD WOMAN: That's all most colored mothers can give freely, a name, without begging, scheming, praying, and saving for it.

BAY: The man got a right to change his name. His! Ms. Allen call you every name in the book 'cept the one your mama give you. You answer to ever one of 'em. I don't hear you complaining 'bout that.

(Old Woman stares at Bay as she arranges peaches in the bowl on the table.)

BAY: *(Calling in a "woman's voice.")* Suzy, Sarah, Sandra, colored girl. *(In his own voice.)* I doubt she know what your real name is. Don't bother you none.

OLD WOMAN: *(Singing.)* Long as I know I'm gonna get my freedom, it's all right. Oh, it's all right.

BAY: And as often as you over there, she must be takin' in all the white folks laundry in the entire city.

OLD WOMAN: You miss me that bad?

BAY: I always do. *(Stares at her.)*

OLD WOMAN: We need the money, Bay.

BAY: *(Defiant.)* I know we need money.

(They stare at one another until Old Woman smiles.)

OLD WOMAN: You know what? I'm goin' to make you a peach cobbler.

BAY: With what? Not with these peaches. *(Picks up a peach and holds it out toward Old Woman.)*

OLD WOMAN: What's the matter with these peaches?

BAY: These peaches too fresh. Every colored man know rotten peaches make the best cobbler. They must. 'Cause whenever you buy fresh, pretty peaches from waaay way out there Ms. Allen way, you put them in a pretty bowl on display 'til they turn rotten . . .

(Old Woman attempts to interrupt him, but he stops her from interrupting by raising his hand.)

BAY: Ripe. Then you serve them to me.

OLD WOMAN: I do not.

BAY: Yes, you do.

OLD WOMAN: Why you trying to pick a fight with me, Bay? *(Beat as she snatches the peach from Bay.)* I went to Ms. Allen's to do laundry.

BAY: *(Gives her a kiss.)* You know I love you and your cobbler. *(He sits back down and continues to fidget with more tinfoil for the TV, paying no attention to her. There is a long pause as she goes about her chores.)*

OLD WOMAN: I don't know what's wrong with you. Like you got up on the wrong side of the bed or somethin'. Ms. Allen pay good money. We need money way these bills come in here. Thank God Ms. Allen got work for me. You want to act like I'm the one crazy. I use rotten peaches to make cobblers. You right, you love rotten peaches way you suck up ever crumb. You a rotten peach-eatin' fool the way you don't bring your head up from the plate 'til it shine like new money.

BAY: What's that you say, Baby?

OLD WOMAN: I said what they saying?

BAY: *(Never taking his eyes off the TV.)* What's that, Baby?

OLD WOMAN: Did they say anything about the injunction yet?

BAY: That's what I'm trying to find out. This damn TV. I can't hear nothin'.

OLD WOMAN: Well, you can see. Just don't touch the TV whatever you do.

BAY: I can't follow this.

OLD WOMAN: You ain't got to hear nothin' to know what's up. *(Walking over to Bay, pointing at TV.)* Look at those white folks faces. If they all frowned up, worried looking, specially Mayor Loeb, King got the injunction stopped. If they grinning like a Cheshire cat sitting pretty on your money, gonna be four hundred years and nine weeks.

BAY: I don't even want to think about that. Please don't say it.

OLD WOMAN: The Lord will make a way, Bay. Just watch they faces. White folks can't play poker worth a damn.

BAY: Specially when it comes to Negroes marching up and down Memphis city streets.

OLD WOMAN: Course they got cause to worry, way colored folks showed they tail last week when King was here the first time.

BAY: *(Chuckling.)* He, he, he, he.

OLD WOMAN: All that running, burnin', and breaking windows, and looting. *(Starts toward kitchen.)*

BAY: We kicked butt.

OLD WOMAN: You mean y'all showed butt. Embarrassed King . . . and yourselves. Police the ones kicked butt. Tanks, dogs, hoses, bloody broken heads. It's a wonder King came back here as colored as y'all acted. It's a testimony to his goodness.

BAY: Y'all?

OLD WOMAN: *(Crossing UL of Bay in his recliner.)* You were right in the middle of it.

BAY: Aw, like it's all our fault.

OLD WOMAN: I didn't say that, Bay, and you know it.

BAY: But you believe it.

(She exits into kitchen to get plates and silverware.)

BAY: Two colored boys died dead collecting garbage. Men with families, children. You think Loeb and 'em compensated they families? Naw. Ain't got no money for food, none for clothing, no way to pay rent and didn't pay no decent wage from the get go. But they don't care about that. *(Gets up, crosses around LC toward kitchen doorway.)* You suppose to be happy they let your colored ass pick up maggots and shit in the street. And when you dead, you just dead. Throw all the rest of your raggedy, naked, hungry family on the fire like they do in India. Hell yeah we looted. Time to loot. I shoulda got myself a new TV. Seem like that's the only way to get one. Sure can't buy nothin'.

OLD WOMAN: *(Coming out of kitchen carrying two plates and silverware.)* What you standing here outside my kitchen for? You suppose to be reading white folks' faces, *(Putting plates and silverware down on table.)* find out if there's gonna be a march Monday. Maybe y'all can redeem y'all-selves.

BAY: *(Grabbing her from behind.)* Redeem myself. No, ma'am. Monday I'm gonna get myself a brand new television.

OLD WOMAN: You gonna end up like Larry Payne. They just buried him the other day. *(Struggling to get free.)* Turn me loose, Bay. You just want to argue.

BAY: *(Kissing her neck.)* No I don't, Baby.

OLD WOMAN: Stop now. *(Pulling away.)* Darn. *(Walks over to table and begins to set it.)* I know you, Bay. After twenty-five years of you. I know when you mad at me.

BAY: What makes you think I'm mad at you? You haven't done anything to make me mad. Have you?

(The lights flicker off and on. Old Woman and Bay look upward Bay crosses DL to the television while Old Woman gets a knife out of the SR side drawer of the kitchen table and crosses UC to bang on the pipes.)

OLD WOMAN: Oh Lord! It's that stupid woman upstairs bootleggin' electricity again. *(Banging on the pipes and shouting toward the ceiling.)* Hey! Hey!

BAY: Aw look, Baby. The TV messed up again. You gonna work some of your magic on it?

OLD WOMAN: *(Crossing back to the table to put the knife back into the drawer.)*

I'm trying to work some of my magic on getting dinner. Ain't but so many tricks I can do in one evening. You ain't lookin' at it anyway.

(Music can be heard from upstairs.)

BAY: Well, I see she's playing music tonight. *(He stands.)* That's better than one of her loud fights.

(She crosses DR of the table.)

BAY: I hope she plays something I like. Something mellow like Aretha . . . or The Supremes . . . or

OLD WOMAN: *(Crossing toward him.)* Or what? You making request now?

BAY: I'm trying to make the most of a bad situation. What's wrong with that? Hell, I'm a expert at it. Story of my life.

(She crosses UR of the table as he screams toward the ceiling.)

BAY: Hey, play "Ain't No Mountain High." Shhhh! What's that song? What's that song? *(He begins to dance.)*

OLD WOMAN: Oh no, I know I got to get out of here now. You got the woman upstairs entertaining you. We got to move. We got to move. If I have to spend another month here, I know I'll die. *(She walks over to the SR wall above the bed, shifts the picture on the wall, and removes the jar of money in the hole-in-the-wall; and crosses DR and sits on the DL corner of the bed with the jar and removes money from her bra as Bay watches her.)* I want a quiet place with a little garden where I can plant string beans and roses or something. Some place where nobody's dog go and pee on it. That ain't too much to ask nobody for. Somewhere where I can have a little porch and some quiet. No noise 'cept birds. But please no pigeons. Pigeon only live in the slum and on the top of courthouses. *(Counts money and stuffs it into the jar.)* Twenty, forty, sixty, seventy-five. Yes. Let's see, with that money you won last night, that makes four thousand and five dollars, Bay. We got enough. I think we finally got enough.

BAY: Seventy-five dollars? Seventy-five dollars? You didn't get seventy-five dollars washing clothes or I need to quit my job hauling garbage and do laundry myself.

(Old Woman sits with jar in her lap, clutching the jar as she looks straight ahead.)

BAY: You did another abortion. *(Stands and crosses UL of the table.)* You done gone fixed some woman.

OLD WOMAN: *(Attempting to quiet him.)* Will you be quiet, Bay. What you wanna do, tell the whole world?

BAY: You promised me you quit. I knew it when you walked in here. You lied to me.

OLD WOMAN: I did quit. I ain't done one in two years. I swear Bay. But we need the money. *(Sits SL chair at table.)* With you on strike, I didn't have no choice.

BAY: Oh go put it on me. You know I had to strike. *(Sits on DR end of the bed.)*

OLD WOMAN: I ain't puttin' it on you. But we got to get some money comin' in from somewhere if we gonna buy a house. Your part-time lifting job and my cleaning and washing clothes barely put food on the table and keep the lights on. Bay, we had to do something, bring in more money. Bay, we can't stay here no more.

BAY: We?

OLD WOMAN: OK, I can't stay here no more. I just want my own place before I die. And I don't want to die here.

BAY: You gonna die in jail, old woman. And I got news for you. Ms. Allen ain't gonna do a day. She gonna put it all on the colored girl. Bet she remember your name then. You gonna lose everything trying to get where? Some greener pastures. Some suburb way, waay out Ms. Allen way where the deer and the Klan play. That light you keep seeing. That bright vision is the KKK in white sheets burning a cross in you string bean and rose garden.

OLD WOMAN: Ain't nothing wrong with wanting something.

BAY: Something wrong with wanting things you can't have.

OLD WOMAN: *(Standing.)* We got $4,005, Bay.

BAY: And what you gonna do with it?

OLD WOMAN: I'm gonna spend it. It's money.

BAY: When you gonna spend it?

OLD WOMAN: *(Confused.)* When?

BAY: *(Loud.)* When?

OLD WOMAN: *(Looking around confused.)* Now! I can spend it now.

BAY: Naw, you ain't. *(Stands and crosses UL of the table.)* Naw you ain't. That money just like them peaches. Just like everything else you got. You save it, and save it and look at it and admire it. *(In a "woman's voice.")* Isn't it pretty, Bay? Isn't it pretty? *(Own voice.)* When it comes down to using it, it's too late. It's rotten or it's gone. *(Grabs jar of money from Old Woman, who crosses DL to recliner and sits on SR arm.)* Ten years. Ten years we been saving. Ten years we sacrificed. Ten years we done without. All the risk you took. Like some crusade. Quit, I told you. Quit 'fore some dizzy woman die or get infected and point at you.

OLD WOMAN: *(Stands and crosses to table.)* I ain't gonna hurt nobody, Bay. What you worried about? Ain't nobody gonna point no finger my way.

BAY: Why not? 'Cause you say so. These the same girls, all some man got to say is "Hey, Baby," legs fly open like the automatic doors at the A & P. *(Crosses UR of table.)* You put your trust in them?

OLD WOMAN: Why not? They trust me. They put they life in my hands, Bay. These. *(Showing her hands to him.)* I help these girls. What you think? *(Puts the jar of money down on the table.)*

BAY: *(Crosses DR to the bed and sits.)* Ah!

OLD WOMAN: Girls come here, ain't got no name, ain't got no life. 'Cause he stole it. She got to pray he marry her and give her his name. Her name don't count. Marry her and make her a decent woman. Marry her so they child ain't labeled a bastard. Never own nothin'. Another generation gone. Girls come here 'cause I will do what her man won't. Give her back her name. Her name! Girls come here 'cause it's either the devil or the witch. *(Sits on the SR arm of the recliner.)*

BAY: And which one are you?

OLD WOMAN: Sometimes I'm one. Sometimes I'm the other. *(Stands and crosses DR and sits next to Bay on the bed and takes his arm.)* I went out to Ms. Allen's do the laundry, like I say. But she asked for my help. Meant getting paid seven dollars for washin' or seventy-five dollars for holdin' some girl's hand.

BAY: So you chose to hold hands.

OLD WOMAN: I didn't lie to you, Bay. I didn't lie to you.

BAY: I can't figure you out. You accuse me of gambling. Wasting money. If I lose, I lose twenty, twenty-five dollars. If you lose they gonna put your ass so far in the ground, you gonna swear they buried you. You gonna roll the dice one time too many, woman. Gonna come up snake eyes looking you dead in your face.

OLD WOMAN: *(Singing as she stands and crosses US of the table, picking up the jar of money and continuing around DL toward the recliner.)* "Long as I know I'm gonna get my freedom, it's all right, oh it's all right."

BAY: You don't hear me, do you?

OLD WOMAN: We can have the house we always wanted, Bay.

BAY: It ain't gonna happen.

OLD WOMAN: Why can't it, Bay? We got $4,005.

BAY: You got $4,005. Your money.

(She sits on the SR arm of the recliner.)

BAY: I wish I could have given you what you wanted. *(He stands and crosses around UC.)* Status, security, nice home with carpet, sectional couch, long stereo, new console TV. But I make $1.40 a hour. This the best I can do here. And here ain't where you wanna be. I'm just a garbage man.

OLD WOMAN: I know what you are, Bay. You my man.

BAY: No. *(Cross around toward her. Points at jar.)* That's your man right there. That money. Only thing you live for.

OLD WOMAN: No, Bay. It's you.

BAY: I can't do what that money do for you. I can't buy you a home. And I ain't the kind of man gonna let no woman, including you, buy me one.

OLD WOMAN: What you talking about? This our money. Yours and mine. We saved it together.

BAY: That's you and Ms. Allen's money. Most of it. Y'all did it. Y'all ain't got no use for men. Kill his children. Man ain't got no say about it. Tell him what to eat, when to eat it. When to shit and what flavor. Where he gonna live and where he gonna die. I've been marching eight weeks up and down Beale and Main Street screaming, I am a man, to every white folk in earshot. Eight weeks wearing a sign so when they see me, they know what I am. I ain't gonna wear no sign in here. Not in here.

OLD WOMAN: I know you a man, Bay. And like a man only way I ever treated you. But right now you acting like a fool. It don't matter who make the money. I know you don't think I want this money more than I want you? *(Bay stares at her.)*

OLD WOMAN: I thought you wanted what I wanted. *(Shoving money at him.)* Here, take the money. Take it. You the man of the house. Do whatever you want with it. Buy a console TV or a new suit or whatever. Here!

BAY: *(Puts jar on the table.)* I don't want it.

OLD WOMAN: Then I don't want it either.

BAY: *(Holds jar toward her.)* You don't want it! You don't want it! *(Opens jar and begins emptying jar, throwing money all over the room.)* Years and years of saving and saving, sacrificing and now you don't want it!

OLD WOMAN: Bay! Bay! What you doing? What's wrong with you?

BAY: *(Continuing emptying the jar.)* We ain't been living. Sacrifice, take chances. Now it don't mean nothing. You don't want it. *(Throwing the money.)*

OLD WOMAN: *(Attempting to stop him.)* Bay, why are you acting this way? What's the matter with you?

BAY: All of a sudden, cold turkey. Just like that. How many times you lied to me just to put some money in that jar? Your jar of dreams. I ain't your man. *(Puts the empty jar on the table. Picks up money and shoves it in her face.)* Here's your man, Washington, Jackson, Hamilton. There's your man.

OLD WOMAN: *(Screaming.)* Stop it, Bay! Stop it! Stop!!!
> *(There is a sudden loud explosion and a flash of light outside illuminating the window. Bay and Old Woman are startled. Smoke begins seeping under the door.)*

OLD WOMAN: *(Yells.)* Oh!

BAY: *(Turning toward the window.)* What was that?

OLD WOMAN: *(Picking up money, meticulously putting each bill in order.)* It's that damn woman upstairs. Maybe you should just move up there.
> *(Bay stands, walks over to window opening the curtains. It is dark outside and an orange glow continues to illuminate the window.)*

OLD WOMAN: Both of you acting stupid around here.

BAY: *(Leans out of the window. Pandemonium can be heard outside.)* What in the hell? *(Shouting.)* What's going on? What happened?
> *(Street sounds, anxious voices, and police sirens can be heard.)*

OLD WOMAN: You want to act a fool. Ain't nothing wrong with wanting something.

BAY: *(Shouting out of the window.)* What? Oh man. You lying. When?

OLD WOMAN: I just wanted us to have a home. That ain't too much to ask for? *(Looks up at Bay then goes back to picking up money. Bay coming back out of window, stands motionless, looking shocked. Old Woman looks up at Bay.)* What's wrong, Bay?

BAY: They killed King. King's dead, baby. He's dead.

OLD WOMAN: What? What are you talking about? Who told you that?

BAY: Colored folks out there gone crazy. It's all over now, baby. White folks gonna have us right back where they want us.

OLD WOMAN: No. This ain't right. This ain't right.

BAY: *(Walking over to TV.)* Let's see if I can find out what the hell happened. *(Beating on TV.)* Come on. Come on.

OLD WOMAN: *(Confused.)* King's dead? How can this be possible?
> *(Smoke continues seeping under the door.)*

BAY: I don't know. I don't know nothing. This damn old ass TV. *(Slams fist on TV.)* Goddamn it. Can you fix this thing?

OLD WOMAN: Something's burning. Something's on fire around here.

BAY: Folks gone crazy out there. Come and fix this TV, you swear will have to do, 'cause we don't have no money buy another one.
> *(Old Woman walks over to window as Bay continues fidgeting with TV.)*

OLD WOMAN: *(Looks out of window.)* God almighty! *(Looks at Bay, screams.)* Bay! Bay, the building's on fire! *(Running from window.)* The building's on fire!

BAY: Fire? Us?

OLD WOMAN: *(Running to Bay and grabbing him by the arm.)* Come on, we got to get out of here. *(Old Woman puts a handful of money in her bra.)*

BAY: *(Looking around.)* Oh my God. There's smoke everywhere. *(Touching door.)* Door's hot. The fire's right behind this door. Come on. We got to go out the window. Now. *(Bay helps her toward and out of the window. Once she's out the window, he starts to follow but steps back into the room, picks up the jar and begins to fill it with the money scattered on the bed and floor.)*

OLD WOMAN: *(Kneeling in the window.)* Come on, Bay. We ain't got time. Smoke's all in here. *(Begins to cough.)* Come on. Leave it. Leave it.

BAY: I'm right behind you. Go head. Go head. I'm right behind you. Go I told you. Go! Go!

(She hesitates and then disappears down the fire escape. Bay continues putting money in the jar as smoke continues to fills the room. He grabs his chest, coughs and gasps for breath as he collapses onto the floor. We can hear Old Woman calling as the sound of fire continues to build.)

OLD WOMAN: *(Offstage calling. Her cries muffled by the sound of the riot.)* Bay! Bay! Come on, Bay, we ain't got time for that. Come on, Bay. Leave it. Leave it. *(Calling.)* Bay! Bay! Bay!

(The lights flicker off and on a few times. They then go off. The only light remaining is from the old TV. Old Woman's voice is heard calling and we hear the last lines from Martin Luther King Jr.'s, "Mountain Top" speech is heard, in total or in part, coming from the TV over Bay's gasps for life.)

"I JUST WANT TO DO GOD'S WILL. AND HE'S ALLOWED ME TO GO UP TO THE MOUTAIN. AND I'VE LOOKED OVER, AND I'VE SEEN THE PROMISED LAND. I MAY NOT GET THERE WITH YOU, BUT I WANT TO KNOW TONIGHT THAT WE, AS A PEOPLE, WILL GET TO THE PROMISED LAND."

(We can hear the sound of fire consuming the building. The lights go to black.)

END OF ACT I

ACT II
Scene One

Twelve years later in a room at the Lorraine Motel Election Day, November 1980. It is about seven o'clock. We see a bed. Flashing red lights can be seen periodically flashing outside the window. The muffled sound of music can be heard in the distance. There are two doors. One leads to a restroom, the other to the outside. There are food containers scattered about the room. A woman, young and sophisticated, sits on the bed wrapped in a blanket rocking nervously back and forth. Although she tries to hide it, she is not feeling well and has a fever. After a brief pause, Old Woman enters from the bathroom drying her hands on a towel.

OLD WOMAN: *(Entering from the bathroom UL, drying her hands on a towel.)* Gal, please stop that rocking. Don't know what botherin' me more, these old arthritis feet and hips of mine or that seasaw back and forth you doing. 'Tween that and all this boogie-woogie ass music, 'bout to go stone crazy. *(Old Woman walks over to SR chair DS of a window, her sweater and coat are over the back of the chair and her large handbag is US of it.)* You got everything you need?

WOMAN: What you mean?

OLD WOMAN: *(Folding the towel and putting it over the back of the chair.)* I'm fixin' to go. It's Election Day. I'm gonna go vote for that Jimmy Carter. Don't know what we gonna do if that movie man gets in.

YOUNG WOMAN: You can't leave me here. Not like this.

OLD WOMAN: *(Putting on her sweater.)* You waited too long for Grandma to help you. Too long. *(From her handbag she takes out a brown paper bag and puts it down on the SR side table by the bed.)* Got a dog and pony show going on up under there. Now I brought you some of my world famous peach cobbler. Enough so you'll have some for your bus ride home . . . or wherever is you headed . . . out of here.

WOMAN: Grandma, please! I can't go home 'til I'm straight. You hear me. I can't.

OLD WOMAN: You gotta go to one of them clinics. They got clinics now. Best I can do, make sure you get on your way.

WOMAN: I can't go to no clinic. You don't understand. They want to put me in the hospital. I can't have no record of this.

OLD WOMAN: You don't have to use your real name honey. Think!

WOMAN: It don't matter who I say I am. They got all them people standing outside picketing with signs. What if I'm seen?

OLD WOMAN: Gal, please. You ain't who they tryin' keep out. Surprised they don't hand you a lollypop on your way in. Well, what you goin' to do? Stay here 'til you have that baby? *(Beat.)* Um hm, you ain't thought that far, have you? Look at you. Look at this place. How long you been here?

WOMAN: I don't know. Awhile.

(Old Woman begins to pick paper plates/boxes from the floor and puts them into the wastebasket UC.)

OLD WOMAN: You can't stay here. *(Beat as she reacts to a sound unheard by the Woman.)* You hear that?

WOMAN: What? *(Beat.)* The music?

OLD WOMAN: Sssssshhhh! No, listen, listen. You can't hear that?

WOMAN: I don't hear nothin'. Old walls, sound just bleeds right through them. This place ain't where you come for peace and quiet. Ain't you ever been to the Lorraine Motel before?

OLD WOMAN: *(Crossing to the window.)* I've only seen this place from down there, looking up. Looks so different from up here. Small. Closed in. Dark. Feel like a thousand eyes on me. Place sure give me the creeps.

WOMAN: Don't nobody know we're here. And don't nobody care.

OLD WOMAN: I know this was 'fore your time, but this use to be the place. Black folk dressed in beads and fur coats. Miss Lorraine, place named after her you know, she kept this place nice. Now this place ain't no more than a whip shack. Nothing but a whip shack now. *(Beat as she looks about room.)* This the last place Martin Luther King saw before he died. Knew they was going to kill him. Stepped right out on that balcony anyway.

WOMAN: Seem to me, if you know somebody out to get you, you'd stay inside where it's safe. I know I would.

OLD WOMAN: Miss Lorraine dead too. She was here that night. Dropped dead right after she heard the news. There ain't nothing but death here.

WOMAN: My grandma say, right before you die, your whole life flashes before you.

OLD WOMAN: Judgment day.

WOMAN: All the mistakes you made. All the regrets. The sins.

OLD WOMAN: *(Crossing toward the bed, resumes picking up trash.)* Think we goin' be like Judas to Jesus?

WOMAN: Betrayed by a kiss.

OLD WOMAN: *(Realizing the Woman has been talking about herself.)* And some silver. People gonna always remember that King died in Memphis. He died right here. Sweet Lorraine. You from Memphis?

WOMAN: No.

OLD WOMAN: Where you from?

WOMAN: Around.

OLD WOMAN: I see. Good a place as any I reckon. *(Flinches from pain and begins rubbing her legs. Sits in the RC chair.)* Calhoun where I from. Grew up in a little rusty shack no bigger than this room.

WOMAN: I was born in Memphis. We moved away when I was twelve. You Okay?

OLD WOMAN: Oh this. This come from standing on my feet all my life.

WOMAN: My grandma's legs use to bother her too. She had sugar. She loved when I'd rub them for her. Took the pain out for a little while.

OLD WOMAN: *(Stands and crosses to bed.)* Your grandma, she here in Memphis? That why you here?

WOMAN: *(Laughs knowing her grandma is dead.)* Naw. She ain't here. Ain't nothing in Memphis for me. Nothing. I got plans. Big plans. I'm on my way to New York City. Do some modeling or get a singing or acting career going.

OLD WOMAN: *(Crosses back to chair and sits.)* I wanted to be a singer too. I use to picture myself sitting on top of Duke Ellington's piano, swinging my big pretty legs.

WOMAN: Well I know I can sing. Act too. Lots of people tell me I got what it takes.

OLD WOMAN: You can't always believe what you hear.

WOMAN: You saying I don't have talent?

OLD WOMAN: *(Walking to Woman.)* I'm saying all that singing and showboating's cute, gotta get somethin' solid under your belt. *(Touching Woman's forehead as though she is trying to fix her hair. Noticing she has a fever, she continues fixing Woman's hair, concerned.)* Come a cold night, your fanny ain't naked to the wind. My mama told me, hanging over a rusty tub full of dirty clothes and hot soap, eyes full of sorrow and hands so wrinkled and small they didn't look human no more. She say, Gal, find a hard working man with a job first, fall in love with him second.

WOMAN: Typical mama. Do as I say, not as I did.

OLD WOMAN: Say, make sure his shoulders are broad and his hand had calluses so thick, pickax couldn't make a dint in 'em. I wasn't seventeen 'fore I sneaked off and married the prettiest man in town. That man was so pretty, I use to sit there and watch him sleep.

WOMAN: Pretty man, huh!

OLD WOMAN: *(Still fixing Woman's hair.)* Prettyyy. He was scared of work though. Had a excuse for everything. I had two boys 'fore I cracked twenty. Wasn't long 'fore I was hanging over a rusty tub full of dirty clothes and hot soap, my eyes full of sorrow and hands so wrinkled and small they didn't look human no more. *(Finds a rubber band to put onto the Woman's hair.)* My mama say, old sheep know the road, young lamb gotta find the way. Lord, she ain't never lied. He ain't no pretty man, is he? Man prettier than you? At least I got a smile out of you. Pretty smile too. Is he married?

WOMAN: *(Gets off the bed and crosses RC US of chair.)* No, he ain't married.

OLD WOMAN: Oh, o', I done hit a nerve.

WOMAN: He ain't married. I said he wasn't married.

OLD WOMAN: Don't take it personal, honey. Just that I did this for so long, I can usually tell. What's the matter?

WOMAN: I'm fine. This just ain't the right time.

OLD WOMAN: *(Moves toward her.)* Why you wait so long? 'Cause if you waiting for him to leave his wife and marry you, got better odds winnin' a snowball fight in hell.

WOMAN: *(Moves around to the DS side of the chair.)* I don't need no sermon, Okay.

OLD WOMAN: Okay, Okay.

WOMAN: I know this a girl. My mama had six girls.

OLD WOMAN: Keep your voice down.

WOMAN: She cursed the day she had each of us. Said a girl child only gonna bring you pain.

OLD WOMAN: Things have a way of working out. The Lord'll make a way.

WOMAN: *(Counter-cross: As Woman moves toward the bed, Old Woman crosses RC US of the chair.)* Now you promised you'd help me. All you did was bring me some pie. What the hell you think I need with that and my life is falling apart?

OLD WOMAN: Come on, put your dress on. I'll help you. Come on, child.

WOMAN: *(Lies back down on the bed, exhausted.)* I ain't going nowhere.

OLD WOMAN: Let's get you cleaned up. *(Picks up dress and puts it on the UR end of bed; then crossing DS of the bed and exits UL into the bathroom. Returns with a damp washcloth and sits on the SL side of the bed putting the cloth on the Woman's forehead.)* Here we go, come on now. Don't that feel better. Child, you 'bout to jump out of your skin. You ought to let me put some hoodoo on him. I'll fix him. He wake up one morning expectin' to find the long ranger, unzip his pants, little Tonto pop out.

(Woman does not react. Old Woman continues to rub her forehead.)

OLD WOMAN: I was standin' at the bus stop one night. I wanted that bus to come, but I was afraid I couldn't lift my legs high enough to get me up on that bus I was so tired. I started praying. Along came a man in a truck so loud and raggedy, sound like fireworks on the fourth of July. He stopped the truck. Say, "Baby, you need a ride?"

WOMAN: Baby!! I know you ain't gonna tell me you got in a strange man's truck?

OLD WOMAN: Well, I looked at his shoulders first. They was broad. *(Stands and puts the wet cloth down on the SL side stand; then crosses DS around the bed and goes toward RC, stops, remembering she'd put the dress on the bed, turns and goes to the bed, picks up the dress then attempts to help Woman into it as she tells her story.)* I looked at his hands. He had so much dirt stuck up under his skin, lye soap wouldn't wash it off. He told me he was a garbage man. A sanitation worker, way he put it. Picked up all of Memphis' garbage. Heavy, rotten garbage. Hauled it all away with his bare hands. *(Extends her hands.)* These. Dead dogs, maggots, spoiled food, used Kotex. All of yesterday's forgotten dreams, bad news, secrets, lies, regrets, sins. Stuff folks want to forget. He carried it all away. Made folks feel clean again. *(Fussing with and buttoning the dress.)* Got paid only pennies for what they pay preachers good money for. All that filth gets under your skin. Gets in your pores, your blood, eats up your soul. Makes you believe you don't deserve nothin'. Makes you believe you no better then the garbage you haul. He smelled like the dump.

WOMAN: And he stunk too? Does this get any better?

OLD WOMAN: He came to see me every weekend for a year. Saved and gave me the money for my divorce. We got married that summer. *(Still fussing with the dress.)* Raised my boys like they was his own. He wasn't no stranger. He was a answer to a prayer. And the prettiest man I ever knew. Mama said, pretty is as pretty does. Lord, she ain't never lied. It's gonna be all right, gal. I know you don't believe it, but it's gonna be all right.

WOMAN: I don't want to be nobody's housewife with no whole lot of kids. I got plans for myself. I don't want to have to wait for some big man with broad shoulders that snore all night to rescue me. I rather be dead. I rather be dead.

OLD WOMAN: Come on, child. Let me take you to your grandma. *(Stands, picks up an article of clothing, folds and packs it into suitcase.)*

WOMAN: My grandma can't help me. *(Turning her face into the covers on the bed.)*
(After packing another article of clothing, Old Woman, stares at Woman, and picks up her coat she has left on the chair, and begins to gather her things.)
WOMAN: *(Noticing her.)* What are you doing? You ain't going nowhere. You can't leave me here.
OLD WOMAN: I don't want to leave you, gal. But I got to get over to the polls 'fore they close. My old man didn't believe in voting.
(Woman stands and snatches the handbag from Old Woman and sits back on bed, clutching it. Old Woman is startled, but tries not to react. Putting her coat over her.)
OLD WOMAN: Said the minute you register they put your name on this hit list. Next thing you know, you dead in a pine box. This will be the first time I voted. First time. Put my best dress on for the occasion. So if they kill me, I'll die respectable, goddamn it.
WOMAN: Ain't nobody gonna kill you for voting. You a crazy old woman.
OLD WOMAN: *(Puts coat down on chair.)* You laugh, but one day you gotta stop running. Stop, turn around and look the monkey in the face. SOB ugly. But his bark worse than his bite. You can't stay indoors, gal. One day, you gonna have to walk out on that balcony.
WOMAN: I ain't got to walk nowhere, except where I please.
OLD WOMAN: You can't stay here, gal. You gone done something to yourself. You sick. You burnin' with fever. Now I'm going to go vote for that Jimmy Carter. I got to do this. You hear me. I didn't know how much 'til I stood in this room. *(Mindlessly picking up and folding an article of clothing.)* Some little ol' white man sitting somewhere got three strands of hair he comb from one his ears t'other. Glasses hangin' way down his nose, britches way down his tail. Don't have no face, but I knowed what he look like. Same little ol' white man call me girl or auntie, all my life. Not allowed to look him in the eye. Say, "Show me your money, girl." Take it. Give me the change he wanna give me. Tell me, "These fresh peaches ain't they, girl?" I say, "Yes, sir, fresh peaches." Smell the rot from the next block. But they fresh 'cause he say they fresh. That's the white man gonna count my vote. My vote equal to his vote. I'm equal to him. He ain't never see my face, but he knowed what I look like. He know I'm lookin' him right in the eye. That's power. Power a scary thing. Power dangerous. Somebody die give me that power. Somebody die right here. *(Points toward window. Puts article in the suitcase. Starts to picks up handbag and coat.)*
WOMAN: Don't go. I can't do this. You been listening to me? I can't do this.

PRESIDENT JIMMY CARTER IN A LANDSLIDE VICTORY. HE'S
PROMISING WELFARE REFORM AND A TURN AROUND TO
THIS SLUMPING ECONOMY. IN OTHER NEWS TODAY THE
AMERICAN HOSTAGES ARE STILL BEING HELD IN IRAN. AND
THE WEATHER FORECAST IS, RAIN, AND MORE RAIN . . . "

Scene Two

*A prison interview room a short time later. There is a large wooden table with
two chairs around it. The window has bars on it. It is raining very hard and
periodic thunder can be heard and lightning can be seen illuminating the
window. The lights come up with the sound of a metal door sliding shut. Young
Woman, now a sophisticated attorney, enters, wearing glasses, smartly dressed
and carrying an attaché and crosses C to the table where Old Woman is seated,
but she stands when she sees Young Woman.*

YOUNG WOMAN: Hello.
   (Old Woman looks up at Young Woman.)
YOUNG WOMAN: I'm . . . *(Puts her attaché down on the floor and sits in the SR
   chair.)*
OLD WOMAN: *(Interrupting her.)* What's the matter? You look like you just
   saw a ghost. I ain't dead yet. I think they trying to put me in the electric
   chair though. You the woman I talked to on the phone yesterday?
YOUNG WOMAN: Yes.
OLD WOMAN: You my lawyer, right?
YOUNG WOMAN: Yes.
OLD WOMAN: You ain't got much to say for a mouthpiece do you?
YOUNG WOMAN: Well. It's not that. It's just that . . .
OLD WOMAN: *(Interrupting her.)* You didn't expect to see a old black woman
   like me standing here charged with murder?
YOUNG WOMAN: I just pictured you a little different. That's all.
OLD WOMAN: You don't read the papers do you? They had my picture plas-
   tered all over 'em. Wouldn't a been a bad picture neither if the words ar-
   rested for murder weren't under it. I always wanted to make the social
   page, but not like this. Mind if I sit down. My feet are bothering me something terrible.
YOUNG WOMAN: Please. Are you okay? I can ask the guard to bring you some
   water and aspirin or . . .

OLD WOMAN: No. No. *(Smiles admiringly at Young Woman.)*

YOUNG WOMAN: I know this isn't exactly the Sheraton, but if you need something let me know.

OLD WOMAN: *(Rubbing her knees and legs.)* No. no, honey. I'm fine. I'm fine. Just old and tired and wanna get out of here's all.

YOUNG WOMAN: This hasn't been no day at the beach, huh?

OLD WOMAN: Took the words right out of my mouth. They got me in one of those holding cells with a bunch of young women. Keep a whole lot of noise going. They 'bout to drive me crazy. *(Continues to smile at Young Woman.)*

YOUNG WOMAN: *(Smiles at her, then opens briefcase.)* I've gone over what evidence and information the district attorney has on your case so . . .

OLD WOMAN: *(Interrupting her.)* I knew you was black.

YOUNG WOMAN: Pardon me?

OLD WOMAN: Even though you didn't sound like it on the phone. When they arrested me, I called my son Thomas. Smart boy. Work for the post office twenty-three years. I told him to find me a good lawyer. Get me out of this mess. You can do that. Can't you?

YOUNG WOMAN: *(Touching her hand.)* I can try my best. Like I told you on the phone, I've only been out of law school a few years. I'm what you call an associate . . . like a junior attorney. But my law firm has a long history of successes and a lot of very good seasoned senior attorneys who will help me on this case. You'll get the best representation. I promise.

OLD WOMAN: Forgive me for staring. I ain't never seen a black woman lawyer before. Not in the flesh.

YOUNG WOMAN: Well, there're more and more of us every year.

OLD WOMAN: A black girl, young . . . and a lawyer. My, my. And work for a firm. Got a suit and a briefcase. I ain't scared to have you represent me neither.

YOUNG WOMAN: What?

OLD WOMAN: Some people think 'cause you female and black . . . don't know your dooky hole from your elbow. Excuse my colorful tongue, but you know what I mean.

YOUNG WOMAN: Yes. Unfortunately I do. But we're not going to let that stop us.

OLD WOMAN: Ain't stopped us before. Ain't gonna stop us now.

YOUNG WOMAN: Yes, ma'am.

OLD WOMAN: I didn't kill that girl you know. Ain't never laid a eye on her before in my life.

YOUNG WOMAN: *(Reaching in her briefcase, picks up papers.)* Well, all the evidence they have against you is purely circumstantial. Meaning evidence not bearing directly on the fact. In this case, her death or the botched abortion that led to it. *(Picks up another paper.)* The Coroner lists the cause of death as septicemia. *(Looks up at Old Woman.)* Infection. She died of an infection. She never stated where she got the abortion or who performed it. All they found on her person that links her to you is a card with your address and phone number. *(Putting papers back on table.)* Circumstantial. Purely circumstantial.

OLD WOMAN: But what does all that mean though? 'Cause she dead and she got my phone number and address in her pocketbook mean I killed her?

YOUNG WOMAN: It boils down to that. They may have some evidence or some reason to suspect that you performed abortions. But they don't have to. She was found in a motel in a black neighborhood she didn't live in. Speculating, she went there to have the abortion or to recuperate and never recovered.

OLD WOMAN: They ain't got no reason to believe I did nothing like that to that girl. I'm just a old woman who minds her business. Don't want no business to mind me. They got somebody say I did it?

YOUNG WOMAN: I don't know. This is all the information I have right here. But if this is it, tomorrow at your arraignment, I will ask the judge to dismiss the charges against you for lack of evidence.

OLD WOMAN: You make it sound so easy.

YOUNG WOMAN: That is the easy part. Hard part starts if the judge denies my request.

OLD WOMAN: Um! Funny how things can affect you. Here it is some young girl come to my neighborhood and die. They want to put me in jail for the rest of my life for it. Why didn't she just go to the hospital when she saw she was feeling poorly. The papers say that girl was more than four months gone. Um! Stupid. Stupid. Stupid. Stupid.

YOUNG WOMAN: Or scared. Or confused. Or just ashamed.

OLD WOMAN: Same thing. If they cause you to lose your life, they all lead to stupid.

YOUNG WOMAN: And abortions are legal now. She didn't have to go to the quote unquote back alley.

OLD WOMAN: Um! Yeah, they legal. But only a handful of doctors do 'em here. Cost so much. Three, four hundred dollars. At least that's what I hear. Some people ain't got money like that.

YOUNG WOMAN: Guess all she had was fifty dollars.

OLD WOMAN: Honey, it cost more than fifty dollars, get yourself set straight waaay back when I was young. Fifty dollars got to be the rate for family and friends. Hundred, hundred fifty at least what it cost ten years ago. Before they made all this legal. So I hear. Ain't never been none of my business.

YOUNG WOMAN: *(Shocked.)* Yes. I suppose you're right. You can't get yourself nothing for fifty dollars. *(Long pause as she gets up from table and walks center stage away from Old Woman, stops, her back to Old Woman.)* Your son Thomas . . . you say he referred me to you?

OLD WOMAN: That's right. He's a supervisor at the post office. Know a lot of people and a regular walking encyclopedia of information. But he got your name from his son Tyrone.

YOUNG WOMAN: Tyrone! If that ain't a player's name, I pray for lying.

OLD WOMAN: Um. Player since the day he was born. Always running to his grandma get him out the trouble. Cold in here. Place show gives me a chill. Looks like it's never gonna stop raining. Like in the Bible, forty days and forty nights. I hate it when it rains like this. Dark and dreary. Sad and lonely.

YOUNG WOMAN: I don't know. I've had some of my most memorable times on a dark rainy night.

OLD WOMAN: Um. It's funny you would say that. I use to love a rainy night myself. The harder the better. Give me a reason to get all cozy. You know what I mean? Me and Bay. Together twenty-five years. We had a fight, day he died. Never got to say I was sorry.

YOUNG WOMAN: I'm sorry to hear that. I didn't know you lost your husband. I was hoping he could give you an alibi.

OLD WOMAN: No, ma'am. He can't help me no more. And all the water in the Mississippi can't put out this fire burning in my heart. You married?

YOUNG WOMAN: Yes. Two years now.

OLD WOMAN: Umm. You still on your honeymoon. No wonder you like a rainy evening. Pardon me for asking, but if you the lawyer, who wear the pants in the house?

YOUNG WOMAN: My husband's a lawyer too. So I guess we both do. How long has your husband been gone?

OLD WOMAN: Um. It's been more than a dozen years. Died on the same day as Dr. Martin Luther King. Hope he went to heaven with him. I hope he had the chance to tell King thank you for everything. Thank you for coming all the way to Memphis. If they acted right in the first place . . . King wouldn't a been shot in Memphis. Wouldn't a died in Memphis. Black folks wouldn't a be so mad they burn down they own buildings where they had to live. Bay and King might be alive today. And I wouldn't be here. 'Cause I'd be in my own home. Maybe have my picture in the paper for grandma of the year. And I'd be with Bay. I'd be with Bay.

YOUNG WOMAN: If only we could see into the future in the first place, we wouldn't get into trouble . . . make bad choices. We wouldn't get on the plane that was going to crash or turn head on into oncoming traffic or stay in a burning building with no way out. We wouldn't love, because the people we love may die. We wouldn't have children, they may disappoint us. We wouldn't love a man that was going to leave us or die trying to get rid of babies we don't want 'cause he's gone, and can't afford, even if he stayed. We wouldn't live, because there's pain in living. Everything hurts . . . eventually. We can only pray for wisdom and make the best choices at that time.

OLD WOMAN: *(Stands.)* I don't need no young woman give me no lecture on life. What you know about it? What you know about anything?

YOUNG WOMAN: I know I'm standing on the shoulders of many people. Hope one day somebody will stand on my shoulders. Bay won. I'm proof of that.

OLD WOMAN: Bay's dead. He's gone. And I'm old and alone. What you know about it? What do you care?

YOUNG WOMAN: I know. I know. And I care.

OLD WOMAN: Care? About what?

YOUNG WOMAN: *(Stands, takes off glasses.)* About you. I'm here to help you. Look at me. Please look at me. *(Beat.)* Grandma!!
(Beat as Old Woman turns and looks hard at her.)

YOUNG WOMAN: The name Lucy means light.

OLD WOMAN: Lucy?

YOUNG WOMAN: It took a long time to find her, but I finally did . . . in a little church in New York.

OLD WOMAN: What you talking about? Found who?

YOUNG WOMAN: I went to law school in New York. New York has a whole lot of churches. Hundreds of them. I must have called fifty before I finally found her . . . Saint Lucy with her plate of eyes.

OLD WOMAN: *(Crossing DR.)* Who told you about Saint Lucy?

YOUNG WOMAN: According to tradition, she was born to noble parents in Sicily. *(Crosses DL of table.)* Her mother arranged for her to marry a pagan gentleman.
(Old Woman turns to Young Woman.)

YOUNG WOMAN: But she refused. She had decided to offer herself and her virginity to God. And so, because she rejected him, he exposed her as a Christian. Seems in 300 A.D. you were persecuted for being Christian. Ironically, the governor sentenced her to life in a brothel. But when the guards tried to take her, they were unable to move her. They tried to burn her to death, but the flames make no impression on her. Finally, they stabbed her and cut her throat. She died in prison. One tradition has her eyes torn out by her judge. In another, she tore them out herself to present them to the man who condemned her. In both cases, they were miraculously restored. Seems whatever blinds you, faith can help you see again.

OLD WOMAN: *(Crosses to the UR corner of table.)* During the strike, you put your cans out if you were against the strike and the city picked up your trash.

YOUNG WOMAN: The police report states that the woman had the abortion about four to five days before she died.

OLD WOMAN: If you were for the strike, you didn't put your cans out. Almost ten weeks of garbage.

YOUNG WOMAN: Somebody had been taking care of her. The room was clean, the bedding, the floor. She was clean. And she could not have had the strength to take care of herself. Somebody brought her food everyday. Somebody took loving care of her.

OLD WOMAN: White folks wondered where black folks was hidin' all that garbage. Course, we wasn't makin' no money. Common sense tell you . . . no money, no groceries, no garbage.

YOUNG WOMAN: Somebody, the desk clerk, the housekeeper . . . somebody had to notice some one coming and going out of that room everyday. Somebody saw something!

OLD WOMAN: I took the garbage out to where I worked. Put it in white folks trash out there in North Memphis, including a empty chitterlings bucket. Nobody questioned a thing.

YOUNG WOMAN: We have to be able to show that the person wasn't you. That you were nowhere near that motel. That it couldn't of been you.

OLD WOMAN: In all that time, Bay never asked where the garbage went. All he knew was it was gone. Poof! Like magic. People want you to get rid of they garbage. They just don't want to know how. *(Counter-cross: she crosses to DL corner of table as Young Woman crosses to the UR corner of the table. She has her back to Young Woman. Long pause.)* I didn't kill that girl.

YOUNG WOMAN: I know you didn't. Stupidity killed her.

OLD WOMAN: Or maybe she did die trying to get from where it's dark, up somewhere where it's brighter. *(Beat.)* You must think I'm a monster.